THE AMERICA SYNDROME

THE AMERICA SYNDROME

APOCALYPSE, WAR, AND OUR CALL TO GREATNESS

Betsy Hartmann

Seven Stories Press

NEW YORK • OAKLAND • LONDON

Seven Stories Press
140 Watts Street
New York, NY 10013
www.sevenstories.com

Library of Congress Cataloging-in-Publication Data

Names: Hartmann, Betsy, author.
Title: The America syndrome : apocalypse, war and our call to greatness /
   Betsy Hartmann.
Description: New York : Seven Stories Press, 2017. | Includes bibliographical
   references and index.
Identifiers: LCCN 2016057014 (print) | LCCN 2017010548 (ebook) | ISBN
   9781609807405 (hardback) | ISBN 9781609807412 (Ebook)
Subjects: LCSH: United States--Civilization--1970- | Fear--United States. |
   Crises--United States. | National characteristics, American. |
   Exceptionalism--United States. | Social psychology--United States. |
   BISAC: SOCIAL SCIENCE / Anthropology / Cultural. | SOCIAL SCIENCE /
Future
   Studies.
Classification: LCC E169.12 .H378 2017 (print) | LCC E169.12 (ebook) | DDC
   973.92--DC23
LC record available at https://lccn.loc.gov/2016057014

Printed in the USA.

9 8 7 6 5 4 3 2 1

For Alistair and the next generation

CONTENTS

An optimist isn't necessarily a blithe, slightly sappy whistler in the dark of our time. To be hopeful in bad times is not just foolishly romantic. It is based on the fact that human history is a history not only of cruelty but also of compassion, sacrifice, courage, kindness. What we choose to emphasize in this complex history will determine our lives. If we see only the worst, it destroys our capacity to do something. If we remember those times and places—and there are so many—where people have behaved magnificently, this gives us the energy to act, and at least the possibility of sending this spinning top of a world in a different direction. And if we do act, in however small a way, we don't have to wait for some grand utopian future. The future is an infinite succession of presents, and to live now as we think human beings should live, in defiance of all that is bad around us, is itself a marvelous victory.

Howard Zinn, "The Optimism of Uncertainty,"
The Nation, September 2, 2004

ACKNOWLEDGMENTS

So many people have helped me in the process of writing this book that I worry, in my usual way, that I have left someone out. First, I'd like to thank my agent and friend Rick Balkin who believed in the book since its inception. He went above and beyond the call of duty by casting his sharp editorial eye on drafts and keeping my spirits up whenever they lagged with his great sense of humor. Special thanks go to publisher and editor Dan Simon, assistant editor and publisher Lauren Hooker, marketing and publicity director Ruth Weiner, and their team at Seven Stories Press. Dan's insightful comments helped me to see and shape the book in new ways, and it has been a pleasure to work with such a dedicated publisher.

For help in developing a deeper understanding of American history I am grateful to Susan Tracy, professor emerita of History and American Studies at Hampshire College, who kindly commented on numerous chapter drafts, lent me books and answered my questions. I just wish I could have put everything I learned from her into the book. Alan Hodder, professor of Comparative Religion at Hampshire, shed light on the Puritans and transcendentalism. I also owe a big debt of gratitude to two great scholars of American history: Paul Boyer and Sacvan Bercovitch, both of whom passed away recently. Their books inspired many of my thoughts, and I wish I'd had the opportunity to thank them personally.

A number of colleagues, friends, and family members gave valuable feedback on the manuscript or parts of it. They include Sue Boyce, Axel Harneit-Sievers, Anne Hendrixson, Nick Hildyard, Peggy Hobbs, Katie McKay Bryson, Kathy Pfister, Rosalind Pollan, Jade Sasser, Sarah Sexton, and Banu Subramaniam. My previous work with Banu and Charles Zerner on our anthology *Making Threats: Biofears and Environmental Anxieties* helped lay the ground for this book. The population chapter benefitted from my long association with dedicated scholar/activists Mohan Rao and N.B. Sarojini in India, The Corner House in the UK, and Hampshire College colleagues Marlene Fried, Anne Hendrixson, and Kay Johnson. Through teaching together and through her books, Kay taught me so much about the tragic human consequences of China's one-child policy. Ongoing conversations with colleagues Michael Klare and Frank Holmquist and disasters expert Ben Wisner have deepened my knowledge of climate, security, and the African context. Lyla Mehta and Melissa Leach at the Institute of Development Studies and Jan Selby in the Department of International Relations at Sussex University in the UK have helped me sharpen my analysis of population, scarcity, and environmental security issues. Simon Dalby has also been an important influence on my thinking.

Hampshire College, from which I recently retired, has always been supportive of my research and writing, and I especially appreciate my colleagues in the School of Critical Social Inquiry, the Civil Liberties and Public Policy Program, and the Population and Development Program for all the help they have given me over the years. I also appreciate my students for keeping me on my toes and hopeful.

Geoffrey Boyce and Sarah Launius taught me a lot about border issues and activism, and Sonia Kruks introduced me to Simone de Beauvoir's views on political purity. Charles Mann provided me with new materials and insights on the history of apocalyptic thinking in environmentalism. Thanks to Amy Diehl for her help in website design.

A fellowship at the Mesa Refuge in Point Reyes, CA in the spring of 2012 allowed me the space to write the first draft of the climate chapter, and that same spring, thanks to Jade Sasser, I was able to workshop my chapter on the atomic bomb at the University of California, Berkeley, Workshop on Environmental Politics.

My mother-in-law Alice Boyce and four friends, Cliff Kuhn, Bill Howley, Sue Leather, and Robert Prasch, all of whom were inspiring thinkers and activists, died while I was writing this book and I hope it honors their legacy.

Many friends and family provided moral support, guidance, and a sounding board along the way. Special thanks to Rosette Gault, who has been there for me since the age of twelve and whose ideas spark my thinking, Corinne Demas, Kathy Pfister, Neil Stillings, Joyce Duncan, Sam Gladstone, Jennie Kitteringham, Ivan Nutbrown, Patty Mintz, Debbie Bernick, Doug and Jane Smith, Greg Lieberknecht, Matthew Roehrig, Jerry Epstein, Fran Deutsch, the members of my writing and political study groups, my father-in-law James E. Boyce, my sister Darcy Hartmann, my mother Martha Hartmann, and my children and their partners, Jamie Hartmann-Boyce and James Sinclair, and Tom Hartmann-Boyce and Melissa Arrambide. My first grandchild Alistair was born while I was writing this book and he has brought enough joy to brighten even the darkest day.

Last but not least, I owe a huge debt of gratitude to my husband Jim Boyce. He has been there beside me every step of this journey, never faltering in his interest, smart advice, and emotional support. He is also a thorough and meticulous editor, and my prose is better for his patient editorial labors of love.

PREFACE

I came of age in the late 1960s, at the apogee of that tumultuous time in American history. In the spring of my junior year in high school, Martin Luther King and Bobby Kennedy were assassinated and revolution convulsed the streets of Paris. A few months later Mayor Daley's police busted the heads of anti-war protesters at the Democratic National Convention in Chicago. When I entered Yale University in 1969, as part of the first class of undergraduate women, breaking that gender barrier seemed tame compared to manning the barricades.

On May Day 1970, demonstrators converged on New Haven to protest against the trial of Black Panther leader Bobby Seale for the murder of an alleged FBI informant. When news broke of the secret US bombing of Cambodia, the protest expanded to include the bloody war in Southeast Asia. Yale's president Kingman Brewster opened the university's gates to feed and house thousands of young people who came from across the country. Meanwhile, the Nixon White House dispatched 4000 National Guard troops to join the ranks of armed state troopers in the city.

The day before the protest was scheduled to begin, President Nixon upped the ante, announcing the invasion of Cambodia and denouncing domestic dissidents in a televised speech to the nation. "My fellow Americans, we live in an age of anarchy, both abroad and at home," he warned. "We see mindless attacks on all the great institutions which have been created by free civilizations in the last 500 years. Even here in the United States, great universities are being systematically destroyed."[1]

Speaking the next day at the Pentagon, he was even blunter. "You know, you see these bums, you know, blowing up the campuses. Listen, the boys that are on the college campuses today are the luckiest people in the world and here they are, burning up the books, I mean, storming around about this issue, I mean, you name it. Get rid of the war, there'll be another one."[2]

The May Day demonstration in New Haven went off relatively smoothly, but things got scarier that night. Street skirmishes drove protesters to seek refuge in our dorms as tear gas wafted through the windows. We got off lightly. On May 4, Ohio National Guardsmen shot four students dead at Kent State University and wounded nine others. Less than two weeks later, two more students lay dead and eleven were wounded at Jackson State University in Mississippi. The killings galvanized a national student strike movement and classes were suspended at many colleges and universities, including Yale. It felt like I was living on the edge of a revolution.

Personal transformations were in the air, too. I became a feminist, and then, after spending a year working in India in 1971–72, a believer in third world peasant revolution. During my last year of college, two close friends, my boyfriend (now my husband, Jim), and I began to talk about going back to the land.

The prospect of nuclear annihilation added to our sense of urgency. For the most idealistic of my generation, the task was nothing less than saving the human race and the planet. We would build sturdy arks to survive the apocalypse. Our music reflected our hopes and fears. In 1965, a tune called "Eve of Destruction," recorded by Barry McGuire, hit the top of the pop charts. I was

14 years old and knew all the verses by heart. At Woodstock in 1969, Jefferson Airplane and Crosby, Stills & Nash both played the haunting song "Wooden Ships," in which a young man and woman from enemy sides stumble upon each other after a holocaust, munch on purple berries, and float peacefully away as others perish around them. "We are leaving, you don't need us," goes its refrain.

The specter of the bomb knit together the diverse utopian experiments of the 1960s and '70s. The 1962 Port Huron Statement that launched Students for a Democratic Society (SDS) captured the mood: "Our work is guided by the sense that we may be the last generation in the experiment with living." If so, why not experiment? Maybe a new revolutionary millennium was to come—maybe it had already been born in Maoist China, still hidden from the world by the bamboo curtain. It was imperative to devise new ways to live in harmony with each other and with nature. We would strike the right balance between manual and intellectual labor, work and leisure, communal solidarity and individual freedom, escaping as much as possible from the capitalist world's cruel hierarchies of class, race, and gender.

On graduating from college, Jim and I received grants to go to Bangladesh, so we put the back-to-the-land dream on hold. Our friends moved to make the dream a reality. They lived rent-free in an abandoned farmhouse in West Virginia until they scraped together enough money to buy 70 acres along with another couple. The house that came with the land had been grand in its time, but now it had no windows, electricity, heat, or running water. It was being used to store hay.

We returned from two years in Bangladesh in serious culture shock and reeling from the political violence we'd witnessed there.

We needed a place to live cheaply where we could write our book about the village. Though we'd grown enormously during our time away, we hadn't outgrown the back-to-the-land dream. Our friends invited us to join them in West Virginia and to build a cabin on their land. When my grandfather counseled against building on property we didn't own, I bristled at his bourgeois values.

And so we bought an old Dodge Dart for $150, packed it with our belongings, and headed to Appalachia in the fall of 1976. After the crowded cities and highways of the northeast, driving into West Virginia was pure liberation. We floated over rolling waves of green hills, and from their crests glimpsed tantalizing views of steep meadows and pastures. The John Denver song, "Take Me Home, Country Roads," was our anthem. It did seem "almost heaven," this West Virginia he celebrated, though his geography was a little off—the Shenandoah River and Blue Ridge Mountains the song extolls are further east in Virginia. It didn't matter. The map we were following led more to a dream than to any specific locale.

Countless others took such journeys. Some went back to the land, others formed urban communes or joined the political underground. The '60s, or whatever one chooses to call the era since it stretched well into the '70s, were heady times. In our youthful zeal to transform the world, few of us realized that we were acting out a much older American apocalyptic tradition. Had we understood this, we might have better prepared ourselves for the political challenges that lay ahead—the rise of Reagan, the collapse of Communism, the new wars on the horizon. Nixon's remark, "Get rid of the war, there'll be another one," proved all too prescient.

Writing this book has taken me on a long journey—back to my past, but also toward the future. My generation's apocalyptic terrors and utopian dreams were my starting point, but I realized that to understand them I had to look much further back in American history. Our apocalyptic mindset was less the exception than the rule.

Today apocalypse is again in the air Americans breathe, blown on a swirling wind of religious prophesies, sci-fi movies, doomsday prepper TV shows, environmental predictions, and worst-case national security scenarios. A young college student recently told me she didn't see any point in having children since the planet is headed toward collapse. To ride out the coming apocalypse in style, a number of super-wealthy American tech executives and hedge-fund managers are buying up land in New Zealand or investing in luxury survival condos in old underground nuclear missile silos. The latter feature sniper posts so armed militia can protect against unwanted intruders.[3] And now we have a president whose apocalyptic rhetoric is calculated to raise fear to a fever pitch. Trump's policies also heighten insecurities about the future. The more his administration slows progress on environmentalism, for example, the worse the long-term impacts of climate change will likely be. While it's hard not to be anxious and pessimistic in the present moment, we need to resist the temptation to become apocalyptic.

In the course of writing this book, I spent four months in New Delhi, India as a Fulbright Scholar. There's so much more there than here to induce doomsday despair—deadly pollution, nightmarish traffic congestion, unconscionable rates of poverty and disease. Not a pretty picture, in other words. Yet people in Delhi seemingly went about their lives without fear that the world would soon end. They didn't shoulder that unnecessary burden. Why do so many Americans shoulder it, then? What's so appealing about the burden that we can't lay it down?

My hope is that this book challenges Americans to think beyond the apocalypse, sparking fresh thinking and opening new windows on the world. In writing it, I have felt the burden of apocalypse slip slowly from my own shoulders. It's a big relief.

Amherst, Massachusetts—December 2016

END TIMES AND
ENDLESS WAR

According to opinion polls, a staggering percentage of Americans accept that the world will end in a battle in Armageddon. In a 2010 Pew poll, 41 percent of respondents said they expected Jesus Christ to return to Earth by 2050. Two years later a Reuters poll found that over one-fifth of the American population believed the end of the world will happen in their lifetime, as compared to 6 percent in France, 7 percent in Belgium, and 8 percent in Great Britain. Another recent poll by the Public Religion Research Institute reported that 49 percent of Americans think that natural disasters are a sign of "the end times."[4]

In the months before the purported December 21, 2012 Mayan apocalypse, the National Aeronautics and Space Administration (NASA) received so many inquiries from children and adults terrified that a rogue planet might crash into the Earth or that the sun might explode that it set up a special webpage to allay their fears. The page received over four and a half million views. On December 22, NASA posted a video it had made in advance, "Why the World Didn't End Yesterday."[5]

Of all the intertwining reasons for our apocalyptic disposition—

reasons I explore in this book—the one that stands out most starkly is our acceptance of the necessity and inevitability of war. In the same 2010 Pew survey, six out of ten Americans saw another world war as definite or probable by 2050. This expectation of war isn't surprising, given that Americans' apocalyptic images and beliefs are derived mainly from Christianity, especially the Book of Revelation at the end of the New Testament which, above all, is about the grotesque violence and crowning glories of war.

The Book of Revelation is "wartime literature." Its author, John, is thought to have been deeply affected by the Roman army's attacks on Judea and its siege and sacking of Jerusalem in the year 70 AD.[6] John himself was banished to the Greek island of Patmos by Roman rulers around 95 AD. In John's macabre vision of the end times, a fourth of the Earth is wiped out, a third of the trees, green grass, and sea creatures are extinguished, and a third of the world's water is poisoned. There are terrible earthquakes, fires, and plagues. Four demons kill a third of all mankind. The Whore of Babylon, a symbol of evil and carnal lust, is assaulted by the seven-headed, ten-horned Beast which strips her naked, eats her flesh, and burns her with fire.[7]

Toward the end of the Book of Revelation, the savior with eyes like a flame of fire, "Faithful and True," rides out on a white horse to lead the armies of Heaven in battle. He is "clothed with a vesture dipped in blood," and on him are written the words "KING OF KINGS AND LORD OF LORDS." He holds a sword in his mouth "to smite the nations" so he can preside over them with a rod of iron and the fierceness and wrath of Almighty God.[8] In the Final Judgment the dead are brought back to life, but those judged to be sinners by their deeds are thrown along with the devil and death itself into the Lake of Fire, burning with brimstone, where they meet the second death of eternal suffering.

Fortunate, then, are those who are judged worthy to live on in the New Jerusalem, a city with streets of gold, gates of pearls, and walls inlaid with gems. There is no need for the sun or moon, since God and the Lamb are the light, and from their throne flows "a pure river of Water of Life, clear as crystal" that nourishes the fruits on the Tree of Life.[9]

This promise of a New Jerusalem for the elect, and the cataclysmic violence against people and nature necessary to achieve that goal, has made the Book of Revelation an ideological tool of conquest and empire from the Crusades onwards. You don't have to be a Christian to be susceptible to John's logic that the perfect end—the New Jerusalem—justifies the bloody means.

Despite the official separation of church and state, religious axioms thread through the fabric of American political culture. Historian Robert Bellah coined the term "civil religion" to describe the religious orientation that the great majority of Americans share. That a Higher Authority guides human affairs, that American history follows a providential path, that Americans are special and exceptional, a chosen people obliged to carry out God's will or else suffer dire consequences, are widely held to be self-evident truths.[10] So, too, is the belief that war is divinely justified.

The Civil War marked a watershed in the evolution of our civil religion. As it metastasized into a total war that targeted civilian populations as well as soldiers—estimates of the number of war deaths have recently been revised upwards to three-quarters of a million people[11]—leaders and clergy on both sides invoked divine authority to justify the slaughter. "Many saw in the unprecedented destruction of lives and property something mystical taking place," writes historian Harry Stout, "what we today might call the birthing of a fully functioning, truly national, *American* civil religion."[12] Patriotism became a sacred duty, as important as adherence to a traditional faith, maybe more so. Civil War deaths created a "republic of suffering" in which "sacrifice and the state became inextricably intertwined."[13]

World War I brought about a major reaffirmation of this civil religion. The nation's turn away from isolationism to global intervention was accompanied by hyperbole about its "starring role as world redeemer" in a continuing war between good and evil around the globe.[14] President Woodrow Wilson proclaimed, "The world must be made safe for democracy."[15] That we are ordained by God or a Higher Authority to be the defender of freedom has been a rallying call in America's cold and hot wars ever since. Our national mission is bound tightly to our military might.

So, too, are our economy and government. In 1961, in his farewell speech to the American people, Republican President Dwight D. Eisenhower famously warned of the growth of the military-industrial complex. It's worth recalling his exact words:

> This conjunction of an immense military establishment and a large arms industry is new in the American experience. The total influence—economic, political, even spiritual—is felt in every city, every State house, every office of the Federal government. We recognize the imperative need for this development. Yet we must not fail to comprehend its grave implications. Our toil, resources and livelihood are all involved; so is the very structure of our society. In the councils of government, we must guard against the acquisition of unwarranted influence, whether sought or unsought, by the military-industrial complex. The potential for the disastrous rise of misplaced power exists and will persist.[16]

Since then, the power of the military-industrial complex has become so pervasive that we have entered an era of what many commentators call permanent or endless war, in which we are always preparing for wars, or fighting them, or both. War has become normal, peace the aberration. "Today as never before in their history Americans are enthralled with military power," writes West Point graduate and military scholar, Andrew Bacevich. "The global military supremacy that the United States presently enjoys—and is bent on perpetuating—has become central to our national identity."[17] The prospect of endless combat induces powerful longings for some kind of ending. Unfortunately, we are more predisposed to imagine the end of the world than the end of American war-making.

FORWARD MARCH OF THE CRUSADES

It is tempting to believe that permanent war began with 9/11 and the George W. Bush administration's launch of the "Global War on Terror." Bush's doctrine of preventive war, giving the US the right to take "anticipatory actions to defend ourselves, even if uncertainty remains as to the time and place of the enemy's attack," did mark a shift in official defense policy.[18] The administration also expanded the theater of war to include the entire world. According to the *9/11 Commission Report*, "9/11 has taught us that terrorism against American interests 'over there' should be regarded just as we regard terrorism against Americans 'over here'. In this same sense the American homeland is the planet."[19]

The Bush doctrine was less a turning point, however, than the culmination of trends that began decades before. It was Jimmy Carter who legitimized ongoing American intervention in the

Middle East to protect strategic energy interests. In his 1980 State of the Union address, he announced what became known as the Carter Doctrine: "Let our position be absolutely clear: An attempt by any outside force to gain control of the Persian Gulf region will be regarded as an assault on the vital interests of the United States of America, and such an assault will be repelled by any means necessary, including military force."[20] Bush Sr.'s first Gulf War flowed seamlessly from this doctrine.

When Reagan came to power in the 1980s, seeking to overcome the supposed defeatism that had set in after the disastrous war in Vietnam, his intention was "not only to rearm the Cold War militarily but to reload it ideologically."[21] His New Right coalition brought together neoconservative policy wonks and hardline career militarists like Paul Wolfowitz and Donald Rumsfeld with the emerging political power bloc of the Christian Right.

It was an odd but effective foreign policy coalition, with Christian Right evangelicals adding an apocalyptic twist. "Their sense of themselves as a persecuted people engaged in a life and death end-time struggle between the forces of good and evil mapped easily onto the millennialism of anti-Communist militarists, particularly those involved in Central America," writes historian Greg Grandin.[22] Central America emerged as a laboratory for testing the coalition's methods of intervention abroad. In Nicaragua, El Salvador, and Guatemala, the Reagan administration supported brutal counterinsurgency operations against progressive leaders and social movements in the name of protecting freedom and spreading democracy.

Today Americans often think of the Christian Right in terms of the "culture wars" it waged, and is still waging, against abortion, sex education, gay rights, the teaching of evolution, and lack of religious training in public schools. Its role in the resurgence of militarism in the post-Vietnam period gets shorter shrift, but may turn out to be their most enduring legacy. Prior to the 1970s, Christian evangelicals hadn't played a major role in American party politics. The hugely popular evangelical preacher Billy Graham was nonpartisan, serving as a spiritual advisor to Republican and Democratic presidents alike. But by the 1980s, Graham's approach was superseded by "a movement built around partisan politics and apocalyptic rhetoric."[23] That movement was led by people like Reverend Jerry Falwell, who drew disaffected conservative white Christians to "I love America" rallies. In 1979 he launched his political organization, the Moral Majority, with the help of Tim LaHaye, a right-wing evangelical who went on to co-author the best-selling (80 million copies) *Left Behind* series of apocalyptic novels.

The Republican Party, already pursuing a strategy of wooing Southern whites, saw in the Moral Majority a route to electoral success.[24] Ronald Reagan became the go-to man. One of the Christian Right's main strongholds was Orange County, California, Reagan's own power base, where it attracted into its fold many evangelical engineers and technicians employed by the defense industries located there.[25]

In the early 1970s, as governor of California, Reagan had already started mining the evangelical vote. For many Christian fundamentalists, the Cold War battle with the Soviets literally signified the coming of the Biblical apocalypse. The Soviet Union was portrayed as the evil Gog, whose invasion of Israel was prophesized to hasten the end times. Reagan declared at a 1971 dinner with lawmakers that Russia "fits the description of Gog perfectly . . . For the first time ever, everything is in place for the battle of Armageddon and the second coming of Christ."[26]

This view of Israel's centrality persists in apocalyptic narratives, though the enemy is now the evil Arabs rather than the evil Communists. The Christian Right provides key political support to hardline Israeli hawks, interpreting the return of the Jews to the region as a sign of the Second Coming. Former House Majority Leader Tom DeLay told a reporter in 2007 that he lived for the Rapture, "and obviously we have to be connected to Israel . . . to enjoy the Second Coming of Christ."[27]

During his two terms in office, Reagan's hardline foreign policy crusade played well to the Christian Right. He beefed up the military-industrial complex, massively increasing defense expenditures on systems like the Strategic Defense Initiative, popularly known as Star Wars, which, despite its name, was meant to enhance America's offensive power. The military underwent significant changes, including the final demise of the citizen-soldier in favor of a professional army and the ascendency of new high-tech strategies of warfare.[28]

Another of Reagan's legacies was the manipulation of public opinion, not only as the so-called "Great Communicator" but also as Commander-in-Chief. In 1983 he set up an Office of Public Diplomacy that brought together experts from PR firms and military psychological operations—"psyops"—to sell the administration's covert wars in Central and Latin America. In an Orwellian twist, the democratically-elected Sandinista regime in Nicaragua was portrayed as "terrorists" and the right-wing Contras as "freedom fighters" who embodied nothing less that the spirit of the American Revolution. The Office even coordinated a national campaign of religious sermons extolling the Contras.

The most pernicious effect of this campaign was the erosion of press freedom. The Office of Public Diplomacy fed the media so many falsehoods about Central America that journalists were forced to spend most of their time fact-checking, rather than

pursuing their own independent lines of inquiry about US intervention in the region. Journalists who didn't toe the Reagan line
were targeted. "It was on the front lines of the Central American conflicts that the Pentagon learned how to finesse the news
at home by controlling reporters at the source," writes Greg
Grandin.[29] The brave war reporting of the Vietnam War era was
over. We live with the consequences.

The "war on drugs" also played a starring role in the militarization of the homeland. Reagan officially launched it in 1982,
though Nixon had already set the ball rolling during his administration. John Ehrlichman, Nixon's domestic policy advisor of
Watergate fame, later made this remarkable admission:

> You want to know what this was really all about? The
> Nixon campaign in 1968, and the Nixon White House
> after that, had two enemies: the antiwar left and black
> people. You understand what I'm saying? We knew we
> couldn't make it illegal to be either against the war or
> black, but by getting the public to associate the hip-
> pies with marijuana and blacks with heroin, and then
> criminalizing both heavily, we could disrupt those com-
> munities. We could arrest their leaders, raid their homes,
> break up their meetings, and vilify them night after night
> on the evening news. Did we know we were lying about
> the drugs? Of course we did.[30]

Reagan turned Nixon's covert campaign into an all-out crusade.
It didn't matter that drug crime rates were declining. Reagan's drug
war, like Nixon's, was less about drugs than about other strategic
goals. In targeting small-time dealers and users, mainly black,
in inner cities, it hid the fact that one of the main conduits for

cocaine and other illegal drugs to enter the country was through smuggling operations run by the Contras and other "freedom fighters."[31] Reagan launched a media campaign to foment racial panic about the dangers of crack cocaine. "Almost overnight," writes legal scholar Michelle Alexander, "the media was saturated with images of black 'crack whores,' 'crack dealers,' and 'crack babies'—images that seemed to confirm the worst negative racial stereotypes about inner-city residents. The media bonanza surrounding 'the new demon drug' helped to catapult the War on Drugs from an ambitious federal policy to an actual war."[32]

The drug war began the full-scale militarization of domestic law enforcement. In 1981 Congress passed the Military Cooperation with Civilian Law Enforcement Agencies Act to facilitate the use of military equipment, bases, and intelligence by local, state, and federal police forces for anti-drug activities. The act eroded a long legal tradition, beginning with the post-Reconstruction-era Posse Comitatus Act, which proscribed the deployment of the military for civilian policing. By declaring drugs a national security threat, Reagan furthered the process of erasing that all-important boundary. To be sure, many police forces were still more interested in solving serious crimes than pursuing minor drug offenses, but Reagan sweetened the deal with large infusions of government cash. Another financial incentive was added in 1984 when local police agencies were given the opportunity to profit from property seized from suspected drug dealers and users. In 1986, with the passage of legislation mandating long minimum prison sentences for low-level drug dealing and crack cocaine possession, the cornerstones of the prison-military-industrial complex were set firmly in place.[33]

From then on, the construction process was fast and ugly. In cities across the country, para-military SWAT teams were deployed to serve drug warrants, breaking unannounced into people's homes, brandishing automatic weapons. Annual SWAT deployments grew from 3000 in the early 1980s to 40,000 by 2001. Community policing was out, military policing was in. The prison industry boomed. President Bill Clinton became Incarcerator-in-Chief, ratcheting up the "wars" on crime, drugs, and undocumented immigrants. His get-tough policies, including federal "three strikes and you're out" legislation that mandated life sentences for minor crimes, swelled the ranks of the nation's prisons. Under Clinton, more people were locked into federal and state prisons than under any president in American history.[34]

Today, the US has the dubious distinction of incarcerating more people than any other country in the world. More than two million people are imprisoned, a 500 percent increase over the last 40 years. The increase is due to changes in sentencing policy, not changes in crime rates, which remain relatively low. More than 60 percent of prisoners are people of color, creating what Michelle Alexander calls "a new racial caste system," as disenfranchisement and stigmatization persist even after release.[35]

Reagan's foreign policy crusade, the militarization of domestic law enforcement, the war on drugs, and mass incarceration prepped the body politic for the homeland security operations launched under George W. Bush. His War on Terror was less a rupture in business as usual than another step, albeit a big one, in organizing the country for permanent war at home and abroad. But there was an important difference between Reagan's crusade and Bush's sequel. Under Reagan the apocalyptic storylines woven into his bellicose foreign policy were largely scripted by the Christian Right. After the Twin Towers fell on 9/11, the apocalyptic nightmares that disturbed the sleep of the anesthetized body politic were diffused more widely. We have yet to wake up from them.

WHOSE TRAUMA?

The events of 9/11 *were* traumatic, especially for the injured, those who lost loved ones, the first responders who came face-to-face with the human tragedy, witnesses to the attacks, and New Yorkers whose city would never be the same. But that very real trauma quickly spilled beyond the circle of those directly affected to encompass the whole country, as if each of us had been deeply and indelibly scarred psychologically. Americans, unlike Europeans, had no modern history of being attacked on their mainland, and Pearl Harbor was a distant memory. But the sense of trauma went beyond the shock of being attacked. Those who were spared the worst were nevertheless encouraged to think the worst, to believe that life in general, and our lives in particular, would never be the same.

I was by no means immune to this mass panic. The subsequent anthrax attacks from New York to Florida only heightened my anxiety. But what really pushed me over the edge was a short article in our local paper about a rental car traced to one of the 9/11 bombers that had been spotted at a nearby nuclear power plant the summer before. The clear implication was that terrorists had been scoping out the plant as a potential target. The reliability of the evidence was debatable for this story and for the other reports that suggested the terrorists had considered targeting nuclear plants,[36] but the article nonetheless triggered the nuclear fears of my childhood, fears that I probe further in Chapter Three. For me, the panic induced by 9/11 got bound up with images of atomic explosions and radiation. We kept emergency supplies in our car in case we had to flee suddenly.

Over time I realized my emotions were getting the better of me, and getting in the way of a sober assessment of the causes and consequences of the 9/11 attacks. I was falling into yet another apocalyptic trap, but how could I get out of it? Looking for answers, I began to study how national security fears are produced, work that culminated in an anthology I co-edited called *Making Threats*. One chapter in particular provided the insight I needed to spring the trap—sociologist Jackie Orr's concept of the "militarization of inner space."

Orr uses the term to describe the "psychological organization of civil society for the production of violence." While US military and civil defense agencies have long been in the propaganda business, after 9/11 the militarization of inner space took a new form "with the language of psychology itself, of emotional and 'inner' experience . . . immediately deployed in public discourse about the attack and its aftermath. A reductive, repetitive discourse of trauma, healing, and recovery displaced the complicated realities of violent historical and political conflict." Instead of a serious reckoning about the high price of our foreign policy in the Middle East, we were encouraged to engage in a kind of "therapeutic patriotism."[37] "Every American is a soldier, and every citizen is in this fight," Bush proclaimed a month after the attacks.[38]

Was the focus on mass trauma a psyops campaign perpetrated by the Pentagon and Bush administration? Maybe, but probably not. More relevant are the ways trauma was already well-planted in the American psyche.

In 1980 the American Psychiatric Association added Post-Traumatic Stress Disorder, or PTSD, to its classification scheme of mental disorders. The PTSD diagnosis grew out of studies of Vietnam War veterans, Holocaust survivors, and sexual violence victims. PTSD became a valuable diagnostic tool for treating people directly affected by serious or life-threatening accidents and catastrophic or violent events, but in popular culture it soon lost its sharper edges and became overused. All sorts of stress and anxiety began to be conflated with trauma and its aftermath. In encouraging Americans to feel traumatized by 9/11, the media drew on this cultural propensity. The effects were widespread enough that the US government's National Center for PTSD issued this correction: "Exposure through electronic media (e.g., televised images [of] the 9/11 attacks on the World Trade Center) is not considered a traumatic event."[39]

It didn't help that government leaders themselves were freaking out. Journalist Jane Mayer traced Vice President Dick Cheney's paranoia in the aftermath of 9/11 to his participation in Cold War nuclear attack drills during the Reagan administration in which he spent days in an underground bunker as part of a secret government team.[40] Other senior administration officials, including the President himself, were frightened sick by daily security briefings based on the "Threat Matrix," an unfiltered list of potential terrorist threats based largely on rumors and unsubstantiated information, whose "catalogue of horrors" and "daily looming prognoses of Armageddon" made policymakers ever more terrified of Islamic extremism.[41]

The result was that the Bush administration came to see terrorism as an "existential" threat, capable of destroying the country and civilization itself. Accompanying this institutionalized paranoia was the fear that if policymakers didn't take all potential threats seriously, then they would be held responsible should one actually materialize.[42] "Not on my watch" became the order of the day. In the throes of trauma, both real and manufactured, Americans were susceptible to the rising apocalyptic alarm coming from the administration, as were most of their elected representatives in Congress.

Predictably, cynicism grew as time wore on. The administration may have been in the grip of paranoia in the first months after 9/11, but afterwards the Bush–Cheney team proceeded to play the apocalypse card for all it was politically worth: the Patriot Act, color-coded terror alerts, birth of the Homeland Security leviathan, the war in Afghanistan, and finally the trump card—the 2003 invasion of Iraq. In retrospect it may seem astonishing that they got away so easily with leading the country into a major war on the basis of blatant lies about connections between Saddam Hussein's regime and Al Qaeda, alongside false claims of Iraqi weapons of mass destruction. Astonishing, that is, until one considers the power of their propaganda machine. George W. Bush may not have had the Hollywood magic of Ronald Reagan, but he turned out to be a master of strategic PR.

In *The Greatest Story Ever Sold*, Frank Rich describes how the Bush administration systematically fed the press false stories, infomercials, and infotainment, all produced at taxpayer expense, to sell the public on the war on terror. A covert Office of Strategic Influence (OSI), that included representatives of the Army's Psychological Operations Command, opened in the Pentagon by the end of 2001. Its mission was to plant "helpful" news in foreign media outlets, with the assistance of PR firms. After it was exposed by the *New York Times* in 2002, the OSI was forced to shut down, but its activities were dispersed elsewhere in the Pentagon bureaucracy.[43] Presaging the Trump administration's manufacture of fraudulent "alternative facts," in a now-famous interview with journalist Ron Suskind a presidential aide—probably Karl Rove—expressed his disdain for what he called the "reality-based community" of journalists who pursue the real facts on the ground. It's "not the way the world works anymore," he declared. "We're an empire now, and when we act, we create our own reality."[44]

In the 1990s, major changes in the news industry had already weakened the "reality-based community" of journalists. With the advent of cable TV and its 24-hour news cycle, the news format shifted from serious reportage to entertainment. The media crafted a "problem frame" to churn out scary stories that would titillate viewers. Echoing the morality plays of a bygone era, this framing highlights dangers and threats, exaggerates the number of people they impact, and touts solutions that typically involve the courageous efforts of the forces of law and order. "Fear is more visible and routine in public discourse than it was a decade ago," media scholar David Altheide wrote shortly before 9/11. "Indeed, one of the few things Americans seem to share is the popular culture that celebrates danger and fear as entertainment organized with canned format delivered through an expansive and invasive information technology."[45]

The same decade also saw the growth of a "military-media complex," featuring increased use of satellites for both military and communications objectives, target-based cameras that bring the shock and awe of aerial bombings straight to your TV screen, and appearances by retired military officers as news commentators.[46] The "embedding" of journalists with military units during the 2003 invasion of Iraq cemented a relationship that had already grown incestuous. *Washington Post* columnist David Ignatius, who has embedded with the US military in Afghanistan and Iraq, wrote about the result: "We are observing these wars from just one perspective, not seeing them whole. When you see my byline from Kandahar or Kabul or Basra, you should not think that I am out among ordinary people, asking questions of all sides. I am usually inside an American military bubble. That vantage point has value, but it is hardly a full picture."[47]

Hardly a full picture, indeed. How little Americans have come to know—or been allowed to know—about the terrible human costs of our invasion of Iraq and its aftermath. Brown University's Watson Institute estimates that from 2003 to 2015 at least 165,000 Iraqi civilians died from direct war-related violence, while twice as many probably died from war's indirect effects on systems that provide food, clean water, and health care, bringing total civilian deaths to about half a million. In the same period, around 8000 American soldiers and military contractors lost their lives.[48]

THE BATTLEGROUNDS OF PERMANENT WAR

The US defense establishment has become so powerful that it operates—in the words of Michael Glennon, international law scholar and former legal counsel to the Senate Foreign Relations Committee—as a "double government," effectively independent of Congress, the judiciary, and the executive branch. In the sphere of national security, constitutional democracy has become more and more a charade.[49] Always looking toward new threats to legitimize its financial and political power, the military-industrial complex generates a constant stream of worst-case scenarios to terrify elected officials, like the rest of us, into compliance.

Preparations for such scenarios are rehearsed again and again by government agencies and their civilian counterparts, sometimes making them seem all too real—especially to those left out of the loop. An anti-terror active-shooter drill at New York's JFK airport, which happened to be held on the very day of the terrorist attack on the Brussels airport in March 2016, took the Port Authority police by surprise, putting officers and the public at risk. In August 2016 a false report of gunfire at JFK's Terminal 8— probably triggered by waiting passengers clapping enthusiastically while viewing the Olympics on an overhead screen—prompted a multi-agency counter-terror response that evacuated two terminals and caused mass pandemonium.[50] Even though the risk of dying in a terrorist attack in the US remains infinitesimally small—one in four million under present conditions[51]—most Americans have become convinced that they or a family member could be next in line.

The fact that the US is now by far the largest military power on Earth reinforces American exceptionalism, the belief that we are a special and superior nation, with an ordained mission to save the world.[52] Yet that heady sense of confidence is hard to sustain when there are few real victories to celebrate in America's permanent war. Soldiers return, not to jubilation in the streets, but to long waits at VA hospitals and mounting casualties from suicide. A recent spate of nostalgic movies about World War II may have done well in the box office, but the bells of freedom and justice ring hollow. The martial music playing in the background instead sustains fears of future terrorist attacks. American exceptionalism has come to mean that the population must be rendered exceptionally afraid. If there were a fear thermometer, Americans would likely be the most feverish people on Earth.

A vicious cycle is in play. Blowback from the war on terror continually throws up new enemies to be vanquished, enemies with twisted apocalyptic ambitions of their own that in turn stoke our fears. Al Qaeda and other jihadi groups had virtually no presence in Iraq until Bush's war plunged the country into chaos, creating a power vacuum for extremists to fill. Today, even George W. Bush says his main regret about the war in Iraq is that it set the stage for the rise of ISIS, the so-called Islamic State.[53]

Pentagon officials describe ISIS as an organization with "an apocalyptic, end-of-days strategic vision."[54] Among the beliefs that ISIS propagates is the prophecy that the Day of Judgment will arrive after Muslims defeat Rome (now a stand-in for Western powers) at al-A'maq or Dabiq, two places near the Syrian border with Turkey.[55] The group's grisly beheadings of infidels and hostages give a medieval cast to its otherwise modern methods of warfare, including advanced weapons systems and the use of social media to recruit new adherents. An ISIS Twitter account, "End of Times Dreams," influenced an American who attacked a Muhammad cartoon contest in Garland, Texas in spring 2015. Social media are particularly well-suited to spreading apocalyptic ideas. Their fast pace compresses time and distance and communicates imminence, and they provide a virtual but intimate reality where people can experiment with transgressive world views.[56]

Domestically, permanent war encourages the tightening of borders and the further militarization of domestic law enforcement. Author Todd Miller describes how Customs and Border Patrol grew after 9/11 into the largest federal law enforcement agency in the country. Previously housed within the Department of Justice, in 2003 the Border Patrol moved into the new Department of Homeland Security, with an expanded mission to protect the country from terrorists and weapons of mass destruction. The $18 billion allocated to border and immigration enforcement in 2012 was more than the combined budgets of all other federal law enforcement agencies. The allocations have been a windfall for the manufacturers of weapons, surveillance technologies, and construction materials, creating a new phenomenon: the Border Security- Industrial Complex.[57]

The border has expanded even as it tightens, becoming an "elastic frontier" that stretches inwards and outwards.[58] The idea of a border *line*, epitomized by the fence between the US and Mexico, disguises the fact that the Border Patrol has extra-constitutional powers in wider border *zones* within 100 miles of our land or coastal boundaries. With the additional integration of local police into immigration enforcement and workplace raids, the security apparatus now extends across the length and breadth of the country.

In partisan Washington, this militarization has been a bipartisan affair. Even as he wooed Latino voters, Obama deported more immigrants than any previous president.[59] If Trump's dangerous rhetoric on immigration is put into practice, he will undo what small progress the Obama administration made on immigration reform—such as Deferred Action for Childhood Arrivals (DACA)—while further militarizing border enforcement and sanctioning mass deportations and rights violations, such as the Muslim ban he ordered only a week after his inauguration in January 2017.

These developments contribute to the further militarization of inner space, bringing the apocalyptic imagery of war to the no-longer-safe homeland. The physical distance shrinks between the embattled desert landscapes of the Middle East and those of southern Arizona. In both places, Predator B drones hover overhead, and checkpoints are manned by men with guns. No bombs have been dropped on Arizona yet, but the forest fires stoked by climate change lend hellish pyrotechnics to the scene. Meanwhile, on the northern edge of the country, post-industrial cities like Detroit and Buffalo come to represent post-apocalyptic wastelands in popular culture. In addition to the war on drugs in such cities, there are now surveillance operations and raids of immigrant communities.[60] These undermine the positive efforts of those communities to revive abandoned neighborhoods and rebuild local economies.

The arming of local police with surplus weapons from the war on terror adds another dimension to the militarization of the homeland. M16s, armored vehicles, night-vision goggles, surveillance aircraft—all may belong to a police department near you. In Ferguson, Missouri they were on display in 2014 against those who took to the streets to protest the police shooting of unarmed black teenager Michael Brown.

Of course, it's not only the state that perpetrates a culture of violence in America. The power of the National Rifle Association to block gun control, even bans on assault weapons, in the aftermath of mass shootings in schools, sparks moments of public outrage that quickly dissipate into despair when nothing really changes. Access to assault weapons turns the actions of homegrown, mentally unstable would-be terrorists from small-scale events into mass murders. Omar Mateen, who attacked the Pulse gay nightclub in Orlando in June 2016, killed 49 people and wounded 53 in the deadliest mass shooting in American history. Even that wasn't enough to overcome the power of the gun lobby. As despair breeds dystopia and dystopia breeds despair, a powerful undercurrent of anxiety is always there, ready to be tapped. What's next, if you can't even be sure your own kids are safe at school?

THE AMERICA SYNDROME

I name our apocalyptic bind "the America syndrome." The syndrome is so normalized that its abnormalities are scarcely recognized. Ideology and psychology have spawned a national pathology of global significance. Although its parts are closely intertwined and the whole is much more than the sum of its parts, one can identify core elements of the America syndrome. These elements don't define *all* of American history nor do we *all* share them. They're dominant traits, not universal ones. I call them the Seven Deadly Synergies:

1. American exceptionalism. The Puritans bequeathed to us the confidence and hubris that we are God's chosen people, called upon to save the world. America is at the center of the moral universe.

2. Belief in a coming apocalypse. Pessimistically, we are headed toward a violent end. Optimistically, a golden millennium awaits us. In either case, history is an unfolding prophecy, and time itself runs on a spiritual clock.

3. Susceptibility to sermonizing. Perfected by the Puritans, a powerful form of political sermon called the "jeremiad" continues to keep us trapped in the America syndrome. It castigates us for our sins and calls for repentance so that we may renew ourselves and fulfill the promise of America.

4. Expansion, occupation, and empire. This land is our land, not yours or theirs. To reach our God-given destiny, war is just and extreme violence justified. To ease moral qualms, we paint ourselves as victims, and the victims as perpetrators. We also see our enemies as racially, ethnically, and religiously inferior to the white Protestant ideal.

5. Exclusion, inequality, and duality. In order for the chosen people to be who they are, they must distinguish themselves from those who they're not. Those who don't conform don't belong, and should be punished or banished. Hierarchies are sanctified by the invisible hand of God as well as the invisible hand of the market. The world is sharply divided between good and evil, friend and foe.

6. Nature as fractured mirror. We project onto nature the tensions and contradictions of our providential mission. Nature is seen as a wilderness to be tamed, a continent to be conquered, an apocalypse over the horizon, and at the same time a sublime landscape where we can escape the wounds of civilization and lift ourselves toward heaven.

7. *Paranoia and anxiety.* Last but not least, we see enemies everywhere. They even lurk inside us in dark and distressing emotions. No matter how hard we try, we can never be pure enough or worthy of our special place in the divine design. In the marketplace where money is worshipped as the marker of status, we are beset with anxiety that we will never have enough of it.

When French political writer Alexis de Tocqueville visited America in the early 1830s, he was struck by how equality of opportunity had led to a feverish acquisitiveness that was never satisfied. No matter how much wealth people had, they wanted more than others had. He found Americans to be nervous, dour, overly hardworking and self-centered, locked up within themselves and unable to enjoy life as fully as their European counterparts. Despite living in a free and bountiful country, they were "serious and almost sad," looking "as if a cloud habitually hung upon their brow."[61] Would de Tocqueville find Americans much different today?

The symbiosis between this anxiety and being a member of God's chosen people—how can one ever measure up?—is a breeding ground for prejudice. When one's sense of internal order and self-control is under stress, as it so often is with sufferers of the America syndrome, there is a tendency to project bad things one feels or fears about oneself onto the Other. This is a classic feature of stereotyping.[62]

In a country that is often at war, internally and externally, the Other is not only an object of hatred and disgust, but an enemy to be feared: the dangerous Red man, Black man, alien immigrant, Muslim terrorist—enemies whose identities change with the times. Paranoia about the enemy covers up fears of our own inner darkness and unworthiness.

Together, these deadly synergies comprise the America syndrome.

As the American empire declines, its ugliest symptoms—flexing our military muscle, tightening up our borders, punishing those who can't measure up—become ever more apparent. In the words of the Italian political philosopher Antonio Gramsci, "The crisis consists precisely in the fact that the old is dying and the new cannot be born; in this interregnum a great variety of morbid symptoms appear."[63] Donald Trump's rise to power has drawn on and reinforced these deadly synergies and morbid symptoms in the body politic. His America First agenda, apocalyptic warnings about how terrorism could obliterate the US, demonization of Muslims and Mexicans, embrace of the white, male conservative Christian mission, Twitter sermonizing, and constant fomenting of fear and anxiety carry the America syndrome to its far-right extreme.

Understanding the America syndrome, where it comes from and what it does to us individually and collectively, is a political challenge of the highest order. In looking critically at it, however, we need to avoid the temptation to create a counter catalogue of equally simple-minded and self-righteous stereotypes, substituting "bad" for "good." Depicting the US as the belly of the beast, or the source of all evil, again situates America at the center of the universe. Whether impossibly good or bad, we are special. For the Chosen People, with the right class, gender, and skin color, being special is not only a privilege but a birthright. But among the Unchosen, too, there is sometimes an affectation or afflic-tion of specialness, especially when identity politics run amok. Righteousness is recast as exclusion and victimhood, a measure of virtue that still remains quintessentially American.

Even with strong cognitive defenses, it's hard to escape the emotional pull of the America syndrome. It's manipulated by politicians, invoked by the mass media, and stoked by jeremiads that make us alternately into sinners and saints.[64] What if Americans could come to understand that we're not so special after all? What if we could train our ears to hear echoes of the jeremiad in political rhetoric across the ideological spectrum, like a recurring phrase in a musical score? What if we could better understand our own history, with all its inanity and profanity, instead of skipping from one myth or parable to another?

Since the roots of the America syndrome lie in the Puritan settlement of New England, learning more about that legacy is a good place to start.

Chapter One

THE PURITANS: PRIDE AND PREJUDICES OF A CHOSEN PEOPLE

"Methinks I see the destiny of America embodied in the first Puritan who landed on those shores, just as the human race was represented by the first man."
—Alexis de Tocqueville, *Democracy in America*[65]

Like most children of my generation, and past and present ones too, I learned very little in school about the Pilgrims. Between their arrival and the American Revolution there was virtually a blank slate except for the usual stories—the fabled landing of the Mayflower at Plymouth Rock in 1620, the first Thanksgiving, and the community's propensity for godliness and hard work, as if the two were synonymous. Even in high school I hardly knew the difference between the original Mayflower Pilgrims and the Great Migration of Puritans to the Massachusetts Bay Colony that began a decade later.

In college I made the common error of confusing Puritanism with Victorianism. My cartoonish image of Puritans was of little men dressed in black with funny hats and even grimmer women in high collar dresses and frumpy white bonnets. I blamed them for much that was uptight and repressed in American culture. Little did I know that richer members of the community wore colorful and fashionable clothes. Or that the Puritans were very much into sex. Within marriage both men and women were entitled to sexual pleasure, and in some colonies male impotence was legal ground for divorce. Some historians argue that women were better off as Puritans than later on.[66]

These false impressions of the Puritans aren't for lack of historical evidence to the contrary. Puritan luminaries kept diaries and wrote histories, like William Bradford's journal *Of Plymouth Plantation* and the later epic penned by Cotton Mather, *Magnalia Christi Americana*, published in 1702. Local records of land transactions and judicial proceedings also shed interesting light on the period. One of my ancestors came over on the Mayflower, a young man named George Soule who was a servant to senior Pilgrim leader Edward Winslow and probably the teacher of his children. George later became a free man and was given land in Duxbury, north of Plymouth, in the 1630s. Family lore has it that George was an exemplary man with an exemplary family, but in writing this book, I discovered local records reveal a more complicated picture. George's son Nathaniel was whipped for "lying with an Indian woman" and was ordered "to pay ten bushels of Indian corn to the said woman towards the keeping of her child." His daughter Elizabeth was punished twice for committing fornication.[67]

That the Puritans were men and women on a religious mission is widely known, but what exactly was that mission and how does it continue to affect us today? Puritanism evolved in the context of the Protestant Reformation that roiled Europe from the early 16th into the 17th century. The Reformation was inspired by theologians like the German Martin Luther and the Frenchman John Calvin who attacked Catholic religious doctrine and the Vatican's worldly power. In England the Reformation led to a long period of social and political upheaval. The Church of England's first break from Rome came when the Pope refused to annul Henry VIII's marriage to Catherine of Aragon so that he could marry Protestant Anne Boleyn. But under the reign of Mary Tudor from 1553–58, the Church again accepted Papal authority. The next split came in the reign of Mary's successor, Queen Elizabeth, but the extent to which the Church was truly reformed remained a bone of contention. The Puritan movement rose to resist continuing Catholic influences in the Church. The Puritans opposed the special vestments and privileges of the Anglican clergy, looked down on their rituals and rites, and rejected manmade images of God and Christ.

For the Puritans, God's relationship with man was marked by two covenants, the Covenant of Works and the Covenant of Grace. In the first, God promised eternal happiness to Adam and Eve if they submitted absolutely to his will. When they broke that covenant, man became guilty of original sin. After the Fall, individual salvation was only possible through the Covenant of Grace by which God redeemed the faithful elect.[68]

At the core of Puritan theology was a profoundly troubling quandary. Drawing on Calvin's doctrine of predestination, the Puritans believed that God determined before you were born whether you were going to be saved or not, but you wouldn't know for sure until you passed into the afterlife. In other words, you might do everything in your power to live as a member of the elect, but would you die as one? Would all your good works be good enough to win a place in heaven? Even the most devout Puritans were plagued with self-doubt, guilt, and anxiety—future hallmarks of the America syndrome.[69] No rosaries or confessionals for them, no discount passes through the gates of paradise. "Seldom has there been a spiritual discipline where so much effort was put into recognizing the worthlessness of one's own efforts," observes historian George Marsden.[70]

The religion drew converts, however, thanks in part to the way its messages were spread. Better educated than many Anglican clergy, and less bound to dry dogma, many Puritan ministers were skillful sermonizers who used the pulpit as a public stage. Whether they employed a plain, logical style of preaching, applying lessons from the Bible to the lives of the congregants, or a more flamboyant, evangelical style, they knew how to reach people. The pulpit also served as a major means of communicating news and providing moral and practical guidance.[71] The Puritans carried this narrative mastery to the New World, where their words would flourish in fresh soil.

The English Puritans split between those who believed it was possible to reform the Anglican Church and those who didn't. The latter, known as the Separatists, broke off all relations not only with the Anglicans but other Protestant denominations as well. Their isolationism led to persecution, and many went into exile in the Netherlands. While they were allowed to practice their religion there, local trade guilds were closed to them. Frustrated by their lack of economic mobility, and wanting to live as Englishmen, a Puritan congregation in the city of Leiden resolved to find greener pastures. After securing financing from London merchant adventurers, 35 members of the Leiden congregation, along with assorted relatives, friends, and non-Separatists with desirable skills, set off for the "New World" on the Mayflower in early September 1620.[72]

So it was that the first Pilgrims to cross the sea to settle in

Massachusetts were members of a small extremist sect driven from Europe because of their own intolerance. Hardly standard bearers of religious freedom, they were more like a utopian community wanting to live apart by its own set of rules. While the Pilgrims loom large in the public imagination—tourists flock to Plymouth Rock and the Mayflower replica and to nearby Plimoth Plantation where actors and actresses with Old English accents skillfully play their parts—the Great Migration to Massachusetts Bay began in earnest only a decade later, in rather different circumstances.

GOD, THE DEVIL, AND THE DEEP BLUE SEA

In many ways, the story of American apocalypse begins with the sense of impending doom in 1620s England. It was a decade of plague, bad harvests, economic troubles, and escalating religious tensions. In 1625 the accession to the throne of Charles I and his French Catholic queen threatened to lead to a Catholic revival, while in continental Europe the bloody Thirty Years' War pitted Protestants and Catholics against each other. Under Charles, even the non-Separatist Puritans began to suffer greater persecution, including threats of imprisonment. The impetus to leave England intensified.

That push—along with the pull of the New World—was often cast in the language of the Book of Revelation. Not only Puritans but many of their contemporaries believed that England had a special role in God's providential design. Its reformed church would help light the way to the new millennium after the "Beast of Catholicism" and the "forces of the Antichrist" were finally defeated. As that possibility came to seem more remote, hopes turned to the New World. While the Puritans still expected the millennium to arrive someday in England, they wanted to prove by their own example that on the shores of New England another world was possible.[73] After securing funding and a royal charter from the newly created Massachusetts Bay Company, wealthy lawyer John Winthrop and other Puritan associates set off across the Atlantic in 1630 on the ship Arbella. In the words of eminent historian Perry Miller,

> [t]he Bay Company was not a battered remnant of suffering Separatists thrown up on a rocky shore; it was an organized task force of Christians, executing a flank attack on the corruptions of Christendom. These Puritans did not flee to America; they went in order to work out that complete reformation which was not yet accomplished in England and Europe, but which would quickly be accomplished if only the saints back there had a working model to guide them.[74]

Aboard the Arbella, Winthrop delivered his famous sermon, "A Modell of Christian Charity," in which he reflected on the rules and values that should guide the new colony. While exhorting his fellow passengers to form a strong community of believers who would aid and support each other, he made it clear from his opening sentence that not all people were created equal. God almighty in his infinite wisdom had made the condition of mankind such that "in all times some must be rich, some poore, some highe and eminent in power and dignitie; others meane and in subjeccion." Winthrop set very high stakes for the mission's success. Joined in a special covenant with God, this new plantation in New England would be like "a citty upon a hill, the eies of all people are uppon us." If the Puritans breached the covenant, through "carnall intencions" or seeking worldly greatness for themselves and their posterity, God would surely visit his wrath upon them. They wouldn't be the only ones to suffer his revenge; their fall would "be made a story and a by-word through the world," which God's enemies would use to "speake evil" about His ways. The Puritans' sins would "shame the faces of many of God's worthy servants," whose prayers would turn to curses against them.[75]

In Winthrop's sermon we see some of the earliest roots of the America syndrome: a notion of community rightfully divided between rich and poor, yet bound together through a covenant with God; ambiguity about worldly success, as the accumulation of wealth and power is part of God's design but also can be sinful and self-serving; and above all, the vision of "the city on the hill." The failure to climb those lofty heights would bring punishment not only to the Puritans themselves but to Christians everywhere. This peculiar hubris—we're so important that our sins have tragic consequences for the entire world—instills, along with a fear of God, an overblown sense of self.

Prior to departure, Winthrop voiced another key element in the America syndrome: the belief that divine mission justifies Occupation. Land the Puritans wanted, and land they would get. Providentially, Winthrop wrote, God had already "consumed the natives with a miraculous plague whereby the greater part of the country is left void of inhabitants." Once in the New World, he wrote back to his wife in England that with smallpox "God hathe hereby cleared our title to this place."[76] The depopulation was real. Historians now estimate that a viral hepatitis epidemic, starting in 1616 through European contact, killed up to 90 percent of the Native population in coastal New England, and that 17 years later a smallpox epidemic claimed the lives of between one-third and one-half of those who remained.[77] Winthrop read these tragedies as opportunity. Other Puritans professed more sympathy, believing that they could help the poor Indians at the same time as they colonized their land. The first seal of the Massachusetts Bay Colony features a noble savage with a bow in one hand, an arrow pointed down in the other, with the caption "Come over and help us."[78]

Come over they did. In the 1630s some 21,000 people made the journey from England to New England, many of them motivated at least in part by religious fervor.[79] While the area around Boston was the epicenter of the Great Migration, the immigrants soon spread outwards, forming the sister colonies of Connecticut and New Haven. While governance differed from colony to colony, the Puritans knit church and state tightly together. In Massachusetts and New Haven, only church members had the right to vote; Connecticut gave the franchise to non-church members who took an oath of loyalty. Becoming a member of the church wasn't an easy feat—joining the community of visible saints required proof of personal conversion and sufficient piety. Members and non-members alike were expected to attend religious services.

The purpose of elections for local officials was to build consensus rather than to build democracy. Members of the Puritan aristocracy were returned again and again to public office. The accepted hierarchy between rich and poor was mirrored by that between the rulers and the ruled. While the Puritans established some important divisions between church and state, giving civil institutions authority over secular matters, for example, in practice the boundaries were porous.[80]

Exclusion lay in store for those who dared to challenge the basic precepts of this theocracy. In 1636 the dissident Roger Williams, who had the audacity to argue that the Indians, not the Puritans, owned the land, and who believed in a bright line between civil and religious authority, was banished to what would become the liberal colony of Rhode Island. Several years later, charismatic religious thinker Anne Hutchinson met a similar fate. Theologically sophisticated, Hutchinson reinterpreted the Covenant of Grace in a way that made individual salvation possible through direct revelation and an immediate relationship with God.

At first Hutchinson enjoyed good standing in the Boston community—she was a skilled midwife, married to a prosperous merchant. But as she expounded her ideas, first in small gatherings of women, and later at larger religious meetings, she encountered increasing hostility from the Puritan hierarchy. They resented not only her religious ideas, but also her power to mobilize other women. To add insult to injury, she had male supporters, too. "You have stept out of your place, you have rather bine a Husband than a Wife and a preacher than a Hearer; and a Magistrate than a Subject," charged Reverend Hugh Peter at her church trial. She was called an "American Jesabel."[81] Like Williams, she was banished with a small group of supporters to Rhode Island. Presaging the coming witch craze, Hutchinson's heresies were blamed for the births of deformed fetuses, including one of her own.[82]

More secular developments also rattled the orthodoxy. Relations with the Indians involved a complicated game of playing one tribe against another. When diplomacy, trading, bribery, and swindling didn't work, violence was the response. In 1636 war broke out between the colonists and the Pequot tribe of eastern Connecticut. The Pequot War—which Winthrop termed a "just war"—is best remembered for the massacre of hundreds of Pequot men, women, and children by English soldiers and allied warriors from the Narragansett tribe near Mystic, Connecticut. Survivors were sold into slavery, with some shipped as far away as Bermuda.[83] Across the ocean in England, the Civil War would soon break out, ushering in the intense military conflicts of the 1640s.

The death of original leaders, such as John Winthrop in 1649, marked the end of the first Great Migration era. The clergy worried that the sense of religious mission that inspired the first settlers was dying out. Church membership was declining as the pursuit of economic growth and territorial expansion increasingly drove the colonial enterprise and other Protestant denominations entered New England. In response, many Puritan churches began to adopt the Half-Way Covenant which allowed the children of any baptized individual to be baptized whether or not either of their parents had been admitted to full communion in the congregation. While there was much controversy over the measure, it ultimately gained sway.[84] On its own, however, it wasn't enough to alleviate the pervasive sense of insecurity.

Many of the occupants of the city on the hill started to develop a stronger fortress mentality, markedly bleak and apocalyptic. The Book of Revelation's forecast of bloody wars, disasters, and persecutions seized the public imagination.[85] Presaging the market success of modern-day apocalyptic bestsellers like the *Left Behind* series, the epic poem *The Day of Doom*, written by Harvard-educated minister Michael Wigglesworth in 1662, attracted a huge readership. Literary demerits notwithstanding, it was the best-selling book in the colonies for almost a century until it was surpassed by Benjamin Franklin's *Way to Wealth*, a collection of corny aphorisms about the benefits of frugality and hard work.

In *The Day of Doom*, sinners awake to all manner of natural disasters: "The Mountains smoak, the Hills are shook, the Earth is rent and torn . . ." Judgment Day awaits them:

> With dismal chains, and strongest reins,
>   like Prisoners of Hell,
> They're held in place before Christ's face,
>   till He their Doom shall tell.
> These void of tears, but fill'd with fears,
>   and dreadful expectation
> Of endless pains, and scalding flames,
>   stand waiting for Damnation.[86]

Generations of Puritan schoolchildren were made to recite *The Day of Doom*, perhaps as a way to scare them into compliance with authority. In the poem, wicked ("flagitious") children suffer the endless pains and scalding flames along with their parents.

Far more eloquent than *The Day of Doom* were the jeremiads delivered over this period by some of the great Puritan masters of the form. They laid the foundation of a literary and political tradition that is central to the America syndrome. The term "jeremiad" is derived from the Old Testament prophet Jeremiah, who chastised the Jews in exile for their sins, exhorting them to repent. Despite the errors of their ways, Jeremiah held firm in his belief that the House of Israel had a special covenant with God, that the Jews were His chosen people, and that their exile from Jerusalem and captivity in Babylon would ultimately end in a second paradise.

Over the centuries Jeremiah's verses proved ripe for contemporary reinterpretation in parables of exile, suffering, sin, and redemption. Before the Puritans, Christian preachers in Europe typically used the jeremiad to warn their audiences of the dire straits in store if they didn't repent and prepare themselves for the next world. On American shores, the jeremiad evolved beyond religious rhetoric to become, in the words of historian Sacvan Bercovitch, "a fusion of social and literary traditions that opened into an interactive network of art, economy, value system, and public ritual."[87]

The typical structure of the Puritan jeremiad began with a Biblical story that elaborated the proper norms, followed by condemnations of the community for not living up to them. It ended on a higher note with a prophetic vision of all the good things to come, as the community *could* redeem itself because of its special covenant with God. The stick of guilt and fear was combined with the carrot of future righteousness and its rewards. Ultimately, the jeremiad offered an upbeat view of history, albeit history that would come to an end in Christ's Second Coming.[88]

One of the most famous Puritan jeremiads was the Reverend Samuel Danforth's 1670 election-day sermon, *A Brief Recognition of New-Englands Errand into the Wilderness*. The "errand" referred at once to the Great Migration from a corrupted Europe to the purity of the American wilderness, the individual pilgrimage from sinner to saint, and the larger Christian passage from Old Testament to New, from Incarnation to Christ's Second Coming. "We have . . . in great measure forgotten our errand," Danforth chastised his audience, comparing their behavior to the folly of the Israelites. But there is hope, because in the end God will deliver: "the great Physician of Israel hath undertaken the cure . . . he will provide . . . we have the promise."[89]

The fact that Danforth delivered this sermon on an election day is no coincidence. The Puritans themselves called jeremiads "political sermons." They were typically occasional sermons, sanctioned by civil authorities, delivered in the course of major public events. Not only did jeremiads reinforce the close bonds between church and state, but they exercised a near monopoly on the shaping of public opinion. Civil magistrates carefully selected the men who would deliver them; afterwards, by order of the General Court, the sermons were published and distributed. Not so dissimilar to the role of mainstream media today, jeremiads contributed to a ritualized political consensus forged by the colony's ruling elite.[90]

Indeed, one of the most important legacies of the Puritans was the transformation of the sermon into a dominant cultural currency. Of the 39,000 known works published in America prior to 1800, sermons were the largest single category, a trend that continued up to the end of the 19th century. "For much of American history, delivering sermons, listening to them, and discussing them were the principal intellectual activities for most people," writes historian Edmund S. Morgan.[91] This receptivity to sermonizing remains a core element of the America syndrome, blurring the boundary between religious and secular domains.

Increase Mather's *The Day of Trouble is Near*, delivered in Boston in 1674, reiterated the jeremiad's classic themes. In the sermon, Mather, one of the era's most powerful clerics, chastised both parents and children for turning away from their religious mission toward the pursuit of worldly gains. But all would be set right when "the children of God *learn* to know more of God, and of themselves too" through the tribulations soon to visit them. "The Lord hath been whetting his glittering sword a long time [over New England]. The sky looketh red and lowring," Mather warned. Because the Puritans, like the Israelites, were God's chosen nation, they would survive the coming crucible. After all, in these "Ends of the Earth" the Lord "hath caused as it were a *New Jerusalem* to come down from Heaven." While God would willingly destroy other wicked nations on Earth, Mather confidently predicted that "God is not willing to destroy us."[92] Mather's sermon proved eerily prescient, for Trouble was indeed near.

THE DIVINE PROVIDENCE OF VIOLENCE

King Philip's War—a bloody conflict that scarcely gets a mention in today's history books—began in 1675, a year after Mather's jeremiad. Philip, whose non-English name was Metacom, was chief of the Wampanoag tribe. In the decades after the Pequot War, the colonists' territorial expansion and appropriation of tribal lands by dubious means had seeded deep hatred among many Native Americans. Struggling to maintain their hold in New England, Philip and his allies began to prepare for war.

King Philip's War was not a minor war. In per capita terms, it took more lives than any other war in American history. One-tenth of the Massachusetts Bay Colony's 5,000 draft-age males were killed, wounded, or captured. The proportion was likely higher among Native Americans. Both sides waged a war of terror against civilians, slaughtering women and children. Half of all the white settlements in New England were burned to the ground; the reach of English settlement in Massachusetts shrank to within 17 miles of Boston. Maine was entirely cleared of white people. To the beleaguered colonists, every Indian was suspect. Christianized Indians were confined to isolated prison camps such as Deer Island off the coast of Boston, where half the prisoners died during the winter from cold, starvation, and disease.

Though it persisted to the north, the war drew to an end in southern New England with the killing of King Philip in August 1676. His corpse was dismembered and his body parts dispersed as trophies. To help pay the costs of war, the colonists sold captured Indians into slavery. That summer, 180 Indians were shipped from Boston to the plantations of the West Indies.[93]

While the violence and carnage of the war were deeply traumatizing, the religious interpretation placed upon it helped the colonists make a certain sense out of the senselessness. Harkening back to Mather, the colonists had learned to know more of God and themselves through this terrible trial. During the war, Puritan clergy held covenant renewal ceremonies calling on colonists to rededicate themselves to the community and to God through prayer.[94]

King Philip's War marked a watershed in the evolution of the America syndrome. The insertion of that bloodletting into the jeremiad's providential framework gave meaning and purpose to war, a logic that still impacts the national psyche today. War is God's will, and while its depredations punish us, they also cleanse; they're necessary for the spiritual purging and revitalization of the Chosen People. God condones the use of extreme violence if it serves divine ends.

With much of the script drawn from the biblical exodus of the Jews, the jeremiad speaks to a community, that, while existing in a special covenant with God, is fragile, persecuted, and unsettled—a community that needs protection from its enemies. Those enemies, in turn, are sent by God to test the community's mettle. In the exodus parable, the community is defined by the existence of enemies. Who are we without the Other?

For the Puritans, the Indians proved the perfect enemy in a number of respects. "New Englanders commonly regarded Indians not simply as a military enemy, but as the agent of divine violence, the instrument by which God punished their sins and urged them back toward righteousness," wrote scholars Andrew Murphy and Elizabeth Hanson. This wasn't an arbitrary choice on God's part, for "a crucial feature of New England's punishment was that it was enacted by the people they had promised to convert, but had in fact led further into sin."[95]

Initially, the Puritans had high hopes of converting the Indians, viewing them as distant kin, members of the Ten Lost Tribes of Israel. But as relations with the natives grew tense, they turned to another biblical parable, the story of the Amalekites who attacked the Jews during their exodus from Egypt. After the Jews ultimately prevailed, God commanded King Saul to finish off the Amalekites. "Now go and attack Amalek," God instructed, "and utterly destroy all that they have, and do not spare them. But kill both man and woman, infant and nursing child, ox and sheep, camel and donkey." God's ultimate intention was to "blot out the remembrance of them."[96]

The Amakelite comparison not only helped fuel colonial atrocities against the Indians during King Philip's War, but also served as a license to genocide for years to come. In a 1689 discourse on "just war", Cotton Mather, Increase's equally prominent son, called for vengeance against the Amakelite Indian murderers "annoying this Israel in the Wilderness." He exhorted, "Tho' they Cry; Let there be none to Save them; But beat them small as the Dust before the Wind."[97] During the settlement of the Western frontier, the same trope was dusted off to justify extermination of the Indians. It was used to rationalize violence against Catholics and Mormons, too.

In the aftermath of King Philip's War, Cotton Mather and a number of his clerical contemporaries grew more explicitly apocalyptic, even to the extent of speculating on the precise date of Christ's return. In his epic *Magnalia Christi Americana*, Mather lauded the Puritans' errand into the New England wilderness as the last conflict with the anti-Christ and the harbinger of the impending millennium. In an early sermon, he set the most likely date at 1697.[98]

The powerful ideological force field in which exodus, apocalypse, and war came together cast political violence as prophetic.

Though they were the most numerous, Indians weren't the Puritans' only enemy. Members of dissenting religious sects faced violent persecution, too. Six Quakers were hanged in Massachusetts, and Catholic priests were threatened with execution. And then there were the enemies within the Puritan community itself—the wicked witches.

WONDERS OF THE INVISIBLE WORLD

Most Americans have heard about the Salem witch trials. The Massachusetts city's witch kitsch makes it a major attraction, pulling in 100 million tourist dollars each year. Salem has multiple witch museums—one boasts a dungeon for the full grisly experience, and a month of Haunted Happenings in October culminates in the Salem Witches' Halloween Ball. The aim is to make witches titillating and fun, and to encourage visitors to take home a sack full of tacky souvenirs. In this rite of tourist consumption, historical memory is not served well.

The first documented hanging of a witch in New England occurred in Windsor, Connecticut in 1647. In the 1650s the number of prosecutions for witchcraft rose, with thirty-five people accused and seven executed. Witch panic spread, reaching its height at the beginning of the 1690s in Salem. By 1692 the Salem courts had put twenty people to death for witchcraft, based mainly on the allegations of hysterical young girls. Nineteen of the twenty were hanged, the other, a brave man named Giles Corey, was pressed to death with heavy stones because he refused to stand for trial. Another 156 were imprisoned, four of whom died in jail.

The tradition of witch persecution was imported from Europe, where between 50,000 and 100,000 victims were executed over the period 1580–1650. As in New England, most were women.

"Witchcraft embodies, in each and every one of its otherwise disparate settings, a basic impulse of misogyny," writes historian John Demos, "a fear, and a hatred, of women so generalized that it crosses all boundaries."[99] This fear and hatred typically centered on women's sexuality, fertility, and healing powers, and combined with distrust of anyone considered deviant from community norms. In New England the majority of women accused of witch-craft were poor and middle-aged. Many came from troubled families and were barren or only had a few children. They were contentious and strong-willed in a society that viewed such traits as a source of unwanted "controversy."

While these characteristics help to explain why certain women were targeted, they don't shed light on the larger social context that fostered witch hunts in the first place. Hysteria needs fertile ground to take root and spread. In the case of Salem, historians have long debated the underlying causes of the panic. From a careful reading of public records, historian Mary Beth Norton concluded that fear of Indian violence played a major role. Many people involved in the trials had once lived on or had family con-nections to the Maine frontier where both sides, colonists and Indians, continued to fight a brutal war of terror against each other. The printed portrayals of witches and Indians were much the same in their Satanic imagery. Others have argued that economic ten-sions between town and country sparked the factionalism that led to neighbor accusing neighbor of hideous crimes.[100] And in the 1970s a biologist even argued that the accusers' hysterical halluci-nations were caused by a poisonous fungus found in cereal grains.

Whatever the constellation of causes, without the collusion of the Puritan establishment it's doubtful that so many innocent people would have been persecuted in Salem. Bypassing normal judicial procedures, the governor of the Massachusetts Bay Colony set up a special court to hear the cases, to which he appointed prominent political and military leaders as judges. Guilty until proven innocent was the rule, and by accepting supernatural "evidence," the judges left no way for the accused to prove their innocence. Only when members of the elite themselves started to be accused of witchcraft would the authorities bring the panic to a close.

As with King Philip's War, the witch hunts were made to conform to the Puritans' apocalyptic philosophy. Panic merged with prophecy. The master of the jeremiad, Cotton Mather, turned his attention to the witch hunts. He brought afflicted young girls into his house to exorcise their demons personally. In one case, a local cloth merchant critically reported, Mather rubbed a girl's stomach while she lay in bed with her breasts uncovered.[101] Psycho-sexual innuendoes aside, Mather threw considerable intellectual and professional weight behind the witch trials. On one notable occasion, he showed up on horseback at Salem's Gallows Hill for the hanging of a Reverend Burroughs, a clergyman accused of being the ringleader of the witches. From the hanging platform, Burroughs gave an eloquent speech professing his innocence and generously forgiving his accusers. His words so moved the assembled crowd that some called for a halt to the execution. But Mather would have nothing of it. From atop his horse, he denounced Burroughs as guilty, arguing "that the Devil had often been transformed into an angel of light." Burroughs was then hanged, and his body was stuffed into a hole in the rocks.[102]

Mather also devoted pen and paper to the matter. New England was so tormented by witches, he wrote, precisely because it was so pious. "Where will the Devil show the most malice but where he is hated, and hateth most?" Obsessed as he was with the coming apocalypse, Mather viewed the Devil's sorcery as one part of the larger suite of calamities converging in the end times. His major work on witchcraft, *The Wonders of the Invisible World*, published in 1693, set out "to countermine the whole plot of the Devil against New England, in every branch of it."[103] At a time when others had begun to ask questions, the book was an extended defense of the trials.

Only later did Mather acknowledge that innocent people had been harmed in Salem and that their survivors might deserve some reparation. Yet he never apologized for his own role in the tragedy. Keeping faith with the jeremiad, he saw the witch craze as another divine test, "an inextricable storm from the invisible world."[104] The errors of the official response could be explained away as part of—not the cause of—that affliction. It was the "invisible world," not the visible world of human agency, which was ultimately responsible for the grave miscarriage of justice. And so the perpetrators were assuaged of guilt, another core feature of the America syndrome.

No one was held accountable for the violence of slavery in New England either. To this day, many Americans don't know that in 1641 Puritan Massachusetts became the first colony to officially endorse the ownership and sale of human beings as property. Governor John Winthrop put his pen to that law, ironically called "The Massachusetts Body of Liberties." He himself owned slaves who worked on his large Ten Hills Farm on the outskirts of Boston, on the grounds of what is now Tufts University. In her study of the forgotten history of slavery in New England, C.S. Manegold reveals that successive generations of the Winthrop family, as well as that of the Royalls (whose money helped build Harvard Law School), made fortunes in the slave trade.

By the end of the 1600s, more than 1200 Native Americans and 200–400 Africans had been enslaved in New England. In 1765, the Massachusetts census showed almost 6000 black slaves. While slaves probably never composed more than 3 percent of New England's population, captive labor sustained the livelihoods and lifestyles of the colonies' better-off inhabitants. The involvement of many of New England's respected merchants in the Atlantic slave trade, particularly their direct links to the slave economies of the West Indies, was vital to the colony's economic growth.[105] Puritan New England may have seen itself as a place apart in religious terms, but in economic terms it was well integrated into America's burgeoning "peculiar institution."

While the clergy interpreted the Indian wars as a spiritual test, the slave bounty they yielded was a more mundane source of labor and cash. The violence of slavery was considered so normal, so acceptable, that it didn't need much in the way of religious justification or jeremiad-style hyperbole. The same was true for the enslaved Africans. This moral invisibility of slavery was fundamental to the functioning of the Puritans' economy and society.

That history is still largely invisible. Even today, prominent politicians invoke Winthrop's speech on the Arbella, "A Modell of Christian Charity," to paint the Puritan errand as a beacon of light and of liberty.[106] That men, women, and children were shackled to the gates of the shining city on the hill is excised from New England mythology. What gets left out of a story can be as important as what gets put in.

GREAT AWAKENINGS

While violence was endemic, the apocalyptic fervor that sustained the Puritan mission wasn't nourished by blood alone. The continued power of apocalyptic thinking in the American imagination owes much to preacher and theologian Jonathan Edwards, who lived from 1703 to 1758. In the words of historian Perry Miller, Edwards was America's "greatest artist of the apocalypse,"[107] a man of extraordinary talent and passion who wed stern Calvinist theology with wide-ranging interests in philosophy and science. He had a deep and almost mystical love of nature. Edwards believed in the imminence of apocalypse, but in nature he experienced the immanence of God's grace. He was a revivalist, breathing new life into the Puritan mission, helping to prepare his people for the next stages of nation-building.

Edwards navigated conformity and individualism in a new American way. He showed how the true believer could stay *on* mission while wandering *off* the beaten track to commune solo with God in the great American outdoors. Locating spirit in nature is a theme that would resonate with later generations of American thinkers, men like Ralph Waldo Emerson, Henry David Thoreau, and John Muir. Edwards was a great artist of the apocalypse because he gave it an ecstatic American aesthetic—a ravishing Beauty to counterpoint the ravages of the Beast.

The son of Reverend Timothy Edwards, Jonathan grew up in the Connecticut River Valley town of Windsor, with an impeccable Puritan ancestry and upbringing. He entered Yale College just before his thirteenth birthday. After serving several years as a pastor in New York, he moved further up the Connecticut River to Northampton, Massachusetts to assist his maternal grandfather, the Reverend Solomon Stoddard. When Stoddard died in 1729, Edwards assumed his job as pastor of one of the largest churches in western Massachusetts. He and his wife Sarah had 11 children; one of their grandsons, Aaron Burr, would become third Vice President of the US. So distinguished was the Edwards' lineage that it was held up as a shining example of inherited character and intelligence in early 1900s American eugenics circles.[108]

Edwards was a prodigious writer. He was also an eccentric. On long horseback rides into the western Massachusetts countryside, he pinned scraps of paper to his clothing to record insights he had along the way. Sometimes by the end of a journey his clothes were covered with these scraps. On returning home, he used this memory patchwork to write down his thoughts.[109]

One of Edwards's earliest mystical experiences occurred when he was home from college on spring vacation and wandering in the fields. Looking up at the sky and clouds, God's immanence came over him: ". . . in a sweet conjunction; majesty and meekness joined together: it was a sweet and gentle, and holy majesty; and also a majestic meekness . . ." Years later he wrote in his spiritual autobiography that he saw God's grace "in the sun, moon, and stars; in the clouds, and blue sky; in the grass, flowers, trees; in the water, and all nature . . ." Sometimes he fell into hallucinatory raptures. Once, while walking in the woods, he had a glorious vision of Christ that lasted "about an hour; which kept me, the bigger part of the time, in a flood of tears, and weeping aloud." He experienced such "an ardency of soul" as to feel "emptied and annihilated; to lie in the dust, and to be full of Christ alone; to love him with a holy and pure love . . ."[110] Arguably, such raptures provided Edwards with momentary escape from the heavy weight of prophetic time. Indeed, the seductive appeal of apocalyptic thinking may depend, in part, on this entertainment of catharsis.

For Edwards, the brighter sides of nature inspired rapture, while its darker sides threatened rupture. Like others of his contemporaries, and many Americans today, he read destructive acts of nature as providential signs and apocalyptic portents. The large earthquake that shook New England in 1727 was interpreted this way. Nearing death, and after making many false predictions, Cotton Mather was convinced that the earthquake finally marked the apocalypse he had been anticipating. "This is it," he is said to have pronounced. "Everything is now fulfilled. This is the end."[111] Better versed in science, Edwards understood that earthquakes could have natural causes, but he saw this one as God's message to the young people of Northampton to mend their sinful and frolicking ways.[112]

During Edwards's lifetime, declining church membership pre-occupied the Puritans. The secular forces of economic growth they had helped set in motion pushed against the confines of rigid religious dogma and control. While Puritanism changed with the times—theologians now saw commercial profit as congruent with providential purpose[113]—the religion wasn't attracting enough new adherents. Measures such as the Half-Way Covenant hadn't brought about enough conversions, especially of younger people. Edwards's grandfather and mentor, Solomon Stoddard, argued for opening baptism and communion to all Christians attending the church who led pious lives. In 1710 he scandalized more conservative clergy by claiming that preaching of the Word could bring about conversion, as long as the minister delivering the message was saved himself.[114]

Edwards followed in his grandfather's footsteps. In 1734 his preaching inspired a major religious revival in Northampton, the beginning of what is called the Great Awakening. Men and women of all ages, genders, and social classes, and even "several Negroes" (Edwards's words—he was a slave owner himself) were born again. Virtually the whole town was swept up in the revival, and Edwards pronounced Northampton an iconic city on the hill. His sermons communicated the egalitarian message that "sweet and joyful" divine knowledge wasn't only the purview of learned men, but that people "of an ordinary degree of knowledge, are capable, without a long and subtle train of reasoning, to see the divine excellency of the things of religion . . ." All could gain spiritual wisdom "more excellent than all the knowledge of the greatest philosophers or statesmen."[115]

The mystical man in the woods, besotted with God's sweet glory, could also preach hellfire and brimstone along with the best of them. With his gift for rhetorical flourish, Edwards raised the jeremiad to new heights of emotional intensity, making him one of America's first great revivalist preachers. His most famous sermon, "Sinners in the Hands of an Angry God," repeatedly conjures terrifying visions of hell. Sinners hang by "a slender thread" above the "great furnace of wrath, a wide and bottomless pit," with the flames of hell flashing around them. In a passage that foreshadows the "humans as burden on the Earth" sermonizing of apocalyptic environmentalists today, Edwards thundered:

> Were it not that so is the sovereign pleasure of God, the Earth would not bear you one moment; for you are a burden to it; the creation groans with you; the creature is made subject to the bondage of your corruption, not willingly; the sun don't willingly shine upon you to give you light to serve sin and Satan; the Earth don't willingly yield her increase to satisfy your lusts; nor is it willingly a stage for your wickedness to be acted upon; the air don't willingly serve you for breath to maintain the flame of life in your vitals, while you spend your life in the service of God's enemies.

Toward the sermon's end, Edwards warned the assembled congregants that some of them might die and go to hell soon, even "before tomorrow morning."[116]

While Edwards democratized the conversion experience and infused it with passion and beauty, he raised the stakes when it came to backsliding. For the ordinary mortal to sustain an inspirational spiritual state wasn't easy. What happened when the catharsis was over and the inner light faded? Was one then damned to eternal hell? For many people prone to what was quaintly called melancholy back then, Edwards's admonishments only sank them deeper into anxiety and depression. It didn't help that he also preached that God's wrath toward wicked men could express itself in inner torment. On June 1, 1735, Edwards's own uncle, Joseph Hawley II, a successful merchant who suffered from mental illness, slit his throat. A rash of attempted suicides followed.[117] The bloom was off the Northampton revival rose.

Yet the rose flourished elsewhere. The Great Awakening was heralded as the harbinger of a new millennium. In 1740, British preacher George Whitefield drew crowds of more than 20,000 to revival meetings in New England. Edwards brought him to Northampton, and he was entertained at Harvard and Yale. Other popular preachers followed as the region was swept up in a new wave of religious fervor. At home, though, Edwards encountered growing opposition from the community as he sought to impose stricter terms of church membership and moral behavior. In 1750 he was relieved of his duties, and moved further west to Stockbridge, where he ministered to an English congregation and a Christianized village of Indians. In 1758 he became president of Princeton University (then called the "College of New Jersey").

Like Cotton Mather before him, in his last years Edwards grew ever more obsessed with charting the course of the coming apocalypse. He kept up with newspapers and jotted down current events—economic, political, and meteorological—that might have apocalyptic meaning. He divided Christian history into seven main periods, culminating in "the consummation at the end of the world . . ." Just before that end, he reasoned, wickedness would be at its greatest height.[118] Edwards and many of his Puritan contemporaries viewed the onset of the French and Indian War in 1754 as part of God's divine plan. As followers of the Puritans' favorite anti-Christ, the Pope, the Catholic French were a perfect enemy. After the English victory in Cape Breton Island, Nova Scotia, Edwards wrote to a Scottish correspondent that "the late wonderful works of God in America" were accelerating the fulfillment of God's plan.[119] Once again, through war, America's spiritual and imperial destinies were intertwined.

In 1902, by which time Calvinism was falling from favor, Mark Twain wrote of Edwards that he was "a resplendent intellect gone mad."[120] But was it really madness that made him teeter back and forth between the ecstasy of conversion and the crucible of hell? Although there may be madness in the apocalyptic method, that doesn't mean those who employ it are crazy. On the contrary, Edwards applied his considerable intelligence to adapting the Puritan mission to changing times. He pushed its walls outward but not down, and allowed more people to fit in. In that sense he was the first real genius of the America syndrome.

Through revivalist conversion, Sacvan Bercovitch writes, Edwards expanded the Puritan concept of a chosen people, opening "the ranks of the American army of Christ to every white Protestant believer . . . He rendered the legend of the founding fathers the common property of all New World evangelicals."[121] The Puritan errand grew to become the American Way. Edwards also forged a new faith in the future, making scientific advance and economic growth part and parcel of God's providential design for the coming millennium. As he blended the secular and the sacred, American commercial ingenuity became blessed indeed. His love of nature made room for beauty, too. Edwards updated the American apocalypse, preparing it for the next stage of the nation's history, the American Revolution, which he didn't live to see. One month after joining Princeton, he died from the side effects of a smallpox inoculation. But his ideas, and those of his Puritan contemporaries, have lived on.

So has their way of sermonizing. The jeremiad may have changed in content since Edwards, Danforth, and the other great Puritan preachers and politicians who employed it, but as a form of oratory, it never went out of date. President Barack Obama excelled at it. The jeremiad can be used for good or ill—Martin Luther King's mastery of the form helped to galvanize the civil rights movement in the 1960s—but even the best practitioners reinforce American exceptionalism, regardless of their political persuasion. "The prophetic narratives of sinfulness and redemption from the right and left share certain traits," writes scholar David Gutterman:

> Both begin with a sometimes unspoken presumption about the special status of the United States. Both look at a contemporary crisis and attempt to reveal the meaning of the crisis by looking backward in order to trace specific historical sins (or causes). Both then explain the crisis as a justified or at least unsurprising response to American sinfulness. Both warn of inevitable horrible future events—unless the United States changes its ways. And finally both offer the promise of a utopian redemption if America is able to overcome and atone for its sins.[122]

The jeremiad serves to contain and confine political dissent by making the solution to American ills nothing short of the fulfillment of the nation's promise.[123] If only we would live up to our ideals, all would be set right.

Chapter Two

UTOPIAN DREAMS, MILLENNIAL MADNESS

The US has experienced two great waves of utopian experimentation—from approximately 1820–1850 and 1960–1980. While the first was more explicitly religious in character, both waves combined a commitment to social reform with the quest for a perfect society, an exceptional American heaven on earth. The parallels between the two have a lot to teach us about the America syndrome.

The word "utopia" was first coined by Sir Thomas More in 1516 in his book by that name. One of Henry VIII's closest advisors, who rose to be Chancellor of England in 1529, More was beheaded six years later for opposing the Reformation. More derived the word utopia from the Greek prefix *ou*, meaning "no," and *topos*, meaning "place." Utopia was no place. He may have intended it as a pun, since *ou* also sounds like *eu*, meaning good. Utopia is thus the good place that is no place. Set on an island off the coast of the New World, More's utopia is a vision of highly regulated com-

munal life with an efficient balance between town and country
and a representative government. Its labor system also includes
slavery.

Utopian visions are powerful precisely because, being nowhere,
they aren't constrained by present reality but rather point the way
to a desirable future. "Utopia's 'nowhereness' incites the search
for it," writes scholar Krishan Kumar. "Utopia describes a state of
impossible perfection which nevertheless is in some genuine sense
not beyond the reach of humanity. It is here if not now."[124]

It is the promise of the millennium that joins utopia and apocalypse together. In the Book of Revelation, the millennium is the
thousand golden, peaceful, and prosperous years, a Heaven on
Earth, when Christ reigns before the final Judgment Day. Other
biblical passages also speak of Jesus's return to build a kingdom
on Earth.[125] Christians differ as to whether the Second Coming
ushers in the millennium or marks its conclusion ("premillennialism" vs. "postmillennialism") and whether Christ's epic battle
with the Antichrist will occur before or after the Second Coming.
Dispensational premillennialism, first prophesized by 19th-century
British theologian John Nelson Darby, preaches that the present
age (dispensation) will end in the Rapture, with the true believers
taking to the sky, and the sinners left on Earth to suffer miserably
through the seven year rule of the Antichrist. After that, Christ
and his raptured armies will return to Earth to battle the Anti-
christ and usher in the millennium.[126]

These differences in timing can have a profound impact on
one's world view. The belief that the dreadful battle will occur
before Christ returns can lead to the acceptance, or even wel-
coming, of current wars, plagues, and disasters as harbingers of
the Messiah's imminent arrival. By contrast, a more hopeful version of millennialism urges believers to prepare for Christ's rule

by creating a more just and equal society. This view helped stoke the fires of the American anti-slavery movement and other social reform movements in the 19th century.

Millennialism extends well beyond scripture, deeply affecting Western secular thought. The roots of modern ideas of progress reach back to the early 17th-century English revival of millennial theory. As the scientific revolution progressed, religious scholars began to frame a redemptive view of history congruent with both natural and biblical laws. The radically new concept of nature allowed for a more optimistic reading of the future human prospect. The universe was not irrevocably evil, but instead was the source of hidden wonders that would ultimately help, not hinder, human progress. The great earthquakes and other cataclysms that lay ahead would cleanse the Earth, preparing the ground, literally and figuratively, for the promised millennium. "The notion of history as a process generally moving upwards by a series of majestic stages, culminating *inevitably* in some great, transforming event which is to solve the dilemmas of society—that is the concept destined to dominate 'modern' thought," writes historian Ernest Tuveson.[127] Seventeenth-century apocalyptic theorists were in this sense the forbears of nineteenth-century progressive philosophers, whether of the Hegelian, Marxist, or positivist variety.

While the millennium provides the big picture, utopias fill out the smaller picture of what a heaven on Earth would look like. You can have one without the other (in the Book of Revelation, John offered very little in the way of a utopian blueprint for the New Jerusalem), but the millennium and utopia often exist in dynamic relationship with each other, sharing in particular an obsession with perfection.[128] The Puritans' conception of America as the city on the hill, as well as later versions of American exceptionalism, were deeply informed by millennial expectations of progress toward perfection—"manifest perfectionism."[129] Belief in the perfectibility of mankind is in turn the foundation upon which utopias are constructed, and along with it a yearning for physical and ideological purity, efficiency, and order.

Utopias enshrine perfection into the quest for a better world. But as the old saying goes, the perfect can be the enemy of the good, as evidenced in many utopian experiments and movements gone awry. Does that mean the search for utopia has no value? Utopian thinkers from Thomas More onwards have challenged us to think beyond the status quo and imagine new forms of living and relations between individual and community, man and woman, rich and poor, town and country, humanity and nature. "A map of the world that does not include Utopia is not worth even glancing at," wrote Oscar Wilde, "for it leaves out the country at which Humanity is always landing. And when Humanity lands there, it looks out, and seeing a better country, sets sail. Progress is the realization of Utopias."[130]

The New World held a powerful allure for utopian thinkers and practitioners. The (fictive) narrator, Raphael Hythloday, of More's utopia accompanies the (real) Italian mariner Amerigo Vespucci on his exploration of the New World at the turn of the 15th century. Vespucci, not Columbus, was the first European explorer to realize he had encountered a new continent, and "America" is derived from the Latin version of his first name. Hythloday stays on and happens upon the island of Utopia after Vespucci returns to Europe. More's tale may draw on Vespucci's accounts of the communal customs of the Natives he encountered, but in the end the utopian appeal of the New World wasn't so much its original inhabitants as their land, taken by the Europeans through disease, depopulation, and dispossession.[131]

A century after More's book, a small band of Pilgrims landed in

Plymouth, Massachusetts, searching for a place to create a closed, religious community in the service of an apocalyptic vision. This became a recurrent theme in the settlement of colonial America as other Christian sects sought the freedom and empty land to realize their ideal societies, under God's guiding hand. William Penn encouraged millennial sects from northern Europe to immigrate to Pennsylvania.[132] Many of these newcomers practiced communal ownership of property. In the case of the Plymouth Pilgrims, who did so for their first three years, that arrangement was necessary for survival. Other sects were driven by their desire to recreate the faith and lifestyle of early Christian communities, inspired by the biblical passage from Acts 2:44–45: "And all who believed were together and had all things in common; and they sold their possessions and goods and distributed them to all, as any had need."[133]

Thus from the very start utopia, apocalypse, millennialism, and communalism were intertwined in the search for heaven on Earth in colonial America. In 1774, on the eve of the American Revolution, the founding members of the United Society of Believers in Christ's Second Appearing set sail from Liverpool, bound for New York. Better known as the Shakers, they would become America's longest-lasting utopian sect.

'TIS THE GIFT TO BE SIMPLE, 'TIS THE GIFT TO BE FREE

Today there are only three remaining Shakers left who live in a community in Maine. But over the group's 200-plus year history, an estimated 20,000 Americans kept the faith. Shaker Villages, now museums, can be found from New England to Ohio to Kentucky. One is located in the western Massachusetts town of

Hancock. Its impressive site, showcasing the Shakers' considerable talent for architecture and design, includes a massive, three-floor Round Stone Barn.

The barn is a model of efficiency. On its top level, wagons delivered hay. They dropped their loads into the central haymow on the ground floor and then circled to exit from the same door they entered, eliminating the need to back awkwardly out of the barn. Dairy cows were housed on the ground floor, facing toward the hay to make it easy to feed them. Their manure was shoveled through trapdoors to the cellar where it was stored for use as fertilizer. The barn's stonework, cupola, and Shaker windows make it a work of striking beauty.[134]

Today, to make ends meet, the Hancock Shaker Village, like many museums, rents its facilities to wedding parties. Its website features a photo of a bride and groom kissing with the barn in the background. Since abstinence was one of the Shakers' central tenets, this image would probably be enough to make their founder, Mother Ann Lee, roll over in her grave.

Mother Ann Lee was a rarity: one of the few women to lead a utopian religious movement in the United States. Born into a poor family in Manchester, England in 1736, she broke with the Anglican Church at a young age to join a sect that was scornfully called the "Shaking Quakers" for their unusual mode of worship, which included speaking in tongues, shaking, and shouting as the spirit moved them. They believed that the end of the world was near, and that Christ was on his way. Ann married and bore four children, none of whom survived infancy. The experience of her children's deaths, coupled with an abhorrence of sex, led her to embrace celibacy. While imprisoned in a Manchester jail in 1770 for heresy, she had a vision of Christ, who revealed to her that the root of all human depravity lay in the coupling of Adam and

Eve. Exalted now as the Mother in Christ and Bride of the Lamb, she became the sect's leader, admonishing all followers to live a celibate life. She decided that the Millennium had begun, and received another revelation that she should emigrate to America to establish the Church of Christ's Second Appearing. That goal she accomplished in the town of Niskayuna, called Watervliet by the descendants of the Dutch settlers and now known as the Town of Colonie, in upstate New York in 1776. From there, the Shaker faith spread through the region.

To achieve their kingdom of peace and perfection, the Shakers adopted four core principles: communalism, celibacy (men and women slept in different quarters), confession of sin, and detachment from the outside world. They believed in the spiritual equality of men and women, though they maintained a strict gendered division of labor, with women focused more on domestic tasks like cooking and cleaning and men on heavier agricultural work. They welcomed Jews and blacks into their settlements, making them one of the more radical groups of their time. As pacifists, they suffered persecution during the Revolutionary War.[135]

When a family joined a Shaker community, parents legally relinquished care of their children to the community. If parents decided to leave, the community had the right to keep the children until they reached adulthood. This led to custody battles, lawsuits, and kidnappings, as happened in Hancock in the mid-1840s when a father made multiple attempts to kidnap his sons.[136] The Shaker effort to break the parent-child bond presaged later conflicts over family structures in other utopian communities. All was not simple and all was not free, despite the lyrics of the Shaker dancing song, "Simple Gifts," made famous by composer Aaron Copland in his orchestral suite, *Appalachian Spring*.

Neither were the Shakers completely detached from the outside world. Their business enterprises networked them into the wider community, where they were exemplars of the self-sufficient, communal ideal. Shaker texts influenced the British utopian socialist Robert Owen's model communities set up in New Lanark, Scotland and later in New Harmony, Indiana.[137] Visitors were common in Shaker villages. Authors Nathaniel Hawthorne and Herman Melville reportedly ran a foot race in the round stone barn when they visited the Hancock community.[138]

By the middle of the 19th century, the Shakers had attracted about 4000 adherents. Their success can't be separated from the larger wave of utopian experimentation in the US that peaked in the years 1820–1850. Many of the experiments were explicitly religious. A Second Great Awakening, beginning at the turn of the 18th century, drew many converts to evangelical Protestantism and marked a definitive break with Calvinism. Through God's love and religious faith, sinners could be saved. All were eligible for God's grace, not just a predestined few.

The Second Great Awakening stoked postmillennialism to fever pitch. To prepare the ground for Christ's Second Coming, society had to be cleansed of sin. This fervor to usher in the new millennial age also galvanized social reformers, utopian socialists, and transcendentalists. As before, the line between secular and religious was ill-defined—for all manner of communities, America was considered the Promised Land. It's impossible to do justice here to the wide diversity of experiments in those times, so my focus is on the ones with clear relevance to the second utopian wave of the 1960s.

BLUEPRINTS FOR PERFECTION

The German philosopher Hegel wrote that America "is the land of the future, where, in the ages that lie before us, the burden of the World's History shall reveal itself . . . It is a land of desire for all those who are weary of the historical lumber-room of old Europe."[139] Yet out of that lumber-room came ideas that galvanized utopians in the United States. Count Henri de Saint-Simon, a French aristocrat who fought in the American Revolution, proposed a benevolent society in which industry and science would be harnessed for the good of the greatest number of people. Even more influential were the ideas of another Frenchman, Charles Fourier (1772–1837), who foresaw a 35,000-year millennial era during which society would be organized into self-sufficient cooperatives called "phalanxes," the Greek word for a rectangular military formation. Each phalanx would ideally contain around 1620–1800 people. According to Fourier, 2,985,984 phalanxes would ultimately cover the globe, and Earth would be transformed into a paradise with the climate of the Garden of Eden. The oceans would turn into lemonade.

In Fourier's division of labor, agriculture and industry would complement each other and the workday would be short, allowing plenty of time for leisurely pursuits. At the end of the year, profits would be apportioned five-twelfths to labor, four-twelfths to capital, and three-twelfths to skill and talent, but there would be no cause for jealousy because people could freely change roles and become capitalists if they so desired. Children would join scavenger groups, called "the Little Hordes," to clean refuse and excrement since they delighted in playing in the dirt. Everything, in fact, was supposed to be delightful. Fourier's elaborate architectural plans for the phalanx included a central Phalanstery with amenities such as a ballroom and a sanatorium.

Fourier's ideas came to America through Albert Brisbane, who as a young man studied social philosophy in Europe. On return to the US, Brisbane published a book called *Social Destiny of Man* in 1840 that summarized the more practical elements of Fourier's design while omitting some of the more outlandish fantasies. The book won converts in the highest echelons of American intellectual society, among them Horace Greeley, the editor of the *New-Yorker*. When Greeley became editor of the *New-York Tribune*, he let Brisbane write a regular column.[140] Between 1843 and 1858, 28 phalanxes were established in both rural and urban areas of the US, drawing in an estimated 15,000 Americans. The philosophy influenced other utopian endeavors as well, such as the Northampton Association of Education and Industry, where radical social reformers, including the well-known African American abolitionist and women's rights activist Sojourner Truth, came together to form a communally-owned and -operated silk mill in the mid-1840s.[141]

While Fourier himself never had the means or opportunity to put his theories into practice, Robert Owen had both. The industrial and educational improvements he introduced in the early 1800s at the New Lanark mills in Scotland, where he was part-owner, established his reputation as one of the most important social reformers of his time. As Owen's ideas grew more radical, and more grandiose, he turned toward America. "I am come to this country," he declared in 1825, "to introduce an entire new state of society; to change it from an ignorant, selfish system to an enlightened social system which shall gradually unite all interests into one, and remove all causes for contest between individuals."[142] Eight years later he announced, with messianic zeal, "I therefore now proclaim to the world the commencement, on this day, of the promised millennium, founded on rational principles and consistent practice." He compared his utopian philosophy to the second coming of Christ, because "Truth and Christ are one and the same."[143]

Like Saint-Simon and Fourier, Owen saw people as the products of their environment. Dramatically transform their environment and humankind would become generous, cooperative, and compliant within a few short years. Malleability and perfectibility went hand in hand. In 1825 Owen and a Scottish colleague, William Maclure, purchased land and buildings that had been used by an earlier utopian community, the German Rappites, in southwestern Indiana. They invited "the industrious and well-disposed of all nations" to join this socialist community, which they named New Harmony.[144] Over 800 people from all walks of life answered the call, including educators, scientists, laborers, and artisans, as well as some people looking for a free ride. The community soon divided along class and factional lines, and Owen and Maclure had a falling out. Life turned out to be anything but harmonious, and the New Harmony community dissolved in a few short years, as did other Owenite experiments in the US and England. However, some of the reformers, including Maclure, stayed in New Harmony, and left an impressive legacy. Maclure founded the nation's first comprehensive co-educational public school system and one of its first free public libraries. Owen's son, Robert Dale Owen, went on to become a champion of universal education and women's rights. Another son, David, established the early headquarters of the US Geological Survey in New Harmony.[145]

Transcendentalism also offered blueprints for perfection, though of a more individualized variety. From 1835–1880, the philosophy held great sway in American intellectual, political, and artistic circles, especially in New England. Among its illustrious proponents were Ralph Waldo Emerson, Henry David Thoreau, Margaret Fuller, and the Alcott family. It became a powerful frame of reference for believers and skeptics alike. Drawing from Western and Eastern philosophy, mysticism, and German and English romanticism, transcendentalism is notoriously hard to define. In his allegorical short story "The Celestial Railroad," Nathaniel Hawthorne caricatures transcendentalism as a horrible giant who

> makes it his business to seize upon honest travelers and fatten them for his table with plentiful meals of smoke, mist, moonshine, raw potatoes, and sawdust. He is German by birth . . . but as to form, his features, his substance, and his nature generally, it is the chief peculiarity of this huge miscreant that neither he for himself, nor anybody for him, has ever been able to describe them.[146]

This vagueness was also transcendentalism's strength. It allowed for a freer range of thought, an unapologetic mingling of reason, sensation, intuition, and spirituality as a way to explore the human condition and its relation to the miraculous patterns and series found in nature. The simplest natural object was worthy of serious contemplation. For both Emerson and Thoreau, the structure of a leaf had much to say about the structure of the entire universe. The whole was not merely the sum of its parts; each part contained within it the whole. In its celebration of connectedness, of the unity of all things, transcendentalism positioned the individual self and soul as the vehicle of enlightenment.

Transcendentalism departed from the mainstream religions of its day, but the work of Emerson in particular bore the imprint of Christian apocalyptic thinking. "No American writer since Jonathan Edwards is more thoroughly steeped in the Christian Bible than Ralph Waldo Emerson," writes scholar Alan Hodder.[147] Like Edwards, Emerson also experienced intense spiritual insights into the other world through his contemplation of nature.

Yet Emerson's apocalypse is not the same as Edwards's Puritan one. For Emerson, Nature, not Christ, is the messiah, and the ultimate consummation isn't the marriage between Christ and his church, but instead between Nature and Mind. And it is through the mind that one achieves revelation, an interior process that ultimately leads to perfect vision. The process is arduous, requiring sacrifice, purification, and emptying the mind of ego in order to achieve an apocalypse of the self. "All mean egotism vanishes," Emerson writes of that moment. "I become a transparent eye-ball; I am nothing; I see all; The currents of the Universal Being circulate through me; I am part or particle of God."[148]

It might seem that such a philosophy would lead one away from engagement with the world in the spirit of a lone yogi meditating in a dark cave or on a high mountaintop. However, Emerson and many of his fellow transcendentalists were social reformers who believed in the need for a moral law. If a fierce Christian God no longer sat in judgment of their deeds, then the God within them did. "Build, therefore, your own world," Emerson exhorted his readers at the end of his essay *Nature*. "As fast as you conform your life to the pure idea in your mind, that will unfold its great proportions. A correspondent revolution in things will attend the influx of the spirit . . . until evil is no more seen."[149] Not all transcendentalists were utopians, but this urge to build one's own world inspired the more experimental among them to do just that, by heading back to the land.

TRANSCENDENTALISM'S WILD OATS

In 1873, Louisa May Alcott, author of the American classic *Little Women*, penned a parody of Fruitlands, a short-lived rural utopian experiment that was led by her father, the innovative educator Bronson Alcott, and the English transcendentalist, Charles Lane. "Transcendental Wild Oats: A Chapter from an Unwritten Romance" peels the romance off the adventure to depict the tensions that ultimately caused Fruitlands, like so many other utopian projects, to fall apart.

Louisa was ten years old when her family moved from the gen-teel town of Concord to the old wooden farmhouse that was to become a communal home in Harvard, Massachusetts, 20 miles to the west. Today it's a quick ride between the two towns, but back then the Alcotts travelled by horse and wagon over muddy dirt tracks, "with the pleasing accompaniments of wind, rain, and hail" as recounted in the parody. Despite inclement weather, "these modern pilgrims journeyed hopefully out of the old world, to found a new one in the wilderness." Louisa cast a reproachful but loving eye on the New Eden fantasies of her father, reserving her more stinging criticism for Charles Lane, aka Timon Lion, depicted as the stern, Spartan fanatic behind the enterprise. He "intended to found a colony of Latter Day Saints," she wrote, "who, under his patriarchal sway, should regenerate the world and glorify his name for ever."[150]

Today the farmhouse is part of a museum complex of other historical buildings, including a Shaker office that was relocated there. At the entrance, a panoramic view of the hills and moun-tains of central Massachusetts and southern New Hampshire greets the visitor. The Fruitlands farmhouse is on low land near a river, without the view. It's painted red, as it was back then, with furnishings representative of the period. It seems comfortable, quaint, even charming, belying the austere order that was once imposed there for seven short months that must have seemed much longer to its occupants.

An impecunious idealist, Bronson Alcott was often short on

funds, and his family had to struggle to make ends meet. He relied on the generosity of others, including his friend Ralph Waldo Emerson, to feed his family and carry on his work. Until he met Charles Lane, his austerity wasn't so much a philosophical choice as a practical necessity. In his teaching practice, Bronson is credited with making important pedagogical reforms in children's education, moving away from rote learning to creative expression. In 1842 he crossed the Atlantic to England where a progressive school called Alcott House had been founded in his name in Surrey. By that time his own school in Boston had collapsed, in part because he had had the temerity to admit the daughter of a fugitive slave. In England he met Charles Lane, businessman and reformer, and the two hit it off so well that they decided to return to Massachusetts together to establish a community founded on their shared principles. In June 1843 they arrived in Fruitlands, accompanied by Bronson's wife Abigail, their four children, Charles's son William, and a few other brave and eccentric souls. Soon they were joined by an English nudist, a hired hand, a refugee from another utopian farm, and a woman named Anna Page—until she was banished for the sin of eating fish at a neighbor's house.

Sin it was to stray from the path of abstemious righteousness set out by Charles and Bronson. The entrance to Paradise is "through the strait gate and narrow way of self-denial," Bronson wrote.[151] Their ascetic code included the refusal of any products that depended on "the degradations of shipping and trade."[152] In an early form of veganism, no animal products were allowed in their diet. They subsisted on raw fruits and nuts, grain, porridge, and unleavened bread. The pleasures of coffee, tea, and alcohol were eschewed in favor of plain water. Clothes were stitched from rough linen, and at first no draught animals were used in farming. Only cold baths were taken, even in freezing weather. After bathing, Bronson followed up by flaying his body with a brush to experience the spiritual ecstasies of mortification of the flesh. Convinced like the Shakers that individual family life needed to cease, Lane espoused sexual abstinence, straining the relationship between Bronson and his wife Abigail to the breaking point.

When it came to travel, however, Bronson and Charles were far from abstemious. At the height of harvest season, they wandered off to preach their gospel along the eastern seaboard. This month-long excursion was ill-timed.[153] "Some call of the Oversoul wafted all the men away," Louisa recounts in her parody, leaving her mother, her sisters, and Charles's son to make a desperate effort to gather the grain crop before a storm.[154]

Inside the house, Abigail was responsible for all the cooking and cleaning, not only for the residents but also for the many visitors who came to see the project. In letters and diaries, she left her own record behind of the bitter fruits of Fruitlands. "They spare the cattle," she wrote to her nephew, "but they forget the women and children."[155] She was acutely aware of her situation and of the inferior position of women in the society at large. After visiting a nearby Shaker community, Abigail wrote in her journal that the women were servile and reserved, while the men were "fat, sleek, comfortable . . ." She went on:

> Wherever I turn, I see the yoke on women in some form or other . . . A woman may perform the most disinterested duties. She may "die daily" in the cause of truth and righteousness. She lives neglected, dies forgotten. But a man who never performed in his whole life one self-denying act, but who has accidental gifts of genius, is celebrated by his contemporaries, while his name and his

works live on, from age to age. He is crowned with laurel, while scarce a "stone may tell where she lies."[156]

Ultimately, it was Abigail who ended the Fruitlands experiment. She encouraged her brother to withdraw his financial support, which then put the farm into foreclosure. After a brutally cold and snowy December, she removed herself and her children to the home of a neighbor in January 1844. Bronson soon rejoined his biological family, while Charles joined the Shakers. There, ironically, he had a change of heart about the importance of family bonds. When he decided to leave the Shaker community in August 1845, they refused to let him take his son. It took three painful years to secure his son's release, during which time he returned to England, where he married and had five more children.[157] Today Fruitlands, like the Hancock Shaker Village, is a venue for rustic weddings, a place to celebrate the nuclear family.

Not far from Fruitlands, a longer-lasting utopian experiment unfolded at Brook Farm in West Roxbury, Massachusetts, about eight miles from Boston. Founded in 1841 by a transcendentalist former Unitarian minister, George Ripley, Brook Farm was to be an egalitarian and self-sufficient community, with no distinction between intellectual and manual work, no hired labor, and a healthy balance between work and leisure. Certainly more fun was had at Brook Farm than at Fruitlands. Its members partook in picnics, plays, masquerades, and boating parties on the nearby Charles River.

At its peak, Brook Farm had more than 70 members. For all the fun, they worked hard, if ultimately unsuccessfully, to make ends meet. They sold farm produce and handmade clothes, charged a fee to visitors, and ran a boarding school that was one of the best known of its day. Ripley tried and failed to woo Emerson to Brook Farm. He had more luck with Nathaniel Hawthorne, who joined Brook Farm during its first year not so much from utopian conviction as with the intention of living cheaply and saving money to marry his fiancée, the transcendentalist Sophia Peabody. Hawthorne soon found the manual labor required in farming was more than he'd bargained for—he was put in charge of shoveling manure—leaving him with little time to write. He wrote to Sophia, "Oh; belovedest, labor is the curse of this world, and nobody can meddle with it, without becoming proportionately brutified. Dost though think it is a praiseworthy matter, that I have spent five golden months in providing food for cows and horses? Dearest, it is not so. Thank God, my soul is not utterly buried under a dung heap."[158] Hawthorne left the farm, and later based his caustic novel *The Blithedale Romance* on his experience.

In 1844, Ripley was swayed by the editor Horace Greeley, a frequent visitor to the farm, and other Fourierist friends, to make Brook Farm into a phalanx. More artisans joined the community, and work began on constructing a giant Phalanstery that could house a hundred members. Brook Farm emerged as the center of Fourierist thought in America, publishing the weekly *Harbinger* that became widely known as a source of radical social and literary criticism. But a lack of funds continued to plague Brook Farm, and in 1846 the unfinished Phalanstery burned to the ground, effectively bringing the project to an end.[159] Now all that is left is the farmland, preserved as a park.

WILDER STILL: THE ONEIDA EXPERIMENT

Of all the utopian experiments of the era, the Oneida Community in New York State did the most to shake up conventional sexual norms. It was the brainchild of John Humphrey Noyes, a prophet and genius to some, a megalomaniac and lecher to others. Born into a well-bred Vermont family in 1811, Noyes underwent a religious conversion in 1831 during the Second Great Awakening and entered seminary, first at Andover and then at Yale. His views proved too heretical for the mainstream church, which revoked his license to preach. He believed that the Second Coming of Christ had already happened in 70 AD when the temple was destroyed in Jerusalem and that the Kingdom of Heaven would soon be reached on Earth. He would show the way to it.

His way was Perfectionism. Inspired by the ideals of early Christianity, Noyes proposed a communal style of life and sexual relations that would bring people into a more perfect communion with Christ. Unlike the Shakers, Noyes wasn't ready to eschew sex along with the stultifying structure of the nuclear family. While conventional marriage was taboo, intercourse most certainly was not. He set about to build a community based on what he called "complex marriage," in which all men and women are married to each other and all property is communal. This is the way it is in the Kingdom of Heaven, he argued, and this is the way it should be on Earth. He believed that individual marriages made people selfish and got in the way of their devotion to the community and to Christ.

Noyes espoused coitus interruptus, male withdrawal before ejaculation. Not unlike Shaker leader Mother Ann Lee, he had been deeply affected by his wife losing four babies in childbirth. Separating sex from procreation had a powerful appeal. To maintain discipline and compliance, he instituted the practice of mutual criticism. Those who erred, ideologically or sexually, had to stand in silence before a committee who discussed their strengths and weaknesses for the good of their character development.

Noyes established his first community in Putney, Vermont in

1844. After being run out of town three years later for adultery, he and his followers relocated to the town of Oneida in central New York State, where the community lasted until 1881. Here he perfected the complex marriage system. Outsiders criticized Noyes for his advocacy of "free love," but in truth love was far from free in Oneida. Access to sexual partners depended on one's position in the spiritual hierarchy. Noyes was at the apex. Just beneath him came the most spiritual male elders, and then the most spiritual female elders. Younger people lower in the hierarchy were encouraged to sleep with their esteemed elders in the hope that some of their spiritual wisdom and sexual prowess might rub off, so to speak. The sexual initiation of teens was another privilege enjoyed by the elders. Consent to any sexual transaction had to be given by both parties, and this was arranged through an intermediary.[160]

Reproduction was tightly regulated, too. Noyes believed that the community should only have the number of children it could support. The elders decided who could procreate (though male continence proved imperfect). Once they were old enough to walk, babies were separated from their mothers and placed in an infant department.

Like many evangelical intellectuals of his day, Noyes took a keen interest in science. "God designs to bring science and religion together and solder them into one," he explained.[161] In 1869 he carried out one of the first eugenic experiments in the US, inspired by developments in animal breeding, Charles Darwin's work, and Frances Galton's *Hereditary Talent and Character*. At Oneida, Noyes set out to breed intellectually, spiritually, and physically superior human beings. He coined the term "stirpiculture" from the Latin root *stirps*—stem, root, or stock—to describe the project. Noyes and a group of elders initially chose the couples who would breed the best children. Eventually a 12-person committee was established for this purpose, headed by Noyes's son Theodore, who became a eugenicist while studying at the Yale Medical Institution. Perpetuating the Noyes' own bloodline appears to have been a top priority. Noyes himself sired nine of the 58 "stirpicults," and 19 more were blood relations.[162] The creepiness of this experiment is a cautionary tale of where obsession with perfection can lead.

In economic terms, the Oneida Community performed better than many others. Membership wasn't automatic, and among those chosen were a number of affluent and well-educated followers. The community diversified from farming into a range of manufactures, including steel animal traps bought by the Hudson's Bay Company. It wasn't lack of money that doomed the project in the end. A leadership vacuum emerged as Noyes grew old, and the younger generation began to rebel against the sexual theocracy. The stirpiculure project, in particular, sowed the seeds of discontent. A reverend at a nearby college also launched a campaign against the community's moral turpitude. When the Oneida Community was legally dissolved in 1881, its enterprises merged into a joint-stock company that went on to become a well-known manufacturer of silverware.[163] America's first utopian era had drawn to a close.

Fruitlands, Brook Farm, New Harmony, Oneida—these were only a few of the many communities that sprang up across the country as revivalism, millennialism, socialism, transcendentalism, and American exceptionalism swirled together in a vortex that swept bright minds, free thinkers, religious zealots, progressive reformers, and social misfits into a utopian frenzy. "The world was not ready for Utopia yet, and those who attempted to found it only got laughed at for their pains," Louisa May Alcott reflects in "Transcendental Wild Oats."

In other days, men could sell all and give to the poor, lead lives devoted to holiness and high thought, and, after the persecution was over, find themselves honored as saints or martyrs. But in modern times these things are out of fashion. To live for one's principles, at all costs, is a dangerous speculation; and the failure of an ideal, no matter how humane and noble, is harder for the world to forgive and forget than bank robbery or the grand swindles of corrupt politicians.[164]

The world had changed by the time Louisa penned those words in 1873. The country had experienced a brutal civil war. It was more populated, more urbanized, and more industrialized than it had been three decades earlier. Land was much more expensive, and economic inequality was rising. By 1890 more than half of the nation's wealth was in the hands of less than 1 percent of the population, a concentration with striking parallels to today.[165] In a world of stark class divisions and mounting labor strife, utopianism seemed out of touch. It would soon be superseded by the socialist materialism of Marx and Engels.

In the *Communist Manifesto*, published in 1848, Marx and Engels critiqued the utopian socialism of Saint-Simon, Fourier, and Owen:

they habitually appeal to society at large, without distinction of class; nay, by preference, to the ruling class . . . they reject all political, and especially all revolutionary, action; they wish to attain their ends by peaceful means, and endeavor, by small experiments, necessarily doomed to failure, and by the force of example, to pave the way for the new social Gospel.

"Duodecimo editions of the New Jerusalem" and "castles in the air" were how they described the utopian experiments of their day.[166] But for all their scorn, Marx and Engels themselves were utopian and millennial in their own way. The inevitable victory of the proletariat, the dawn of a classless society, the transformation of human nature through revolution, the end of history as we know it—these Marxian precepts have more than a little of a Heaven-on-Earth edge. While they didn't offer much of a blueprint for what communist society would look like, Marx and Engels held a quasi-religious faith in the wheels of history rolling inexorably toward a communist outcome.[167]

My generation of idealists and dreamers could have learned important lessons from our earlier utopian forbears had we known more about them. Instead we were mostly ignorant about the past and all about creating a new future. When my husband Jim and I set off for the green rolling hills of West Virginia in the fall of 1976, we were steeped in a heady mix of revolutionary fervor, nature nostalgia, nuclear dread, and the conviction that, with a little help from our friends, we could break the chains of traditional gender and family norms. We thought our pioneering spirit was very special indeed. "There is no adventure greater than ours," wrote Raymond Mungo, a founder of Liberation News Service and a rural Vermont commune called Total Loss Farm. "We are the last life on the planet, it is for us to launch the New Age, to grow up to be *men* and *women* of earth, and free of the walking dead who precede us." [168]

APPALACHIAN WINTER

Just about everyone who lived through the utopian experiments of the sixties and seventies has a story to tell. It usually ends sadly or badly. Once we arrived in West Virginia, it didn't take long for our dreams to dim, like a lantern running out of kerosene. Fixing the old house enough to be able to make it through the coming winter took more time and money than anyone anticipated. The balance between work and leisure tilted off the scales: we all worked incessantly. While Jim and I built a cabin, in order to earn money the two other women took emotionally arduous jobs as social workers while the two other men worked construction. Their commutes took an hour or more each way, mostly on unpaved roads. Back on the farm, the crops needed tending. Our survivalist ethic dictated that we can or freeze enough vegetables to last through the winter ahead. The closest we came to communing with nature was bathing in the muddy stream that ran alongside the property.

Things went downhill, fast. We hayed the meadow with a mule-drawn rake, but at the end it began to rain and the haystack rotted. The relationships between the two couples we lived with turned sour. One couple was into transcendental meditation—they were trying to learn to levitate—and the other couple resented them for spending 45 minutes a day doing this instead of working on the house. The kitchen became a battleground. Tempers flared despite group meetings and self-criticism sessions. There was hollering in the holler.

Jim and I, just back from living in a Bangladesh village where people fought, made up, and fought again all the time, didn't see the writing on the wall. We devoted ourselves to building our little cabin on the hill. With meager savings, we did everything the hard way. We dug the pole foundation by hand and used uneven rough-cut lumber for the frame. Neither of us knew anything about construction, but we read how-to books and the others shared their skills. As the weather got colder, we upped the tempo, hoping to move in before the first snowfall. But there was a glitch—the chimney pipe for our wood stove was back-ordered and still hadn't arrived. On top of that, we hadn't had time to lay in a supply of firewood. Ever optimistic, we moved our possessions into the cabin before heading east for Christmas and to do some work in Washington on human rights issues in Bangladesh. We would install the chimney when we got back, and at last have a place of our own to sit down and write. Hadn't that been the idea in the first place? I wish we'd known then about Hawthorne's time, or lack of it, at Brook Farm.

While we were gone, the mountain weather turned even nastier. The snow was two feet deep when the firewood supply ran out for the main house. Chainsaws seized up in the ice and mud. The two couples quarreled over who would go out to saw down some trees and drag the logs back with the mule. Afterwards our friends phoned to tell us they had decided to split up the farm. We only went back to pick up our things. It wasn't the end of the world, but for us it was the end of a dream, the end of an era.

The back-to-the-land movement was losing steam by the mid-1970s, and many dreams were dying like ours. At its peak in the late 1960s, there were tens of thousands of communes throughout the country, with several hundred thousand young people living in them. No one was keeping count, and many were small, informal, and short-lived like ours, but the phenomenon was big enough to get the attention of the mainstream press. In July 1969, *Life* magazine ran a cover story, "The Commune Comes to America," with glossy photos of hippies in rural Oregon frolicking in various stages of undress.[169]

Rural communes were only part of the scene. Communes sprouted up in America's cities, too. While communes were "fabulously heterogeneous," they weren't very racially and class

diverse.[170] It's become almost a cliché that the movement was pre-
dominantly white and middle class. There's truth to this, but the
characterization conceals the important role that radical politics
and Black Power played in the period. The Black Panther Party
created urban communes in an attempt to fold collective living
into a broader vision of liberation. Communal norms, including
gender equality, ended up clashing with the hierarchal, male-dom-
inated system of party leadership. But in working to meet the
needs of the surrounding black community, the collectives left
behind an important legacy. In Oakland, California, the Pan-
thers established a free health clinic and the Oakland Community
School, which became a national model for community-based
education.[171]

The utopian wave of the 1960s crested higher than its 19th century antecedent, but it broke faster, too. Today the traces it left
behind are obscured by stereotypes of naked hippies, big-breasted
earth mothers, and drugged-out rock stars, and the musical score
has been mercilessly appropriated by corporate advertisers. But
beneath the hype of shallow recollections, the experience yields
many insights about how easy it is to fall into the traps of the
America syndrome and how hard it is to get out.

A New World beckoned in the '60s, but how new was it really?
Most of us weren't fully aware of the baggage we took along with
us on our utopian journeys. Our backpacks were jammed full of
American mythologies that ultimately weighed us down. Those
who made the pilgrimage to the countryside were steeped in the
Jeffersonian rural idyll, an agrarian myth that has helped to define
the boundaries of American belonging. "Those who labour in the
earth are the chosen people of God, if ever he had a chosen people,
whose breasts he has made his peculiar deposit for substantial and
genuine virtue," Thomas Jefferson professed in the early 1780s. "It

is the focus in which he keeps alive that sacred fire, which otherwise might escape from the face of the earth."[172]

The Jeffersonian rural idyll depended on an abundance of "vacant" land for farmers to cultivate. While Jefferson himself expressed some hope that Native Americans might be assimilated into his model, the very existence of "vacant lands" depended on expropriation of their holdings. Moreover, there was little understanding among white Americans of Indians *as farmers*; their agricultural practices were largely neglected or misunderstood.[173] Jefferson maintained that blacks, once freed, should be deported; immigrants from the wrong sorts of countries weren't to be trusted either. As tiller of the soil and protector of civil virtue, the yeoman farmer ideal was male, Anglo-Saxon, and heterosexual.[174]

That the chosen people were also a chosen race had lethal consequences. President Andrew Jackson justified the Indian Removal Act of 1830 on the grounds that inferior natives should give their "unused" lands to rightful Anglo-Saxon inheritors. "What good man," he asked, "would prefer a country covered with forests and ranged by a few thousand savages to our extensive Republic . . . ?"[175] From the Trail of Tears beginning that year, when southeastern tribes were forced to move beyond the Mississippi to Indian Territory, to the campaigns of displacement and slaughter that continued throughout the century, Native American lives and livelihoods were decimated in the colonization of the western hemisphere. Mexicans were similarly perceived as a "mongrel race" that must make way for the Anglo-Saxons, an ideology which helped to rationalize the seizing of lands from Mexico in the Mexican War of 1844–48.[176] In the frontier myth that became a staple of American culture, war against the savages came to be seen as redemptive and regenerative, enshrining violence as a formative part of white male American identity.[177]

Parts of the back to the land movement, especially in the western part of the country, drew uncritically on the frontier myth and celebrated the macho outlaw tradition of the Wild West.[178] At a time when the feminist movement was gaining strength, this celebration of frontier masculinity, and docile, hard-working, homesteading femininity, served to reinforce conservative gendered divisions of labor and power.

It was only by ignoring the violent history of land appropriation and western expansion that our generation of yeoman farmers and pioneers could fully embrace the romance of our chosen people mission. As Janferie Stone, a veteran of the movement, writes, "We were North Americans out to retrace our history, ironically replicating all the impulses and misperceptions of European ancestors when they came to this land. Like them, we thought that the lands we came to homestead were 'empty.'"[179] Yet at the same time we venerated and celebrated what we thought was cool in Native American cultures, often naively appropriating their philosophies and spiritual practices in our search for alternative community and consciousness.

Our negative views of the corruptions of urban, industrial life also bore the imprint of a longer American tradition. The rural idyll coexisted uneasily in the 1800s, as it did in the 1960s, with the realities of rapid economic and technological change. The 19th century industrial revolution elicited hope in the future—Americans were special and would industrialize differently than the Europeans, turning technology to positive ends—but also nostalgia for a paradise lost. The forward march of progress inspired a new literary and artistic school, the American Sublime, celebrating regeneration through Nature. "The more rapidly, the more voraciously, the primordial forest was felled," Perry Miller writes, "the more desperately the poets and painters—and also preachers—

strove to identify the unique personality of this republic with the virtues of pristine and untarnished, of 'romantic,' Nature."[180] Pristine American nature was seen as the height of aesthetic perfection, an Eden from which a falling away was tragically inevitable. That inevitability was often shaded in apocalyptic hues, as it was in the 1960s, too. The American Sublime lived on in us.

For better or worse, many '60s communes tried to break down the walls of the nuclear family, whether through non-monogamous sexual relationships or joint child-rearing. As in the 19th century, the desire to create radically new ways of living together was infused with the mythology of human malleability and perfectibility. This aspiration didn't adequately take into account the frailties and varieties of human nature. Nor did it adequately factor in differences in upbringing and values. Sexual jealousy, envy, anger, competition, depression, hurt, and pain destroyed many communities. Communes not only attracted high-minded idealists, but also "freeloaders, cranks, and low-lifes—and often enough of the latter, unfortunately, to bring it all crashing down."[181]

There were so many lessons we could have learned from the communal experiments of the 19th century, lessons that might have tempered our ridiculously high expectations of ourselves and others. We might have realized that it's not so easy to bridge the divide between manual and mental work, or to build an egalitarian society on just one farm or commune. We might have learned that inequalities between men and women don't evaporate overnight, and when male prophets have their heads in the clouds, it's women like Abigail Alcott who hold up more than half the sky. We might have understood that breaking with the traditional family is no easy task and that new sexual regimes can be exploitative and explosive. We would have been warned that the quest for purity and perfection can lead in perverse directions, from the austerity imposed at Fruitlands to the sexual hierarchies and eugenics practices at Oneida.

Hawthorne's transcendental giant cast a shadow over the '60s communal movement, too. Though the more politically minded drew inspiration from Thoreau's sojourn at Walden Pond and doctrine of civil disobedience, Emerson's transparent eyeball better fit the mood of the times. Dilating the pupils with LSD or other hallucinogens allowed a liberating disembodiment, a free-floating sense of ecstatic communion. The resulting fanciful visions also came at a high cost—not just bad trips, but lost time, and blind spots with larger and longer political repercussions.

MORE THAN MEETS THE EYE

In 1964, a band of Merry Pranksters, as they called themselves, including novelist Ken Kesey and an assemblage of counterculture icons, from the Beat generation's Neal Cassady to Grateful Dead guitarist Jerry Garcia, traveled by bus across the country, holding acid parties along the way—a journey immortalized in Tom Wolfe's book, *The Electric Kool-Aid Acid Test*. Two years later, Kesey joined forces with a maverick countercultural entrepreneur named Stewart Brand to organize the three-day Trips Festival in San Francisco, a multimedia psychedelic extravaganza with rock music, light shows, slide projections, and sound system experimentation, all designed to blow the mind. It was one of the first big hippie gatherings of the era. The techno-effects were provided by USCO, the US Company, which was in the business of creating "theatrical ecologies" in a collaborative and interdisciplinary work style not so different, it turns out, from that of cutting-edge Cold War research labs at places like Stanford and MIT.

At first glance, this may seem like an unlikely coupling. But "the swirling scene at the Trips Festival, and Brand's role in it," writes Fred Turner is his book *From Counterculture to Cyberculture*, "represented a coming together of the New Communalist social ideals then emerging and the ideological and technological products of cold war technocracy."[182] The stereotypical picture of the military-industrial complex as inhabited by highly regimented bureaucrats in dark suits belies the fact that in its research labs scientists had begun to cross disciplinary boundaries and put their minds together in an entrepreneurial, non-hierarchical environment to develop new technologies like the bomb, weapons delivery systems, and the computer. For the top brains, it was a free-wheeling and exciting professional existence.

Brand and his fellow New Communalists, as Turner calls them, shared a similar culture of collaborative invention. They were also linked to the Cold War technocrats by an affinity to systems theory and cybernetics, emerging fields which posited that ecological, biological, and mechanical systems were self-regulating, responding to feedback in "patterns of ordered information in a world otherwise tending to entropy and noise."[183] From the natural sciences and engineering, systems theory spread to the study of social systems. Society was thought to function along similar lines to organisms and machines, with the world as a whole seen as a giant information web.

Brand encountered systems theory as an undergraduate at Stanford, where he studied evolutionary biology with Paul Ehrlich, author of *The Population Bomb*, whom readers will meet again in Chapter Five. Another powerful influence on the New Communalists was Buckminster Fuller, best known for designing the geodesic dome, though he had previously designed shelters for the military. Fuller believed that by understanding the rules of natural systems, the "Comprehensive Designer" could deploy technology to overcome scarcity and build a well-balanced and harmonious society. He was a descendant of the transcendentalist Margaret Fuller, the most influential woman in Ralph Waldo Emerson's circle and a well-known feminist author in her own right. "When I heard that [Great] Aunt Margaret said, 'I must start with the universe and work down to the parts, I must have an understanding of it,' that became a great drive for me," Fuller recalled.[184] Like transcendentalism, systems theory assumed a highly patterned and interconnected universe, in which human and natural systems are analogues.

In 1968 Brand founded the *Whole Earth Catalog*, a book that became the bible of the commune era. The outside cover featured a picture of Earth taken from space. On the inside cover was this statement of purpose:

> We *are* as gods and might as well get good at it . . . [A] realm of intimate, personal power is developing—power of the individual to conduct his own education, find his own inspiration, shape his own environment, and share his adventure with whoever is interested. Tools that aid this process are sought and promoted by THE WHOLE EARTH CATALOG.[185]

The tools it promoted spanned the gamut from practical "small is beautiful" technologies for rural life to the big ideas of Buckminster Fuller and other countercultural gurus, including Brand himself. The catalog was at once an ode to individualism and a node for networking. Eclectic as it was, however, the politics of the New Left and issues of gender, race, and class were conspicuously absent from the catalog. The "long hunter" and "cowboy nomad" celebrated in its pages is white, male, smart, and rather full of himself. He may be into saving the planet, but he doesn't care all that much about saving other people.[186]

Turner tells the story of how the New Communalists' interest in cybernetics eventually bloomed into the embrace of the personal computer and the capacity of the digital revolution to transform the world. In 1985 Brand and a fellow entrepreneur founded the Whole Earth 'Lectronic Link, or The WELL, one of the first networked virtual communities. As the would-be hunters and cowboys of the '60s moved into cyberspace to conquer the new electronic frontier, they brought with them their collaborative work style, libertarian individualism, and techno-utopian visions.

This approach resonated with sections of the ascendant New Right. Newt Gingrich and his Progress and Freedom Foundation advocated for information technology along with government downsizing and market deregulation. It also meshed well with novel corporate strategies of flexible labor and outsourcing. Less hierarchical management structures were part of the package, but for many workers, computerization, instead of liberation, brought increased exploitation.

Brand began to work with executives from corporations like Royal Dutch/Shell, Volvo, and AT&T. He launched a consulting firm, the Global Business Network (GBN), in 1987. Over time, the GBN began to consult for the US military, and the relationship between the New Communalists and the military-industrial complex came full circle. Today Brand's techno-utopianism takes the form of advocacy for geoengineering and nuclear power as remediation for climate change. To highlight the benefits of genetic engineering, he also has launched a "de-extinction" project to recreate the passenger pigeon, a once-prolific species that was driven extinct a century ago.[187]

These legacies of '60s utopianism shouldn't blind us to other more positive ones, however. The *Whole Earth Catalog* may have been on the bookshelf of most rural communes, but there was plenty of other reading matter, too. Many people, after getting high on drugs or meditation, came back down to earth and put their boots on to protest the war in Vietnam, institutionalized racism, and the despoliation of the environment. "Many communards were active in organized resistance to the social order by fighting logging companies, defending family farms, building food co-ops, organizing demonstrations, assisting military resisters, or simply offering refuge or R&R to other activists," writes Jesse Drew, a veteran of the times.[188]

Not far from where I live now, Sam Lovejoy, then a resident of the Liberation News Service communal farm in Montague, Massachusetts, cut down a weather tower on the site of a proposed nuclear power plant in 1974. The tower's purpose was to test wind direction in the event of a radioactive release. His act helped to galvanize the national anti-nuclear movement.[189] Women fought back against conventional gender norms. In California's Mendocino County, a rural women's collective produced a national magazine, *Country Women*, which provided advice on feminist consciousness-raising along with practical farming.[190]

As communes disbanded, some people stayed on in the area, becoming part of the fabric of local communities. On the farm in West Virginia, our college friends settled in, built a new house, and became active in local and state-wide organizations to support the arts and build a post-coal energy system and economy. The other couple moved away, selling their half of the land, including our cabin, to survivalists who paid in gold because they didn't believe in paper money. They now graze goats on the hillside.

Many people regard their communal history not as a crucible but as a stepping stone. Their utopian dreams and millennial madness may have abated, but not their desire to change the world, a desire that has been passed down to their children.[191] Real lessons were learned. Many of those who remained active in left politics were better able to tease apart Marxism's profound insights about the nature of class society from its millennial promise of the victory of the proletariat and the establishment of a classless paradise. That communist utopianism can come with high costs—from the genocide under Pol Pot in Kampuchea to Maoist authoritarianism—helped spur this rethinking, too.

Today many alternative agriculture and food justice and sovereignty movements are much more attentive to connecting city and country, and more attuned to the politics of race, class, and gender in the US and overseas. Urban farms help to organize around multiple issues—a clean environment, health, jobs, education, and youth development. Their vision is both practical and hopeful.

As historian Howard Zinn put it so well, "Revolutionary change does not come as one cataclysmic moment (beware of such moments!) but as an endless succession of surprises, moving zigzag toward a more decent society. We don't have to engage in grand, heroic actions to participate in the process of change. Small acts, when multiplied by millions of people, can transform the world."[192]

EARLY DAYS

So where does this journey lead us? Do the risks of utopian dreams outweigh their benefits, especially when combined with millennial madness? In the pursuit of a new and better world, is it possible to escape the America syndrome so intricately connected to our quest for perfection?

People aren't perfect. They never have been, and never will be. The French philosopher Simone de Beauvoir once warned of the dangers of "moral purism" in politics, arguing that we should instead embrace the ambiguities of human existence and the inevitability of conflict and failure when people work together.[193]

In some circles today, ambiguity is a dirty word. Sections of the American Left have retreated into narrow identity politics, strict political correctness, and the moral purism that de Beauvoir decried. There's more than a touch of utopianism and millennialism, not to mention exclusion, in this latest variant of perfectionism. Rather than reaching out to others in solidarity, there's a tendency to collapse inwards, focus on personal or group victimhood, overuse the trauma diagnosis, call out and shame those who don't conform or agree, and create "safe spaces" where everyone has to abide by a certain set of implicit and explicit rules that often amount to a kind of self- and collective-policing. The problem is not so much that people need safe places where they can feel comfortable and free of hostility—they do—but that spaces where differences of opinion and political conflict take place (the classroom, for example) are then considered *unsafe*, and must therefore be surveilled and policed. One wonders if there is also a touch here of the militarization of inner space.

Instead of such universal policing, the political moment calls for a practical and inclusive radical optimism like the kind expressed in the inscription on the side of Scotland's Parliament building: "Work as if you live in the early days of a better nation." Not the worst nation, not the best nation, not the nation Donald Trump says he wants to make great again or the nation Hillary Clinton said was already great. Just a better one.

And lest one occasionally slip into an apocalyptic funk, as it's all too easy to do, it's worth reminding ourselves that we have survived far worse times, like the nuclear madness of the Cold War.

Chapter Three

BOOM AND DOOM: THE MAGIC OF THE ATOM

I was born in 1951, the year that atmospheric tests of nuclear weapons began at the Nevada Proving Ground, later renamed the Nevada Test Site, 65 miles northwest of Las Vegas. The Atomic Energy Commission made no public announcements about the tests, even though they were powerful enough to light up the night sky over Los Angeles and San Francisco, and tourists came to Las Vegas and other nearby towns to witness the mushroom clouds.[194] The November explosion of the so-called "Dog" bomb was the first time American soldiers conducted field exercises in conjunction with an atomic test. The army used them as guinea pigs, making them witness the blast from about six miles away and then move in closer for "defensive" maneuvers.

Thanks to the Nevada Test Site, and other locations around the world where the Americans, Soviets, British, French, and Chinese exploded atomic bombs into the atmosphere, we all carry radioactive residues in our bodies.[195] According to a 2001 US government report, if you've lived in the contiguous United States any time since 1951, all organs and tissues of your body have received some radiation exposure from nuclear fallout because of its lasting effects on the environment. Your degree of exposure isn't just a question of proximity to test sites, but also of which direction the wind happened to blow the day of the test or where it happened to rain. Maps of radiation exposure show higher densities around Nevada and neighboring states, but hotspots are sprinkled throughout the country. The government report estimates that excess cancer deaths from fallout exposure are likely to be the highest in persons born in 1951 because on average they received higher doses of radiation than people born either earlier or later.[196]

From that perspective, 1951 is not a terribly auspicious birth year, but I was lucky in other ways—lucky to be born, in fact. In 1942, at the age of 19, my father was one of the first students to drop out of Princeton University to join the war effort. He became a marine dive bomber pilot, flying more than 80 missions in the Gilbert and Marshall Islands in the Pacific. His plane was hit a number of times, but he made it home alive. Shortly after he returned to the US in late 1945, he proposed to my mother, who was in graduate school at Iowa State University. They settled back in Princeton, where my father completed university on the GI Bill and then became a history teacher at a local prep school. Sometimes my parents spotted Einstein sailing on Princeton's Lake Carnegie. My mother bore three healthy daughters, of whom I'm the youngest.

A year after my birth, we moved to Wilmington, Delaware, where my father got a better-paying teaching job. Three years later, my mother developed malignant thyroid cancer. While it's impossible to pinpoint the cause, she was doubly exposed to nuclear contamination. Thyroid cancer is one of the most common cancers associated with fallout exposure, since radioiodines such as Iodine-131 concentrate in the thyroid gland. A 1997 National Cancer Institute study estimated that exposure to Iodine-131 from the Nevada tests alone led to between 11,300 and 212,000 additional thyroid cancers in the US.[197]

Risks of exposure were higher for those who worked directly with radioactive materials in the nuclear weapons complex. While my mother was studying agricultural economics at Iowa State, her best friends there, including my godmother, were doing secret research for the Manhattan Project at the university's Ames Laboratory. Beginning in 1942, the lab developed new methods for producing high-purity uranium. In the process, it generated radioactive dusts at extremely high levels. There was little in the way of personal protection, engineering controls, or radiation monitoring to protect workers, though my godmother's job was to test the scientists' urine to gauge their exposure. Over 60 years later, the Department of Energy finally established a Former Worker Medical Screening Program for the Ames Laboratory, with possible compensation for 22 types of radiation-induced cancers. Thyroid cancer is on the list.[198]

So where did my mother's cancer come from? Fallout? Or exposure at Ames where she shared an apartment with my godmother and dated a Manhattan Project scientist before my father swept her off her feet? Was there radioactive dust on their hands or clothes or in the food they ate? Was she just genetically predisposed to cancer? Or could it be all of the above?

While I'll never know the exact cause, I do know something about the effects. In the 1950s such things were not talked about openly with children, and my mother's diagnosis was a carefully kept secret from my sisters and me. But no matter how tight the container, fear has a way of seeping out. When my mother went to Boston for her

operation, I came down with the flu. One of my first memories is of
our favorite babysitter giving me a stuffed cat toy as I lay in bed recovering from fever. All through childhood I clutched that cat at night,
even after its fur and button eyes fell off and it looked like a blind old
alley cat that had been in one too many fights.

Fortunately, my mother survived. Life went on, though a sense
of danger remained, a slight whiff of death that hung in the air.
It was like in an upscale nursing home where they do everything
they can to keep the floors and patients spotlessly clean, yet visitors can still smell the presence of the Grim Reaper. In our house
he hid in the shadows, but I knew he was there. Many years later,
my mother told me that, after her operation, her goal in life was
to survive until I turned 16.

When I look back now, I see my childhood in a kind of chiar-
oscuro. When I was seven we moved to Dallas, where my father
became headmaster of an elite boys' school. Affluence surrounded
us. The campus was a gigantic playground, and we swam in the
pools of millionaires, diving into sky blue chlorinated water and
coming up for air in a world baked white by hot sun and racial
prejudice. That incredible whiteness of being made my fears seem
all the darker by comparison. I struggled for mastery over them by
reading mysteries and then imagining and enacting my own as if
I were Nancy Drew.

When I got old enough to analyze myself—in those heady college years when we stayed up late into the night discussing Freud
and Jung—I latched on to my mother's cancer as the source of my
early fears. But there was still a sense of a darker, deeper mystery
left unsolved. It wasn't until recently that I came to realize the
Grim Reaper of my childhood wore more than one hat. I carried
within me not only the fear of losing my mother, but of losing the
whole world in a nuclear holocaust.

How does one unbury one's nuclear fears, inspect them, catalogue them, perhaps put them to rest? There's no easy answer, but sometimes something comes along to cast a little light. While researching the Nevada Test Site, I stumbled on a government photograph taken during a 1952 bomb test that shows two Marines lifting their hands to touch the mushroom cloud.

The caption reads, "The atomic cloud formed by the detonation seems close enough to touch, and tension gone, Poth and Wilson do a little clowning for the camera."[199] The irony is that although they weren't close enough to touch the cloud, its radioactivity was close enough to touch them. Is that the metaphor I'm searching for—the bomb as magic show, with its illusions become delusions? The tricks up the atomic magicians' sleeves not only steered us toward apocalypse then, but still delude the American body politic now.

ILLUSIONS AND DELUSIONS

Strictly speaking, the hidden history of the bomb is not hidden any more. Plenty of good books by good historians painstakingly deconstruct our national nuclear myths. The problem is few of us read them. On the nuclear tourist trail, most of the public history on display is unapologetically uncritical. The basic message is that it's good the Cold War is over, but we should be grateful that the nuclear balance of terror kept us safe.

If all you knew about the atomic bomb you learned from the introductory video *The Town that Never Was* at the Bradbury Science Museum in Los Alamos, you'd think the brilliant Manhattan Project scientists just brought American soldiers home to the waiting arms of pretty women. The killing in Hiroshima and Nagasaki isn't shown, or even mentioned, in the video, much less in the museum's displays. At the Titan Missile Museum outside Tucson, you can descend into the underground control room of a decommissioned Minuteman intercontinental ballistic missile (ICBM) that could deliver nuclear bombs, but that's as deep as the history gets. Visitors are encouraged to feel awe and nostalgia for the clever engineering and the loyal soldiers who worked shifts underground, always at the ready to destroy the world. At the museum's perimeter fence, white Border Patrol trucks wait between desert forays against one of our latest national security threats—poor Mexican migrants.

There are better museums, like the National Museum of Nuclear Science & History in Albuquerque, which has a display about the bombing of Japan, including the burnt remains of a three-year-old victim's tricycle. Arguments for and against the dropping of the bomb encourage viewers to ask the question of whether it was necessary. This museum is the exception, however. The rule is not to question.

That lack of questioning brings us to the first magic trick, the "no choice" illusion: The US had to drop the bomb on Hiroshima and Nagasaki in August 1945 to end World War II and spare hundreds of thousands of American soldiers from a deadly invasion of Japan. I grew up believing this. I was taught that thanks to the bomb, my father didn't have to return to the Pacific. We had used a weapon of mass destruction to save ourselves from destruction—we had to do bad in order to do good.

If more Americans knew there were other options of ending the war, they might be less inclined toward apocalypse. Other choices *could* have been made. While historians still debate whether those other choices *should* have been made, the historical record shows that the fatal and fateful act of dropping the bomb wasn't inevitable. Even President Harry Truman, who called the destruction of Hiroshima the "greatest day in history" and claimed that he never lost sleep over it, knew he had made a *decision*.[200] The decision was less about saving American lives than about punishing Japan, justifying the enormous costs of the Manhattan Project, displaying American power, and letting our erstwhile Soviet allies know who was boss.[201]

Many World War II American military leaders later admitted that we didn't have to drop the bomb. The official US Strategic Bombing Survey of 1946 came to the conclusion that Japan would have surrendered before the end of 1945 without the bomb, without the entrance of Russia into the Pacific war, and even without the threat of an invasion.[202] In 1963, former General and President Dwight Eisenhower wrote that, when he learned from the Secretary of War Stimson that the bomb would be used, he became depressed and voiced "grave misgivings." The Japanese would surrender soon, so that "dropping the bomb was completely unnecessary" and "no longer mandatory as a measure to save American lives."[203]

A second choice also lay within Truman's decision to drop
the bomb—the deliberate selection of civilian targets. Truman
claimed that Hiroshima was targeted because it was a military
base, and he wanted to avoid as much as possible the killing
of civilians.[204] Although Hiroshima had an army base, it was a
city of 350,000 people, 140,000 of whom died. Nagasaki had
270,000 inhabitants, and 70,000 died. The Interim Committee
that advised Truman on the bomb rejected the idea of a demonstration blast, and bombing a less populated area of Japan
apparently wasn't considered. Instead the committee looked for
targets that had many wood-frame buildings in close proximity
to each other, since they would be more vulnerable to the blast
and ensuing fires.[205]

What's extraordinary about the "no choice" illusion is its
staying power. Despite the wealth of scholarship dismantling its
myths and the blunt statements by men who executed the decision to drop the bomb—even "bombs away" Air Force General
Curtis LeMay later admitted it wasn't necessary, saying he did it
"because President Truman told me to do it"[206]—in the minds of
most Americans, the official narrative of my childhood still stands
as sacred truth and we owe Japanese civilians no apology.

In 1994, to mark the upcoming 50th anniversary of the
bombing, the US Postal Service designed a mushroom cloud
stamp with the words, "Atom bombs hasten war's end, August
1945." After protests from the Japanese government, President
Clinton withdrew the proposed stamp, but he refused to apolo-
gize for the bombing.[207] The Smithsonian National Air and Space
Museum planned an extensive exhibit for the anniversary, but its
content was censored when the curators dared to raise a few questions about the A-bomb decision.[208] The remains of a watch and
a child's melted lunchbox, found among the ruins of Hiroshima,

were excluded from the exhibit, lest they remind visitors of the flesh-and-blood people who perished that day.[209]

The second magic trick, the illusion of distance, depends on this censorship of the bomb's human impact. I grew up exposed to vivid pictures of the Holocaust's human toll, haunting images of emaciated concentration camp survivors and mass graves of crumpled skeletons. These lessened the distance between me and the millions who died. I saw and felt the horror of the Holocaust, knew it was evil, found hope in the words "never again." But the bomb wasn't about bodies, it was about a far-off mushroom cloud, more a force of nature than a human creation, eerie and even beautiful like the blue northers that roiled the big Texas sky.

Why didn't I see the bodies?

The abstraction was calculated. As Nagasaki's mayor remarked during the postage stamp controversy, the image of the cloud prevented people from seeing that beneath it "hundreds of thousands of noncombatant women and children were killed or injured on the spot."[210] Most Japanese survivors have no memory of seeing a mushroom cloud because it would have been visible only from high in the sky or miles away. At ground zero, all they saw was a blinding flash.[211] What happened to civilians was kept carefully from us, censored in fact. When pictures of the bombing were later shown to the American public, they were panoramic views of the destruction, burned buildings but not charred bodies.

It wasn't that the photographic footage didn't exist. Japanese photographer Yamahata Yosuke took pictures of the dead and wounded in Nagasaki a day after the blast. Initially, a few photographs of the carnage found their way into the American and Japanese press, but as the US began its military occupation of Japan, most of the visible evidence was seized and locked in a vault so as not to disturb "public tranquility."[212] The extent of radiation injuries was also kept hush-hush.[213]

With the end of American occupation in 1952, suppressed photographs and films of the atomic victims finally became available in Japan. But they remained largely unseen by American viewers until much later. Not until the late 1960s was film footage that had been confiscated by the American occupation authorities finally released.[214] If Americans had been exposed to those pictures earlier, as they were to the terrible realities of the Holocaust, might "never again" have come to include the atomic bomb as well? "Never again" has a healing finality to it, a moral assertiveness that helps keep apocalyptic fears at bay. Instead, the mushroom cloud carried another message: "always possible."

Shielding Americans from awareness of the bomb's impact on the Japanese prepared the way for the third magic trick, the illusion that the perpetrator is the victim, a key element of the America syndrome. How better to avoid moral responsibility for one's crimes than to assume victim status? The vacuum created by the censorship of the Japanese reality left a void in the American imagination which was filled by government propaganda that the bomb was coming to get *us*. The Atomic Energy Commission (AEC) distributed frightening images of atomic attacks on major American cities, including a glowing nuclear fireball above the New York skyline.[215] While this made it even easier to forget the suffering of the Japanese, it also made the apocalypse seem more imminent, coming soon to a war theater near you.

Not only the government engaged in these tactics. Well before the nuclear arms race between the Americans and the Soviets, popular media conjured up nightmarish scenarios of atomic death and destruction on US soil. In November 1945, scarcely three months after Hiroshima and Nagasaki, *Life* magazine ran a spread on "The 36-Hour War," a grim depiction of an atomic attack on 13 American cities, complete with realistic drawings of the ruins left behind. New York is pictured as a tangled mess of radioactive debris, with only the two iconic marble lions of the Public Library left standing watch.[216]

Initially, it wasn't clear who our actual enemy was. In *Life*'s 36-Hour War, the attackers are an unspecified hostile force operating from Africa, of all places. But once the Soviet Union detonated its first atomic bomb in 1949, the new enemy had a face. Already terrified and titillated by atomic thrills, many Americans fell under the spell of the fourth magic trick, the Great Satan illusion. Whatever moral ambiguity might have existed in the immediate aftermath of the war, it was now lost in the latest battle between the forces of Good and Evil.

The Christian dualism that underpins the Great Satan illusion is a potent element in the America syndrome. Add the God/Satan binary to the bomb and the result approaches a kind of national psychosis. This dualism provided important psychological scaffolding for the Cold War and the nuclear arms race, and became a defining characteristic of the age of American empire.

In his book on fear and faith in the arms race, Sheldon Ungar describes how the bomb came to be perceived as a mystical, quasi-religious entity, provoking powerful feelings of awe and transcendent power on the one hand, and dread and fear on the other. These aligned well with the country's civil religion: Only the Chosen People have the superior moral and spiritual qualities to own and control the bomb. As President Truman put it in 1945, "The possession in our hands of this new power of destruction we regard as a sacred trust."[217]

When the Soviets muscled into the action in 1949, it didn't take long for most Americans to view them as the diabolical foe. Indeed, the existence of precisely such a foe was necessary to create the public fear that sustained the American drive for nuclear supremacy. Periodic moral panics that Satan was about to overtake us—during the Korean War, the Soviets' Sputnik satellite launch, and the Cuban missile crisis—raised the background level of nuclear anxiety into near hysteria and fueled escalation of the arms race. The bomb became the only guarantor of the "American way of life," our shield against evil Soviet Communists who threatened the very foundations of our national identity, including that other sacred trust of ours, the "free market."[218] So strong was fear of Communism that a 1961 Gallup Poll found that, given the choice between fighting an all-out nuclear war and living under Communist rule, a whopping 81 percent of Americans chose war. In Britain, the corresponding figure was only 21 percent.[219]

For those working directly on the bomb, apocalypse became a way of life. In her early 1980s study of Amarillo, Texas, home to the Pantex nuclear weapons plant, A.G. Mojtabai found an extraordinary level of literal belief in the Christian apocalypse among plant employees as well as town inhabitants at all rungs of the social ladder. Rather than disarmament, they put their faith in the Rapture.[220]

Of course, not everyone succumbed to the Great Satan delusion. The non-believers included my own secular, liberal family. God might or might not exist—Unitarian Sunday school left it up to us to decide—and there was never any scare talk of Satan. My parents weren't fervent anti-Communists either; they believed in civil liberties and political pluralism and despised Joseph McCarthy. The message I received at home wasn't so much that the Soviets were evil, but that we had to beat them at their game. I still remember when my parents woke me up on a brisk fall night in 1957 to see Sputnik, the first satellite launched into space, twinkling across the sky. I'd never been outside in the middle of the night and the experience was more fun than scary. We were in a race with the Russians! I understood races—I loved to run and I loved to win. A whole generation of schoolchildren was Sputni-kized that night. Study hard and the country can catch up. Run, run, run. I internalized the message well into my teenage years. Wanting to help save the world, I studied Russian and strived to get good grades. Even as it began to dawn on me that the race was absurd, I kept running and running.

In Sputnik's aftermath, federal money poured into education, scientific research and development, defense reorganization, and the space program. A fictive "missile gap" between the Americans and Soviets was manufactured to justify the expenditures. The military-industrial complex that President Eisenhower had so presciently warned about was birthed and fattened, even over some of his own objections.[221] All for the race—but what lay beyond the finish line? Who would win when the end game was mass annihilation on both sides? In the face of such questions, it was no easy matter for the government to sustain public confidence in the crazed competition with the Great Satan. But one more magic trick lay up its sleeve: the illusion of atomic utopia as the counterpoint to nuclear Armageddon. Thanks to atomic energy, the New Jerusalem would be bathed in eternal light.

For every immanent doom forecast by the Cold Warriors, there was also the promise of a New Jerusalem only a few more steps away. It wasn't hard to sell. After all, the postwar years saw the spectacular rise of American consumer capitalism: the economy was booming, living standards were improving, Madison Avenue and the middle class danced in step. The bomb became an edgy part of the mix. In his book *By the Bomb's Early Light*, historian Paul Boyer describes how entrepreneurs and advertisers quickly seized on its sex appeal. The radioactive dust had barely settled in Hiroshima when "Atom Bomb Dancers" performed in burlesque shows in Los Angeles. *Life* magazine ran a full-page picture of "The Anatomic Bomb," a new MGM starlet who was featured lying languidly by a swimming pool, soaking up the rays. In 1946, when the US began nuclear tests in the South Pacific, the first bomb dropped on the Bikini islands sported an image of Rita Hayworth painted on its side, and a French designer coined the name "bikini" for a skimpy new bathing suit. For the kids, more wholesome items like the atomic bomb ring were available for 15 cents plus a Kix cereal box top from General Mills.[222]

In the aftermath of the Bikini tests, however, the public became warier of radiation effects. In the 1948 bestseller *No Place to Hide*, David Bradley, a physician employed by the Radiological Safety Unit in the islands, wrote powerfully about the ecological damage caused by the bombs and their impact on the displaced natives. The bomb started to lose its sex appeal.[223] As Americans began to shed some of their tasteless innocence, Cold Warriors found a new strategy to sell the bomb: the "peaceful atom" that would usher in a fantastic new energy millennium. Appealing to the American dream of eternal abundance, the AEC and corporate partners like General Electric launched a public relations campaign in the late 1940s that included exhibits, comic books, movies, and school textbooks about the wonders of the atom, focusing on its potential as an inexpensive and clean energy source. The 1948 high school study unit, *Operation Atomic Vision*, informed students that with nuclear power,

> You may live to drive a plastic car powered by an atomic engine and reside in a completely air-conditioned plastic house. Food will be cheap and abundant everywhere in

the world . . . No one will need to work long hours. There will be much leisure and a network of large recreational areas will cover the country, if not the world.[224]

In 1953 President Eisenhower delivered his famous "Atoms for Peace" speech before the UN, and in 1957 the world's first nuclear power plant went online in Shippingport, Pennsylvania.

As AEC Chairman David Lilienthal openly acknowledged, there was a symbiotic relationship between nuclear weapons and the atom's peaceful uses: they were two sides of the same coin.[225] Some scientists went even further, promoting nuclear bombs as tools for massive earthworks such as the construction of canals and harbors. In 1957 the AEC initiated Project Plowshare to investigate such possibilities, and a year later H-bomb guru Edward Teller launched Project Chariot, a plan to dig a deep water harbor at Cape Thompson in northwestern Alaska by means of thermonuclear bombs. The ostensible purpose was bringing economic development to the region, but the real motive was to test the latest weapons and, once again, to show the Soviets who was boss.[226]

While Project Chariot was ultimately foiled by resistance from the region's Inupiat inhabitants as well as critical work by scientists and ecologists (some of whom the government then blacklisted), the utopian promises of nuclear energy lived on. In the 1960s and early 1970s, more than a hundred nuclear power plants were constructed across the country. Their formidable financial costs gave lie to the claim of cheap energy abundance, and in 1979 the near-disaster at Three Mile Island gave lie to assurances of public safety. Despite the massive accidents at Chernobyl in 1986 and Fukushima in 2011, there is still talk of a "nuclear renaissance," this time in relation to climate change.

Together the five illusions—that there was no choice, that there were no tangible bodies, that the perpetrator was the victim, that the Soviet enemy was Satan, and that the atomic bomb held within it the promise of a New Jerusalem of plenty—helped put the country in an apocalyptic mood. Ask almost any one of us who grew up in those years what it was like and we'll tell you about the bomb drills at school—how we had to "duck and cover" under our desks or in the hallways, hands crossed behind our heads as if forcing ourselves to bow and pray. And then next we might tell you about the bomb shelter a neighbor built in his cellar. Drilled into us from an early age was the belief that we could survive a nuclear attack, a prospect that raised a disturbing existential question: Would we want to if our family and friends died and the world around us was destroyed?

GIMME SHELTER

If I were to draw a map of nuclear tourist territory, I'd highlight Highway 285 in New Mexico with glow-in-the-dark ink. Where the highway crosses from Texas into New Mexico, it skirts the town of Carlsbad. Famous for its remarkable caverns, Carlsbad also has the distinction of being near the Waste Isolation Pilot Plant (WIPP), one of the world's few underground dumps for permanent disposal of transuranic radioactive wastes, including plutonium, generated in the research and production of nuclear weapons.

Arriving by truck from over 12 government facilities, the waste is stored 2000 feet deep in a salt rock formation. The route from Los Alamos follows Highway 285 south through Santa Fe, with a new bypass built to keep the trucks out of the city center. Since plutonium is one of the most poisonous substances on Earth, taking over 24,000 years to lose just half of its radioactivity, one of the WIPP's challenges is how to communicate the site's dangers to generations in the distant future who may not speak our languages. The WIPP has consulted with linguists, scientists, science writers, and anthropologists to come up with communication strategies for people who may live in a future as distant from the present as the present is from the Stone Age. One of the solutions is a pictograph showing a skull and crossbones on cans of poisonous chemicals.[227]

The WIPP is not the only underground nuclear wonder along Highway 285. About 30 miles north of Carlsbad is the small town of Artesia, with a population of less than 12,000. Its main claim to fame is the now deserted Abo Elementary School, the first—and, as far as I know, the only—school to be built entirely underground to serve a dual purpose as school and fallout shelter. Designed to withstand a 20-megaton blast ten miles away, the reinforced concrete slab above the school doubled as the playground. I visited it on a parched day in March 2011. You can't go inside, so I stood on top. Apart from a national historical register plaque and a statue of an eagle with one wing missing, there's not much to see.

There's more history here than meets the eye, however. Abo was a tomb prepared for the living dead. The zombie apocalypse has nothing on Abo. A 1963 *Saturday Evening Post* article titled "Nuclear-age School: New Mexico students pursue knowledge underground," began with this vignette:

> Betsy Anne Hart, a fourth-grader in Artesia, New Mexico, learned something new at school the other day. "Mother," she burst out when she got home, "did you know there is a room for dead people at our school?" Having a morgue on the premises is just one of the things that makes

Betsy Anne's school unusual. For Abo Public Elementary School, named for a nearby oil formation, is the only school in the nation which lies entirely underground—and which doubles as a fully equipped fallout shelter.[228]

While students appreciated the air conditioning, and teachers found students to be "less rambunctious" with no windows to distract them, other features of the school elicited negative responses. As a bomb shelter, it contained enough space and provisions for only 2,160 people. Once that limit was reached, the 1,800-pound steel doors would be bolted shut. The other ten thousand or so people in Abo would be out of luck.

This worrisome math didn't escape the notice of Abo's students. Sixth-grader Martha Terpening told the *Post* reporter, "What I'm afraid of is that my mother is a teacher and she would be safe, but my daddy works at the post office and he wouldn't have any place to go." Studying underground also fostered other nuclear fears. "You think a lot about the danger while you're here," one boy confided. "Sometimes I have the feeling that fallout is coming now—that it is out there now—and then I go out and it isn't."[229]

That Artesia was selected as the location for the school-cum-shelter isn't surprising. The Trinity Site, where the first atomic bomb was exploded in 1945, lies 100 miles to the west on the White Sands Missile Range. Closer by, just up Highway 285 toward Roswell, Atlas nuclear missile silos dotted the landscape, placed there by the Strategic Air Command in the early 1960s. The region was a Cold War epicenter, a potential target. Artesia's terrorized residents agreed to the school, while in Roswell many people displaced their nuclear fears onto UFOs and space aliens. Roswell now hosts the International UFO Museum and Research Center, another must-see on New Mexico's nuclear tourist trail.

My husband took my picture there with the model of a space alien who looked like a cross between Casper the Ghost and ET.

The Abo school is an extreme example of the shelter craze that seized the country in the early 1960s. Before then, the government's civil defense preparations centered on the evacuation of city dwellers into rural areas as a short-term response, and suburbanization as a long-term strategy, to reduce likely nuclear death tolls amid major urban targets.[230] Released in 1951, the *Duck and Cover* booklet and animated film featuring Bert the Turtle ushered in an era of bomb drills in schools across the country. A pamphlet called *Survival under Atomic Attack* instructed adults on how to protect themselves by sheltering in a culvert or their cars.[231] In a particularly macabre exercise, New York City school officials experimented with giving pupils dog tags so their bodies could be identified after an atomic blast.[232] But with the development of the even more powerful hydrogen bomb, increased knowledge about fallout, and then the introduction in the late 1950s of ICBMs that reduced warning times to 15 minutes, it became more obvious that Bert the Turtle could no longer safely hide under his shell.

Civil defense officials had started some promotion of home shelters in the 1950s, likening nuclear attacks to survivable natural disasters like hurricanes, earthquakes, and tornadoes. But few home shelters were actually built—by March 1960 there were only an estimated 1500 nationwide.[233] Then in the summer of 1961 the Cold War suddenly heated up. When Khrushchev threatened to kick the Western allies out of Berlin, President Kennedy responded by raising the specter of a nuclear response. In July he called for a $207 million initiative to fund public and private fallout shelters, claiming that "the lives of those families which are not hit in a nuclear blast and fire can still be saved—*if* they can be warned to take shelter and *if* that shelter is available."[234] The

Cuban missile crisis the following year brought the world even closer to the brink of destruction.

The home shelter business took off. It was a shady business, complete with scam artists making quick bucks off people's fears. Across the country, shopping centers and trade shows sported models. By 1965 the number of shelters in American homes had risen to about 200,000, but then the craze died out. Historian Kenneth Rose describes the reasons for the demise of the home shelter: The 1963 nuclear test ban treaty eased superpower tensions. A well-designed and well-stocked shelter was too expensive for many families. Psychologically, many people were resistant to the idea of burrowing underground like moles. And a national conversation about "shelter morality" brought up uncomfortable issues, like whether or not you would "Gun Thy Neighbor" if he or she pleaded to be let in. Added to these was a sense of mental fatigue from accommodating so long the prospect of Armageddon.[235]

Even if most Americans didn't burrow in shelters, the *idea* of the bomb shelter burrowed deep into many of us. Scholars have analyzed the ways Cold War civil defense reflected and reinforced the dominant stereotypes of the time. The families depicted in bomb shelter propaganda and advertisements were invariably white and middle class, with father and son doing the construction and mother and daughter laying in the provisions.[236] The nuclear family for the nuclear age.

I came across my first bomb shelter at the age of 10 or 11, in a shopping center a few miles from our house in the burgeoning suburbs of north Dallas. There in the parking lot, a pod-like model was on display, complete with a mannequin nuclear family. The attractive mom was serving a tray of what looked like TV dinners. By the time of the Cuban missile crisis, rich classmates of mine had their own bomb shelters outside town on their daddies' ranches. I wasn't exactly jealous of them—I suffer from claustrophobia—but there was something that fascinated me about shelters, their doll-house quality, as if they were made for play, for setting the mannequins in motion.

The image of the mommy mannequin stayed with me for a long time. I'd seen ones like her before in glittery Dallas department stores, where like giant Barbie dolls they offered up their nubile bodies to be clothed in the latest fashions. Mannequins were about buying, not dying, but the two became connected in my mind. It was as if the spectacle of the bomb and the spectacle of consumerism were two sides of a coin. Inside the bomb shelter, food and water would surely run out—I was old enough to make that calculation. But outside, while the world still existed, affluence beckoned like the Christmas star.

I didn't know then that mannequins were also used in experiments at the Nevada Test Site, where the army constructed mock towns and suburbs to see the effects of the blasts. The mannequins who populated them were always white and well-dressed. In a perverse form of product placement, in one test they sported clothes donated by the J.C. Penney corporation.[237] A 1953 issue of *National Geographic* featured a piece on how "Nevada Learns to Live with the Atom . . . Sagebrush State Takes the Spectacular Tests in Stride." In one photograph, a well-heeled female mannequin is driving a Cadillac—lucky for her, the bomb only buckled the top of the car. In another, a "winsome" female dummy, a classy robe slipping provocatively off her shoulders, sits smilingly intact in a cellar shelter.[238]

The '50s zeitgeist was of course weird and unsettling in other ways, too. Women who had joined the formal workforce during World War II were pushed back into an overdetermined domesticity. Television came to supersede radio as a form of enter-

tainment, and we were brought up on *Leave it to Beaver*, Mickey
Mouse, the black stereotypes of *Amos 'n' Andy*, and the routine
slaughtering of Native Americans and Mexicans in popular West-
erns. Paranoia spread that Communists and perverts were hiding
under every bed. Along with the Cold War, there was a hot war
in Korea. Independence struggles were waged across the globe,
from Cuba, to Algeria, to Vietnam. We were taught to fear the
dangerous forces let loose by decolonization.

Underneath the surface of things, one could also sense the ice
cracking, culturally and politically. Alternative music, art, and
literary scenes flourished while the civil rights movement started
to shake up the foundations of our segregated society. But of all
the many influences on us, what really punctuated our childhood psyches was the flaming red exclamation point of nuclear
apocalypse.

NUCLEAR ABNORMALITIES

In the first decades of the Cold War, remarkably little attention
was paid to the bomb's psychological and emotional effects on
children, or for that matter on adults, except as they pertained to
the efficient execution of civil defense strategy. The government
tried to strike a careful balance between scaring the public enough
to take civil defense seriously and keeping them from panicking,
or even worse, rejecting nuclear weapons altogether.

The psychology profession offered a helping hand in the propaganda operations needed to establish this "nuclear normality,"
an early example of the militarization of inner space.[239] In the
mid-1950s, the National Security Council and the Federal Civil
Defense Administration enlisted prominent psychiatrists on a
panel to study how to prepare Americans to accept the risk of a

nuclear attack. In its 1956 report, the panel recommended "less emphasis on the symbols and images of disaster," since drawing attention to the possibility of annihilation could cause the public to be "attuned to the avoidance of nuclear war, no matter what the cost," a pacifist response that would weaken support for the government's policies. Instead the authors recommended a patriotic call to "our pioneer background and inheritance [which] predispose us to count hardships as a challenge and fortify us against complacency."[240] The choice of words was ironic, for public complacency was exactly what they were aiming for.

It wasn't until the early 1960s that a few true pioneers in the psychology profession ventured to learn how children were experiencing the nuclear threat. One of them was Sibylle Escalona, a researcher and clinician associated with the prestigious Menninger Clinic in Kansas. Her best known work was on the emotions and play of infants. In 1962–63, Escalona and her colleagues conducted a survey of 311 New York City area schoolchildren between the ages of 10 and 17 to assess their views of the future. Even though the survey made no specific reference to war, more than two-thirds of the students, who were drawn from varied socioeconomic backgrounds, mentioned it. "All the people will die and the world will blow up," wrote one. Even those who didn't think war would happen imagined a grim future—for example, one in which everyone was forced to live underground. Only a few perceived the danger as coming from Communism; the vast majority of the kids saw the problem as nations and people just needing to get along better. "I wish Russia and Cuba [would] be our friends," wrote a ten-year-old in what was a common refrain.[241]

Psychologist Milton Schwebel at New York University's School of Education conducted similar research. A peace activist, Schwebel helped to found the field of peace psychology. He led a fight against a New York State plan to build bomb shelters in schools; his efforts brought praise from Eleanor Roosevelt.[242] In 1961–62, Schwebel and his colleagues surveyed about 3000 students, mostly of high school age, in the New York City area, upstate New York, and suburban Philadelphia. The questions they asked were more directed than Escalona's open-ended ones: Did students think there was going to be a war? Did they care? What did they think about fallout shelters?

The researchers found that students cared deeply about the threat of nuclear war. Indeed, students described "the nightmarish horrors with such vividness" that one might think they had read accounts of Hiroshima survivors.[243] Most believed that shelters should be available to everyone, and they worried about being separated from their families during an attack. Many wished for peace. "Time and again," Schwebel wrote, "the students described their universe as a highly uncertain one, its people greedy and irrational, its future questionable. Their great hope lay in the fact that no nation could win and that rational people would not choose suicide, or that, at least conflict would be postponed until they had a chance 'to live', i.e. to work, marry, have children."[244] While most functioned normally in their day-to-day lives, these fears gnawed at them, and some turned to denial. Schwebel's conclusion was that the threat of nuclear disaster should be a focus of "therapeutic collective action"—by helping to build a more peaceful world, students would feel more secure.[245]

What was the reaction to these remarkable studies? The silence was deafening. For more than a decade, no other researchers touched the topic. Was this because the young people were voicing truths and fears that government and society wanted to avoid? Or because the psychologists themselves couldn't deal emotionally with the subject, since they too were afraid to plumb the depths of nuclear fear, worried as they were about their own families' safety?[246] It wasn't until the late 1970s that attention returned to the issue, when the American Psychiatric Association Task Force on the Psychosocial Impacts of Nuclear Developments surveyed over a thousand high school students. They found "a profound dis-ease and uncertainty about the future and a considerable amount of general pessimism" in student attitudes about nuclear war, civil defense, and survival.[247]

The election of President Ronald Reagan in 1980 brought the Cold War to another boiling point, as US nuclear policy shifted from the status quo of MAD, mutual assured destruction, to the demented Strategic Defense Initiative, popularly known as "Star Wars." In 1983 Reagan announced the government's plan to build a ground- and space-based missile defense system that would protect the country from nuclear attack. In reality, Star Wars was more about a first strike offense than a last ditch defense. If we could attack the Soviets first and protect ourselves from a counter-attack, we could win a nuclear war. And if a few Soviet bombs managed to penetrate our shield, we could tough it out. As T.K. Jones, Deputy Under Secretary of Defense for Strategic and Nuclear Forces, advised: "Dig a hole, cover it with a couple of doors and then throw three feet of dirt on top . . . It's the dirt that does it . . . [I]f there are enough shovels to go around, everybody's going to make it."[248]

Reagan's belligerence galvanized anti-nuclear resistance. The same year that he announced the Star Wars initiative, the widely viewed TV film *The Day After* graphically represented what life would be like for a family in Lawrence, Kansas in the aftermath of an atomic bomb. Fears of a nuclear winter enveloping the globe sent shivers up the spine. In the US and Europe, anti-nuclear movements gathered supporters and gained strength.

This sparked a new wave of research on children by psychologists and educators. In addition to undertaking student surveys, groups such as Educators for Social Responsibility and the Union of Concerned Scientists created curricula and sponsored dialogues in schools where children could voice their concerns about nuclear war.[249] Anti-nuclear curricula in the schools drew the ire of conservative hawks. The 1983 Congressional hearing on *Children's Fears of War*, conducted by the Select Committee on Children, Youth, and Families, provides a window on how this aspect of child psychology became politicized. A Republican representative from Virginia denounced anti-nuclear curricula as a form of "political indoctrination." A Kansas psychiatrist testified that it could lead to the "devitalization" of America and induce in students despair, hopelessness, and unwillingness to support the military. He offered a different explanation for rising symptoms of psychological distress among children:

> As you know, family life in our society is deteriorating at a terrifying rate. The divorce epidemic is the major factor for this deterioration, but the mass exodus of women from the home, often due to economic pressure but also and probably largely to the seductive but false drumbeat of the women's lib movement are major determinants . . . The developing child pays the highest penalty for the breakup of the home, the part-time or pathological home.[250]

Prominent anti-nuclear psychiatrists, including Robert Jay Lifton, together with three eloquent students from Iowa, New York, and California, offered opposing views.

I was in my early thirties at the time of that hearing, living in England, soon to become pregnant with my first child. At the time, the sense of impending apocalypse was very real. I remember sitting around with my husband and friends and worrying about the risk of nuclear war in Europe. On the wall of our apartment we had a mock movie poster of *Gone with the Wind*, picturing Ronald Reagan holding Margaret Thatcher in his arms with a mushroom cloud in the background. "The Film to End all Films," the caption read, "The Most EXPLOSIVE Love Story Ever." And below the picture: "She promised to follow him to the end of the earth. He promised to organize it."

Such gallows humor helped—just as Stanley Kubrick's brilliant film *Dr. Strangelove* had helped in the 1960s—but I found real therapy, as Dr. Schwebel had recommended two decades before, in collective action. I marched with thousands of protestors against cruise missiles in Amsterdam in 1981, alongside a contingent of Dutch soldiers in uniform who were cheered when they joined the rally. In 1983 I marched with a million people in London in the Campaign for Nuclear Disarmament's protest over the siting of American cruise and Pershing II missiles in England. Almost every day brought news of inspiring actions at peace encampments, such as the famous women's camp near Greenham Common in England where tens of thousands of women joined hands around the Royal Air Force base's perimeter fence. Back in the US, the nuclear freeze movement attracted many new supporters, including Democratic Party leaders. The sense that we were finally waking up from the nuclear nightmare was empowering. And the historical record suggests that the anti-nuclear movement really was powerful—it helped to push the Americans and Soviets toward disarmament.[251]

With the end of the Cold War, the potential for nuclear Armageddon receded from public consciousness. There has been little research about its lingering psychological effects in the baby boom generation. Is the bomb at the root of some of my generation's pervasive anxieties? Does it continue to influence our relationships with people, nature, and death? Does it make us more susceptible to apocalyptic fears? To speak in generational terms is surely to over-generalize, but the times you grow up in matter and never stop mattering. They churn the water you swim in, steer the direction of the currents, make it easier or harder to come up for breath.

Of all the psychologists and psychiatrists who have written on the human dimensions of the nuclear bomb, Robert Jay Lifton's work remains the most relevant today. In the early 1960s, Lifton was the first American to study the psychological legacy of the bomb in Japanese survivors. He went on from there to study its effects at home, becoming a powerful professional and political voice against nuclear weapons.

Lifton uncovered a number of influences. The fact that the bomb was shrouded in secrecy gave it the special power of forbidden knowledge, especially for children. Adults developed psychic numbing as a defensive measure against the ever-present threat of mass annihilation. Indeed, the continued existence of the nuclear weapons complex depended on a high degree of collective numbing. When fear periodically broke through, it often led to feelings of resignation, cynicism, and a bleak view of the human species. "Well, what is so special about man?" is how Lifton describes the syndrome. "Other species have come and gone, so perhaps this is our turn to become extinct."[252] One hears this same refrain today among those despondent about climate change. For many, the bomb represented the final triumph of the machine over humanity, Frankenstein on nuclear steroids.

But numbing and cynicism weren't universal reactions. Some people were keenly aware that they were leading a double life:

going about their day-to-day business when at any moment they and their loved ones, and maybe the whole planet, could be obliterated. In the best of circumstances, the radical absurdity of this contrast inspired political art and organized action against the bomb. "It is when we lose our sense of nuclear absurdity that we surrender to the forces of annihilation and cease to imagine the real," Lifton wrote.[253]

The bomb profoundly shaped human relationships with nature too. Images of mushroom clouds and nuclear devastation intensified painful feelings of separation from the ideal of a healing and eternal nature. As explored before, the desire to overcome that separation helps to explain the lure of the 1960s back-to-the-land movement. With a doctrinaire emphasis on self-sufficiency, many back-to-the-landers embraced survivalist strategies, acting "as if the bomb had already been dropped."[254] Writer Janferie Stone vividly captures the mood:

> The communal movement must be posed against our sense of the world as a terminally dangerous place. Our dreams were reft by images of nuclear holocaust; we were the generation who had practiced hiding under our desks in the Cuban Missile Crisis. We had bomb shelter visions of a world that, if poisoned, might begin anew. Humanity, nuclearly cleansed, tutored by destruction, might do better in such a future . . . We thought that in a community of scale we could pick up the pieces, we could create if not a new society then an *On the Beach* fulfillment of each day that we had yet to live.[255]

The search for purity took other forms as well. No doubt there were many reasons for getting high on drugs, or meditation, or both, but one was a yearning for transcendent, peak experiences as a counterweight to the prospect of atomic extinction. "When the structure of existence is threatened, people seek to do more with or to their bodies, to extend the experience of their total organisms," observed Lifton.[256] For writer Norman Mailer, the radical experientialism of the nuclear age was gloriously embodied in the macho figure of the "hipster" or "the American existentialist" who confronts death, divorces himself from society, and sets out on "that uncharted journey into the rebellious imperatives of the self."[257]

The prospect of the bomb dropping also functioned as a metaphor of escape from the boring routines and existential malaise of everyday life. "The malaise has settled like a fallout," wrote Walker Percy in his novel *The Moviegoer*, "and what people really fear is not that the bomb will fall but that the bomb will not fall."[258]

Among those who chose to tow the government line and embrace nuclear weapons, the result could be a retreat into fundamentalism. Some made sense of the world through rigid categories of good and evil, a nostalgia for the past, and religious convictions about the future. For others of a more secular persuasion, the bomb created a sense of "radical futurelessness," sowing doubts about the authenticity and endurance of individual achievement.[259]

But of all the psychological effects of the bomb, Lifton saw our changed relationship with death as the "most fundamental psychic deformation."[260] The bomb turned what would otherwise be our normal fears of death—or rather our fears of normal death—into grotesque images of nuclear annihilation, creating profound anxiety about the end of not only our own lives, but of life itself. One of the major psychological challenges of our times, then, was to reclaim "plain old death" and separate it from the insanity of nuclear holocaust.[261]

Many of Lifton's insights ring true in my own experience: growing up with the sense of a double life and the absurdity of it all, seeking a purer relationship with nature, doubting the value of my own achievements, fearing death as a violent cataclysm. In a country of abundance, I shared the pervasive but irrational fear of scarcity, maybe rooted in the anxiety that food, water, and fresh air would run out in the bomb shelter and nothing would grow in the barren world outside. In the end, the mannequin mommy, no matter how pretty and resourceful, could only offer me an empty tray. Lifton didn't write about this particular fear, but I believe it haunts my generation much as the Great Depression haunted our parents.

If I were lying on a therapist's couch, she or he would tell me that you can't blame all of your problems *just* on the bomb. Likewise, historians would remind us that we can't isolate the bomb's impact from the wide drive for American military supremacy after World War II. True enough. But even so, the bomb itself casts a long shadow, accounting in no small measure for the endurance of apocalyptic thought in other realms.

The bomb still threatens world peace, too, even though the prospect of an all-out nuclear war thankfully has diminished. Political instability in Pakistan casts doubt on the safety of its nuclear facilities, North Korea remains a nuclear wildcard, and the open secret that Israel has the bomb ups the ante in the Middle East. Poorly protected sites in the former Soviet Union raise the specter of terrorists acquiring nuclear materials.

Between them, the US and Russia now possess almost 95 percent of the world's nuclear warheads. The US has nearly 5000. Despite hopeful pronouncements early in Obama's tenure, the important diplomatic effort to prevent Iran from developing the bomb, and his historic visit to Hiroshima in 2016 in which he called for a world without nuclear weapons, Barack Obama did less to cut the nuclear arsenal than his predecessors Bill Clinton and both Bushes. Over the next 10 years, the US government plans to spend at least $570 billion—the price tag could rise to a trillion—for new nuclear weaponry and related programs, including 12 new nuclear-armed submarines that can carry up to 1000 hydrogen bombs between them. The government's latest Nuclear Posture Review still holds open the possibility of using nuclear weapons in response to nuclear, biological, or chemical weapons deployment by countries that are judged to be in non-compliance with nonproliferation obligations.[262] Donald Trump's cavalier statements about nuclear weapons are frightening, to say the least. Also alarming is a Pentagon advisory board's recent suggestion that the US increase its stock of lower-yield nuclear weapons for possible "limited use" in regional conflicts.[263] Disarmament, in other words, has a long way to go.

Meanwhile the specter of the bomb continues to work its political magic. "We don't want the smoking gun to be a mushroom cloud," National Security Advisor Condoleezza Rice memorably warned in 2002 as the Bush administration ramped up fears of Iraq's supposed weapons of mass destruction. This ostensible threat helped soften up the American public for the invasion of Iraq the following year.[264]

BEYOND ARTESIA AND AMNESIA

In summer 2014, national headlines about Artesia, New Mexico caught my eye. Six hundred mothers and their children seeking asylum from drug war-related violence in Central America were imprisoned in a federal immigration detention facility only a few miles away from the site of the Abo underground elementary school.[265] "We will send you back," Obama's Homeland Security Secretary Jeh Johnson warned the incarcerated women and children when he visited the facility.[266] A lawsuit before the federal District Court in Washington charged officials in Artesia with "egregious" violations of due process, including lack of access to lawyers and rushed video-teleconference deportation hearings.[267] The detention facility has now been shut down and the mothers and children coming over the border have been imprisoned elsewhere.

Perhaps it's not surprising that Homeland Security set up an immigrant detention center in the bleak nuclear landscape of southeastern New Mexico. During the Cold War, the government claimed to be protecting Artesia's children from the enemy. In 2014 Homeland Security claimed the nation needed protection from the immigrant children they were rushing to deport.

Meanwhile, the real threat to security in the region lies 30 miles down the road at the WIPP nuclear waste dump. It, too, made national headlines in 2014 when a chemical reaction caused a radioactive leak that traveled up the mine shaft into the open environment. It turns out a container of nuclear waste from Los Alamos National Laboratory was improperly packaged with an organic brand of kitty litter that can generate high heat, instead of the usual inorganic product.[268] At first the accident's seriousness was downplayed, but it forced the closure of WIPP—it's only just been reopened in January 2017—with the cost of clean-up perhaps topping $2 billion, making it one of the costliest nuclear accidents in US history. A new ventilation system needed to be put in place, and 35 percent of the underground area was contaminated. Meanwhile, in nuclear facilities like Los Alamos and the Hanford Site in Washington state, nuclear waste destined for WIPP has gotten dangerously backed up. Originally, the Energy

Department calculated that one such incident might occur at the WIPP facility every 200,000 years. This one happened only 15 years after its opening and the cause was something as simple as the wrong kind of kitty litter.[269] It was just lucky that only one barrel was contaminated.

And so the deadly gift of the Manhattan Project keeps on giving. The probability of human error underscores the continuing mortal danger posed by the nuclear weapons complex. Nuclear near-misses—and there have been many—turn up the volume on apocalypse. Journalist Eric Schlosser uncovered a January 1961 incident in which two hydrogen bombs were accidentally dropped by a B-52 bomber over North Carolina when the plane broke up in mid-air. Had it not been for one final low-voltage switch, one of the bombs would have detonated, creating a blast 260 times stronger than the bomb that obliterated Hiroshima.[270] In more recent days, the Air Force has been rocked by revelations of cheating on proficiency tests as well as safety and code protection violations among members of nuclear missile launch crews.[271] The scandals hardly inspire confidence in the system designed to secure our weapons of mass destruction and prevent their inadvertent deployment.

One of my last stops in New Mexico was the office of Tewa Women United, an indigenous women's organization in the town of Española, not far from Los Alamos. There I spoke with Beata Tsosie-Peña, the coordinator of the group's environmental justice program. Tsosie-Peña knows firsthand about the ongoing health threats to tribal communities posed by waste from Los Alamos, including elevated cancer rates. She participated in a project of the US Centers for Disease Control and Prevention (CDC) that documented for the first time the exposure of area residents to high levels of radiation. The preface to the CDC's final report features a poem by Tsosie-Peña. She calls for a time of healing for "the good of all future generations":

> Let us share the stories that have never been told
> And release the pain not even a century old
> No longer shamed by accusations of ignorance
> Let our diverse voices be our deliverance . . .[272]

Remembering the past, and believing in the future, can be a powerful antidote to apocalyptic despair. Beata now campaigns for transforming Los Alamos from a nuclear lab to a site of environmental restoration and research into renewable energy.

The bomb was never a *given*. Its development was, and is, a conscious choice by national security officials. Stripping the bomb of its magic and inevitability positions it differently. We *can* rid the world of the scourge of nuclear weapons if we choose to do so. As the history of the Cold War shows, sanity backed by the force of collective action can prevail. That may not be enough to rid the mind of apocalyptic fears, but it's a helpful start toward deliverance.

Chapter Four

THE CHURCH OF MALTHUS

The ancient Okewood Church nestles in a shady grove of oak, beech, and hazel trees. Although it's not very far from London's Gatwick airport, the journey there takes you back in time. When a friend drove me to Okewood 10 years ago, we got lost more than once on back country roads and narrow lanes. I'm not a religious person, but when we finally parked the car and found the grassy path leading to the churchyard, I felt like I was on a pilgrimage. Some say the 13th-century church is built on the former site of a Druid temple and then a Roman villa. Over the centuries, its fate has vacillated between ruin and restoration, and today it appears slightly off-kilter, like a boat buffeted too long by strong winds. It's still open for Sunday services, though.

Charmingly Old World though it is, not many tourists seek out Okewood Church unless they happen to be admirers or critics of the Reverend Thomas Robert Malthus. Okewood's main claim to fame is that Robert Malthus (he went by his middle name) served as its curate in the last decade of the 18th century before going on to become the father of the "dismal science" of economics.

Malthus came from a cosmopolitan landed family. His father

Daniel was what today we would call a liberal intellectual, an optimist who believed in the capacity of mankind to improve through education and scientific and technical progress. He was a friend of the philosophers Jean-Jacques Rousseau and David Hume. He sent his son to Cambridge University to study mathematics, where Robert distinguished himself. He also encouraged him to take orders in the Anglican Church as a way to make a living, since, as a younger son, Robert wouldn't inherit the family property.

Robert's first post was at Okewood. Most of his parishioners were poor and illiterate, living in cramped huts and surviving on a diet of bread and little else. Their children suffered from stunted growth. Despite these miserable conditions, Robert noted from studying church records that the number of baptisms was much higher than the number of burials—births in the area greatly outnumbered deaths. This disparity evidently sparked his concern about the evils of population growth.[273]

Malthus reckoned that, if left unchecked, human population grows in a geometric progression: 1, 2, 4, 8, 16, 32, 64, 128, 256, etc.; while food production at best follows a linear arithmetic path: 1, 2, 3, 4, 5, 6, etc. This condemns humanity to a constant battle to provide adequate sustenance for its numbers. "The race of plants and the race of animals shrink under this great restrictive law," Malthus wrote, "and man cannot by any efforts of reason escape from it."[274] Only the afflictions of hunger, poverty, disease, and war keep human numbers in check by increasing death rates, with some help from moral restraint or "vice" (infertility caused by venereal diseases) in reducing birth rates. Even though some forms of birth control existed in his time, the conservative Malthus had little truck with it. In his eyes, the poor especially were doomed to live in a state of perpetual deprivation because of their fertility. They were responsible for their own misery.

Was it a form of filial rebellion that he reached conclusions so much more pessimistic about mankind than those of his optimistic father? While Daniel must have argued with Robert, in the end he encouraged his son to put his ideas on paper. The result, *An Essay on the Principle of Population*, first appeared in 1798, and he expanded on its themes in later editions. Because Malthus presented his conclusions as inexorable laws of economics, the field acquired its lasting sobriquet as the "dismal science."

Malthus took on prominent progressive thinkers of his time, men like the Marquis de Condorcet and William Godwin who had more faith in human reason, altruism, and agency, and believed it was possible to build a more equitable and peaceful world. Malthus derided them for locating the causes of misery and vice in human institutions. He insisted that the "deeper-seated causes of evil" are "the laws of nature and the passions of mankind."[275] This passage from his *Essay* sums it up:

> That the principal and most permanent cause of poverty has little or no *direct* relation to forms of government, or the unequal division of property; and that, as the rich do not in reality possess the *power* of finding employment and maintenance for the poor, the poor cannot, in the nature of things, possess the *right* to demand them; are important truths flowing from the principle of population . . .[276]

That is, the rich owed nothing to the poor, and the poor had no right to expect better.

Malthus left Okewood Church after a few years and ultimately abandoned his career as a clergyman to become the chair of political economy at a college that trained colonial officers of the East

India Company. The school of thought he founded has much in common with a fundamentalist religion, however. The idea that human population growth must inexorably outstrip resources, and that it is the major cause of hunger, poverty, environmental degradation, and war, has become a veritable article of faith. From its demographic twist on the doctrine of original sin to the threat of apocalypse that awaits mankind if it doesn't heed its commandments, Malthusianism preaches hellfire and brimstone in the guise of science.

Like most religions, it has developed orthodox and reformist wings. At one extreme are militants who would not only welcome a die-off of a significant part of the human race, but want to hasten it. Some feel compelled to take the matter into their own hands. In 2010, a deranged young man named James J. Lee strapped bombs to his body and held three employees hostage at the headquarters of the Discovery Channel, outside Washington, DC, because he believed the channel wasn't doing enough to raise the alarm about human overpopulation and animal extinction. The police shot and killed him.[277]

More moderate are the "neo-Malthusians" who believe in the central tenet of the faith—the evils of population growth—but espouse contraception as a technical fix. This denomination of the Malthusian "religion" holds great sway today in the American environmental movement, where it co-exists, sometimes easily and sometimes not, with other beliefs. Often a double standard comes into play: on their own home turf, environmentalists may clearly identify the institutions responsible for ecological harm: the dirty factory, the toxic dump, the government bureaucrats soft on polluters. But when it comes to poorer communities, and poorer countries, they see "too many people"—too many dark-skinned young people especially—as the root of the problem.

You don't have to be a card-carrying member of the "Church of Malthus" to be influenced by it. Ask almost any American, liberal or conservative, young or old, man or woman, and you'll find the belief that overpopulation is a big problem. That more people equals more resources consumed is just common sense. In the baby boom generation, fear of overpopulation often occupies the same subliminal zone as the residue of nuclear terror. It may not be a coincidence that the "population bomb" captured the American imagination at the height of the Cold War, although it has a longer history.

Malthusianism is like a religion not just because of the canonical nature of its beliefs, but because of its tremendous institutional clout and public relations power. Money speaks too loudly in the US, and with the backing of some of the wealthiest families in the country, the "Church of Malthus" has managed to spread its message far and wide.

In criticizing Malthusianism, I'm not suggesting that increases in the number of human beings have *no* impact on the natural environment or human society. Rather, the relationship is complicated, varying over time and from place to place. It is mediated by a host of other factors—economic, political, and cultural. The relationship between population growth and human and environmental health can be negative, positive, or non-existent. It's not subject to one universal logic or law.

What makes Malthusianism so dangerous is not only its claim to universalism, but its appeal to apocalypse. In the policy realm, from family planning to the environment to national security, it convinces many otherwise well-meaning people that it is morally justified to curtail the basic human and reproductive rights of poor people at home and abroad in order to save ourselves and the planet from otherwise certain doom. This sense of emergency fosters an elitist moral relativism, in which "we" know best and "our" rights are more worthy than "theirs." It harkens back to the Puritan days, when the chosen people judged natives and slaves as less worthy, less human than themselves. The costs of this ideology are especially high for the women targeted by population control programs that are designed to reduce birth rates as quickly and cheaply as possible, using coercion if necessary.

In recent years, a more politically-correct variant of population control has taken hold among many young, college-educated women in the US. Rather than blame poor women for overpopulation, they blame themselves. Lisa Hymas, senior editor at the environmental blog Grist, proudly identifies herself as a GINK— green inclinations, no kids. "The population problem is all about *me*," she writes, "white, middle-class, American me. Steer the blame right over here . . . Far and away the biggest contribution I can make to a cleaner environment is not to bring any mini-me's into the world."[278] In a curious narcissistic twist, she pins responsibility for the world's ecological ills on her womb and those of other women like her. Her piece is accompanied by an image of a blond, blue-eyed white woman looking at herself in the mirror. Blondes may have more fun, but they shouldn't have any children.

The right-wing war on women's rights in the US targets female fertility and sexuality too, but in a different way, by seeking to deny women access to contraception and abortion. Anti-choice forces have invoked the worst abuses of eugenics and population control to paint all family planning programs as evil. In an effort to appeal to African Americans, they argue that abortion is black genocide. Billboards appeared in African American neighborhoods in the Atlanta area in 2010 featuring a picture of a sad-looking black boy with the caption, "Black Children are an Endangered Species." An anti-abortion website address was also provided. The billboards, cooked up in a secret meeting between representatives of the Georgia Right to Life organization and the state's Republican Party, were intended not only to restrict abortion, but to split the African American vote.[279]

At first glance, it may seem strange that politicians who care little about poor children, black or white, when it comes to funding health care or education, nevertheless oppose their mothers having access to birth control and abortion. It might seem more logical for the Right to join the neo-Malthusians in supporting population control, rather than opposing it. But the woman in the home—pregnant if not barefoot—remains a potent symbol of patriarchal social order, the bedrock of conservatism. Abortion is such a loaded issue in the US because it is freighted with this heavy political baggage. Besides, many Americans see no problem with espousing inconsistent views. So one can defend the rights of the fetus, but deny the rights of the child.

In the national debate on population, it's easy to get locked into an either/or binary: population control on the one hand, or the anti-abortion movement on the other. In speaking over the years against population control, I've been accused of being an agent of the Pope, as if there is no middle ground. Like many advocates of reproductive rights, I support access to safe, voluntary contraception and abortion—not as top-down tools of social engineering, or purported ways to avert planetary doom, but because they are vital to women's health, autonomy, and freedom. I have dedicated much of my adult life to the struggle to attain reproductive rights for all women. My journey down this road began in a small village in Bangladesh.

MATTERS OF LIFE AND DEATH

In the mid-1970s, my husband and I lived for nine months in a village in northwestern Bangladesh, gathering the material for our book, *A Quiet Violence*. Though the land was lush and fertile, times were hard. The country was recovering from its bloody 1971 independence war from Pakistan and a more recent manmade famine. In 1974, monsoon floods had damaged crops in some parts of the country, and grain merchants took advantage of the situation by hoarding rice to drive up prices. The new government was too callous, or too corrupt, to do anything about it. Meanwhile, the US government, in its Cold War wisdom, was holding up food shipments to Bangladesh to punish it for selling raw jute, the fiber used to make burlap bags, to Cuba.

While many people in the village suffered during this period, young children were most at risk. They were more vulnerable not only to prolonged malnutrition, but also to endemic diarrheal diseases caused by lack of clean water. When we lived in Bangladesh, one in four children died before reaching the age of five. My nearest neighbor had borne 11 children. Six had died. High rates of infant and child mortality were factored into the villagers' grim calculus of survival. Needing children to help in the home and the fields, and sons to care for them in old age, parents had to have many children in order to ensure that a few would survive. The resulting surplus of births over deaths was not the cause of the villagers' poverty, but rather a symptom of it.

As time went on, the villagers taught us about the real causes of poverty: unequal land distribution; lack of education, health care, and other public services; political repression; patriarchal social relations that forced girls to marry early and denied opportunities to women—the sorts of human institutions to which Malthus turned a blind eye. When villagers went hungry, it wasn't because of absolute scarcities of food, but because they lacked the land on which to grow it or money with which to buy it.

As I grew closer to the village women, many wanted to know why I didn't have any children yet. When I told them about birth control, they were eager to get it. Some women were ready to stop childbearing altogether, while others wanted to space their pregnancies to protect their health. Many men were supportive of their wives using birth control, too. The problem was that none was available. We visited the family planning office in the nearest district town and asked them to visit the village. The family planning workers showed up once, but they treated the village women with contempt and left behind a few cartons of birth control pills with no instructions on how to use them.[280]

Some years later, after we had left Bangladesh, international aid donors pressed the government to launch a massive sterilization campaign to drive down birth rates. The logic was Malthusian and the methods draconian. The country's fledgling health care system was skewed toward sterilization as the top priority; the job security and salaries of government health workers depended on achieving sterilization targets. Poor people received cash payments, funded by the US government, if they agreed to be sterilized. In some parts of the country, starving women were denied food relief unless they produced a certificate showing that they had been sterilized. In others, the army forcibly rounded up men for vasectomies.[281] So much for the access to voluntary family planning that the villagers I knew had sorely wanted.

I was living in England at this time, where I was part of an international network of scholars and aid workers concerned about development and human rights in Bangladesh. At that point in my life, I had no idea that population policy was to become cen-

tral to my political and professional career. The network asked
me to write about the sterilization drive, and after that, one thing
led to another: first articles and pamphlets, then a book on the
global politics of population control, *Reproductive Rights and
Wrongs*, and eventually my job as director of the Population and
Development Program at Hampshire College for 26 years. Malthus has haunted me every step of the way. If I were superstitious,
I'd believe his ghost still roams the world. While his influence has
sometimes waned, today, with climate change and economic woes
weighing us down, his ideas are back in vogue.

Writing as he did at the end of the 18th century, perhaps Malthus can be excused for not foreseeing the remarkable advances in
agriculture and industry that were about to unfold in his native
land, or predicting that living standards in Britain would steadily
rise, unhindered by population growth. Economic historians
Douglass North and Robert Thomas have argued that, far from
being a curse, population growth in fact was the prime mover
behind Europe's technological revolutions and that it "spurred
the institutional innovations which account for the rise of the
Western world."[282] Whatever the role of population growth in
making it happen, the simple fact is that, from Malthus's time
onwards, global food production has grown faster than human
numbers, an outcome that the Reverend never thought possible.

This is not to say that there haven't been local exceptions, or
that the picture is entirely rosy. In our era, we face many challenges
in providing enough food for everyone in the world: land degradation, the competition of biofuels for cropland, dependence on
expensive oil-based inputs, climate disruptions, the proliferation
of affluent meat-intensive diets, and the exodus of labor from rural
to urban areas, to name a few. Meanwhile, financial speculation in
food crops has increased market volatility, leading to price spikes.

The main concern today is not so much the pressure of human numbers on food supplies, but the impact rising food prices will have on people already living on the margins.[283]

Perhaps Malthus should also be forgiven for misunderstanding demography in assuming that population would always grow exponentially unless held in check by starvation, disease, or war. The world witnessed a huge increase in human numbers in the last century, when the population rose from 1.65 billion in 1900 to 6.1 billion in 2000. But that era of rapid growth—sometimes dubbed the "population explosion"—is over now. As living standards have risen, the world has undergone a "demographic transition" to smaller families. In country after country, declines in death rates have been followed by falling birth rates. During this transition, populations increase while people gradually adjust their fertility to improved life circumstances.[284] Better living standards, improved access to education, health care, and social security, and rising costs of raising children, urbanization, and improvements in women's status, including employment opportunities outside the home, all encourage smaller family size.[285]

What is the role of family planning programs in the demographic transition? Certainly, once people want fewer children, contraceptives can help them achieve their desired family size, and thus affect the timing and speed of fertility decline. Family planning, especially the provision of safe abortion services, can also help in reducing high rates of maternal mortality. Globally, unsafe abortion causes 13 percent of all maternal deaths. But important as they are, contraceptives are not the driving force behind the demographic transition. Broader social and economic changes are.[286]

Moral qualms aside, it might seem that forcing or pressuring people to have fewer children could help jumpstart the demographic transition. The Bangladesh sterilization drive is an example of such logic at work. But coercion often backfires by giving *all* family planning services a bad name long after a particular campaign is over. An emphasis on sterilization also ignores the fact that many people want temporary methods of contraception that can help them space pregnancies. Child spacing is also good for women's and children's health. Meeting people's genuine needs for safe, voluntary family planning services is a far more effective—and moral—strategy in the long run.

The Bangladesh population picture is very different today from that of 40 years ago—but not because of the sterilization drive, which thankfully came to an end relatively quickly. The average number of children per woman in Bangladesh has plummeted from near seven in 1970 to around only 2.2 today and is projected to drop further.[287] Bangladesh is approaching replacement level fertility—the average number of children born per woman at which a population replaces itself from one generation to the next, not counting migration. The global estimate for replacement level fertility is 2.1 children per woman. People are having fewer children in Bangladesh because of a whole constellation of factors, including dramatic reductions in infant and child mortality, and the spread of education, urbanization, and women's employment in the formal labor force. Access to voluntary family planning is complementary to these processes.

When I teach classes on population, I ask students to look back several generations in their own family histories to chart the changes in childbearing patterns. No one family history is exactly the same, but most can easily see the trend toward lower birth rates that accompanies social and economic development. In my own case, my maternal grandparents had four children, my parents had three, and my husband and I have two. Exploring the how and why of falling fertility in the US helps shed light on similar patterns that have occurred, or are now occurring, all over the world.

On a global level, birth rates began falling in the 1960s, dropping quickly in subsequent decades. Today the average global family has about 2.5 children. This figure masks differences among countries. In sub-Saharan Africa, there are 19 countries where women have five or more children on average, but in that region, too, fertility rates are declining. The main impediments to Africa's demographic transition remain the unconscionably high rates of poverty and infant and child mortality due to low public investment in health and education. In many other countries, most notably in East Asia and Eastern Europe, fertility rates have fallen well below replacement level. The UN estimates that the current world population of 7.3 billion will reach 9.7 billion in 2050 and 11.2 billion in 2100 before it levels off. The 11.2 billion projection may be too high, however—the population could peak at a lower figure of 9.5 billion instead.[288]

The main reason we will add two to four billion more people to the world's population before it stabilizes is because a large share of the population, especially in developing countries, is young and approaching childbearing age. Even though most of this younger generation will have small families, there will be an increase in the number of couples having children. This demographic momentum will peter out as birth rates decline to replacement levels. In fact, many demographers now worry about the aging of the population—how will shrinking numbers of young people support growing numbers of the elderly?

The more immediate task in front of us is to plan for two to four billion additional people in environmentally sustainable and socially equitable ways. This can be done, but it will take ingenuity, innovation, and political will. Take the case of urbanization:

today over half the world's population lives in urban areas, and this proportion is likely to rise. Whether increased urban population growth is sustainable or not will depend on critical political and economic choices in city and regional planning. Will cities privilege private cars or clean and green public transport? Will new housing be energy-efficient? What steps will be taken to preserve the water supply? Will gentrification be held in check so lower wage workers can actually live near where they work? Can fairer taxation policies be put in place to ensure adequate funds for public education, health, and other social services? In coastal cities, what infrastructural changes are necessary to protect people from sea level rise?

There's a very important difference between acknowledging the very real challenges posed by population growth and sinking into doomsday despair that the planet can't possibly support that many people. Barring major catastrophes—thermonuclear war, an asteroid strike, the plague of all times—the planet will have to support growth. The question is not if, but how. Cooler minds need to prevail, but unfortunately in many quarters they don't. After many years working in the population field, I've come to understand that, while Malthusian ideology feeds apocalyptic fears, the broader apocalyptic mindset provides the hothouse environment in which Malthusianism thrives. It isn't enough to point out that Malthus was wrong on empirical grounds or to challenge his theoretical framing of the population issue. To get to the bottom of the co-dependent relationship between the apocalyptic psyche and his dismal vision, one has to look more closely at what gives Malthusian prophets and prejudices such enduring appeal.

SCIENTISTS AND SAVIORS

Like any fundamentalist religion, the "Church of Malthus" has its high priests. Some of them resemble TV evangelists who warn of Armageddon while raking in the bucks. There is the same brow-beating and chest-thumping; the same scare tactics, doctrinaire absolutism, overblown egos, and savior complexes; the same compulsive craving for a following. Preaching the population apocalypse can be both seductive and lucrative.

The first time I came face to face with a population prophet was in February 1993, when I was invited to Stanford University to debate biologist Paul Ehrlich, author of the 1968 bestseller *The Population Bomb*. Ehrlich's book made him a media star, and he appeared on Johnny Carson's popular TV talk show 20 times. Like the Puritan preacher Jonathan Edwards, Ehrlich skillfully deployed the jeremiad formula to recruit a following of true believers. He was also one of the first, but hardly the last, environmentalist to tap directly into the Book of Revelation, associating the threat of overpopulation with the Four Horsemen of the Apocalypse: War, Famine, Pestilence, and Death.[289] In a favorable review of his book, *Natural History* magazine noted that, while most scientists don't go around "roaring like Old Testament prophets," it was OK for Ehrlich to do so, since "the world is in worse trouble than we thought."[290]

Worse trouble indeed! *The Population Bomb* warned that the battle to feed all mankind was over—over and lost—and that, in the 1970s, hundreds of millions of people around the world would inevitably starve to death. Famines in poor countries would ignite wars. In one of Ehrlich's scenarios, 100 million Americans would die from Chinese dirty bombs; in another, years of famine would strengthen Soviet influence in Mexico and Latin America, and nuclear war between the superpowers would destroy the northern two-thirds of the planet.[291] Ehrlich advocated coercive population control. When a new edition of the book came out in 1983, he argued that the US government should have supported an Indian government proposal in the 1970s to sterilize compulsorily all men with three or more children: "We should have volunteered logistic support in the form of helicopters, vehicles, and surgical instruments. We should have sent doctors . . . Coercion? Perhaps, but coercion in a good cause."[292]

When I met Ehrlich in 1993, he seemed to have mellowed somewhat—he no longer explicitly advocated compulsion—but his Malthusian faith remained solidly intact, despite the failure of his previous predictions to materialize. In his own eyes, he hadn't been wrong, just prematurely right. Moreover, he maintained that his doomsday predictions had helped galvanize the kinds of action that prevented them from occurring.[293] Even now, Ehrlich is still in the business of prophesying doom. In 2015 he told the *New York Times* that what he wrote in the 1960s was relatively mild. "My language would be even more apocalyptic today," he said. He likened letting women have as many babies as they want to allowing everyone to "throw as much of their garbage into their neighbor's backyard as they want."[294]

The debate between Ehrlich and me was on his home turf of Stanford, at a symposium organized by medical students at the university. They had been inspired to hold the event by a controversial article published by the British public health professor Maurice King in the prestigious medical journal, the *Lancet*. In it, King argued that in poor countries with unsustainable population pressure, public health services shouldn't engage in "desustaining measures" such as giving children suffering from diarrhea the simple treatment of oral rehydration. Instead the children should be left to die to reduce the population in the interest of the greater good.[295] King's proposition caused a major ruckus in the international child health community—I was told that at one meeting, the head of UNICEF and King came to actual blows. Apocryphal or not, this story testified to the intensity of the controversy provoked by King's proposed final solution for the Third World poor.

The Stanford medical students found King's argument compelling enough to invite him to speak at the symposium, too. And so two prophets were there that day in pristine Palo Alto: Ehrlich, who had a tall, craggy presence, and King, older and more diminutive, with wild white hair. I felt like a fish out of moral water. It didn't help that the moderator of the debate turned out to be a good friend of Ehrlich's—the more neutral moderator who was initially invited had been disinvited, I discovered later. The deck was stacked, but I had spent a long time preparing my argument, lacing it with facts and figures, whereas Ehrlich clearly hadn't bothered, relying on a simple diagram and a few stock phrases. He went ballistic when I had the audacity and ammunition to challenge him. I almost felt physically threatened. The moderator did little to calm him down, and the audience kept silent during his tirade, except for one brave young woman who shouted that he was being abusive. The final insult he hurled at me was that I came from a small college with "a small library."

When it was over, I felt if I could get through this, I could get through just about anything. But I was disquieted, too. Something had been going on that was deeper than just a battle of ideas. Over time, I have come to realize that debates about population are not just about numbers and impacts, but also about the authority of the scientists who are self-proclaimed experts.

There's an interesting parallel in this respect between the nuclear and population versions of the coming apocalypse. As the US became a superpower in the last century, science held an exalted social status as our key to technological innovation, material prosperity, and military superiority. The nuclear bomb was the apogee, the awe-inspiring response of American science to the threat of fascism and then of Communism. But even as the bomb cast the scientists of the Manhattan Project in a savior-like glow, its terrible destructive power sowed doubt as to the inevitability of progress, nowhere more than among atomic scientists themselves.

In his book *By the Bomb's Early Light*, historian Paul Boyer points to the role played by atomic scientists in the immediate years after Hiroshima and Nagasaki in trying to prevent the bomb from ever being used again. Joined together in the Federation of Atomic (later re-named American) Scientists, several thousand became politically active, trying to forge preventive national policies and international cooperation. The movement was sustained by "a prevailing belief among scientists and non-scientists alike, that a commitment to science almost automatically gave one a global perspective and a unique ethical vantage point," Boyer writes.[296] Capitalizing on media attention and deploying skillful public relations, the scientists achieved unprecedented visibility on the national political stage. "What a physical scientist says on almost any subject is thought more important than what anybody else says," wrote the University of Chicago anthropologist, Robert Redfield.[297]

Although a few counseled otherwise, the majority of the scientists consciously played on fears of atomic obliteration to drive home their points. "Only one tactic is dependable—the preaching of doom," a nuclear scientist told the *New Yorker*.[298] However effective this strategy may have been in the short run, in the long run it backfired. Ironically, the scientists' invocation of apocalypse helped to fuel the rise of anti-Communist hysteria, and the ideology committed to American nuclear supremacy ultimately won the day in Washington. The scientists' movement never died out—many spoke out boldly against the Cold War—but it never enjoyed the mainstream legitimacy that it had in the immediate post-war years. Many scientists, including Robert Oppenheimer himself, became victims of anti-Communist persecution.

Can we read the population bomb narrative as a wannabe story? There are striking parallels between Ehrlich's rallying call and the earlier one of the nuclear scientists. To start, there is the bomb itself, a real tangible threat in the nuclear case, a sensationalist metaphor of destruction in the other. Both threaten to spell the end of the world as we know it. Fear sells, and it gets you on stage, into the press, maybe even into Congressional hearings. This is not to say that Ehrlich made a cynical calculation to imitate the nuclear scientists. Rather, I suspect that his missionary zeal grew from longing for the kind of social relevance and reverence they received, something that is harder to get if you spend all day in the biology lab.

The appeal of the population bomb scare may also reflect the projection of Cold War nuclear fears onto more comfortable terrain. Controlling human numbers seemed more doable than nuclear disarmament. The target was the world's poorest people, not the weaponry of mass destruction in the hands of the super-powers. The baby boomers' apocalyptic nightmares found a rich new source of imagery. Writer Joyce Maynard recounts that, when she first read *The Population Bomb*, she felt the same rush of dread that she experienced during the Cuban missile crisis: "Not personal individual fear, but end-of-the world fear, that by the time we were our parents' age we would be sardine-packed and tethered to our gas masks in a skyless cloud of smog."[299]

Don't get me wrong—the impulse of scientists to do something about the miserable condition of the planet has many positive aspects. If they occasionally climb too far out on an apocalyptic limb, perhaps it's understandable, even if inadvisable. The real problem is hubris. Just because someone is a scientist doesn't mean they automatically possess an understanding of society. On the contrary, scientists may know little about the moral dilemmas and political complexities that bedevil human affairs. Few social scientists would claim expertise in physics or conservation biology. Why do we grant natural scientists, like Ehrlich, such authority when it comes to analyzing social phenomena like global population dynamics?

Part of the answer may be that the scientists are saying what we want to hear. In a nation fixated on the apocalypse, doomsday predictions stir dark but titillating passions. But something else is going on, too. It has to do with the politics and economics of why certain scientists make a big splash in the public arena, while others do not.

At the same time that Ehrlich was spreading alarm about the population bomb, Barry Commoner, a respected professor of biology at Washington University in St. Louis, was taking on the twin problems of nuclear testing and environmental pollution. His 1971 book, *The Closing Circle: Nature, Man, and Technology*, argued that pollution in America was growing far faster than population, due to changing industrial and agricultural processes. In the drive to increase productivity and profits, he warned, corporations were turning a blind eye to the dangers of new technologies and synthetic chemicals.

Commoner also had a fundamentally different approach to population dynamics than Ehrlich, a comparison explored in Ian Angus and Simon Butler's book, *Too Many People?* Unlike Ehrlich, Commoner understood that birth rates decline with improved living standards. "Pollution begins not in the family bedroom, but the corporate boardroom," he told an audience at Brown University. Commoner directly challenged Ehrlich's views. Appearing on a panel with Ehrlich at a 1970 meeting of the American Association for the Advancement of Science, he declared, "Saying that none of our pollution problems can be solved without getting at population first is a copout of the worst kind." Commoner and Ehrlich continued their battle in the pages of the May 1972 *Bulletin of the Atomic Scientists*.[300]

Commoner never won the same wide audience as Ehrlich, however. One reason is that the population bomb had big money behind it. While Commoner and Ehrlich argued their cases, Dixie Cup magnate Hugh Moore was funneling millions of dollars into overpopulation propaganda. His Campaign to Check the Population Explosion paid for prominent ads in major American newspapers. One warned, "The ever mounting tidal wave of humanity now challenges us to control it or be submerged along with all our civilized values."[301]

In 1970, concerned that the first Earth Day wasn't doing enough to spotlight population, Moore's campaign targeted hundreds of college radio stations nationwide with a free radio program featuring Ehrlich and his Sierra Club ally, David Brower. He also funded the publication and distribution of 330,000 folders, leaflets, and pamphlets about the population bomb. Allan Chase argues in his tour de force, *The Legacy of Malthus*, that Moore's intervention played a major role in undermining the anti-Vietnam war movement by turning social activists into population control fanatics. "By 1970, thousands of earnest and idealistic Americans of all ages were swapping their 'End the Killing in Vietnam' buttons for more modish buttons bearing the words 'People Pollute,'" he wrote.[302] I was an undergraduate at Yale that year, and I remember the appearance on campus of Zero Population Growth (ZPG), an organization Ehrlich helped to found. Its first college chapter was at Yale. On a campus roiled by the war and racial politics, ZPG's message seemed beside the point, but within a few years, its presence was commonplace. In population education more generally, Malthusian models drawn from conservation biology, ecology, and cybernetics came to dominate.

MODEL TRAPS

Malthusian models are first drilled into most Americans in high school, if not in earlier grades. State standards for high school social studies mandate teaching about "the explosion of population growth." Biology and environmental studies textbooks teach that population growth is overshooting the carrying capacity of local ecosystems and the entire planet.[303] My daughter's high school biology textbook illustrated this issue with a picture of cattle overgrazing the land, placed side by side with a photo of a starving African child. "Either we will voluntarily reduce our birth rate or various forces of environmental resistance will increase our death rate," the text warned ominously.[304] When I recently asked a first-year class of American college students what they had learned in high school about population, the most common reply was that it grows exponentially. Well, it doesn't.[305]

The concept of "carrying capacity" has taken deep root in the nation's schools as well as in the wider culture. Few people are aware of the foundations of this foundational concept. The term dates from the mid-1800s shipping industry, when it referred to cargo size. Several decades later it was applied to range and game management. Beginning in the 1940s and 1950s, American biologists began applying it to human populations. One of the first was famous ecologist Aldo Leopold, who wrote in 1941, "Every environment carries not only characteristic kinds of animals, but characteristic *numbers* of each . . . That number is the carrying capacity of that land for that species." Leopold maintained that "self-limiting mechanisms" keep those numbers in check. Echoing Malthus, he ventured, in the case of humans, that war might be one of those mechanisms. "If so," he asked, "why not call a moratorium on human increase?"[306]

Leopold's notion of carrying capacity drew upon a mathematical model developed earlier by biologist Raymond Pearl. Pearl's model maintained that all populations follow a S-shaped curve, growing exponentially until they meet environmental resistance and then tapering off.[307] In the 1953 textbook *Fundamentals of Ecology*, American ecologist Eugene Odum made the S-curve standard academic fare. He called the upper level, at which no further population increase can occur, the "saturation point" or "carrying capacity." To prove his point, Odum relied on laboratory studies of "fruit flies, flour beetles," and "other convenient organisms."[308] According to geographer Nathan Sayre, these studies signified a turn in ecology toward the mathematical modeling of physics and chemistry, an ecology that often bore little relation to the complexities of population–environment interactions.[309]

In a 1948 bestseller *Road to Survival*, ecologist William Vogt also deployed the term "carrying capacity." He painted an apocalyptic picture of population pressures outstripping food production and degrading the natural environment. "There is little probability," he wrote, "that mankind can long escape the searing downpour of war's death from the skies . . . [I]t is probable that at least three-quarters of the human race will be wiped out."[310] The book invoked ugly stereotypes of backward Chinese peasants, over-breeding Indians, and feckless indigents who should be paid to be sterilized.[311]

The carrying capacity concept has many flaws. For one, it assumes that population growth is the primary cause of environmental degradation. "If the long-term carrying capacity of an area is clearly being degraded by its current human occupants," Ehrlich argued, "that area is overpopulated."[312] By this logic, the land degradation caused by a uranium mine on a sparsely populated Native American reservation is a sign that the area has too many people!

Environmental problems often have much less to do with sheer human numbers than with unregulated pollution and resource extraction, unsustainable industrial and agricultural practices, and militarism. Today, the US military alone produces an estimated 5 percent of global greenhouse gas emissions. Nine hundred of the US Environmental Protection Agency's 1300 Superfund toxic sites are abandoned military bases and weapons manufacturing and testing sites.[313]

Carrying capacity doesn't consider critical questions of technological choice. In energy, for example, there's a huge difference between a dirty coal plant and wind mills and solar panels. Moreover, humans are not simple per capita units whose numbers can be equally multiplied to account for environmental degradation. Carrying capacity's greatest sleight of hand is the way it obscures differences in resource consumption between rich and poor, as well as interconnections among villages, towns, cities, regions, and countries through trade and governance. It ignores the examples of cultures, past and present, that live in greater harmony with the land. And it fails to acknowledge that people are capable of either learning from history or of making an ethical commitment to safeguard and improve their environments.[314]

The same shortcomings are evident in the Malthusian I = PAT equation coined by Ehrlich and scientist John Holdren in the mid-1970s. "IPAT," as it is called for short, measures the human impact (I) on the environment as the product of population (P), consumption per person (A, for Affluence), and environmental degradation caused by technology per unit of consumption (T, for technology). The equation frames the population debate in terms of the relative weight of the three factors, each of which is bad for the environment by definition. In the words of environmental writer Patricia Hynes, "So entrenched is IPAT that critics and advocates alike debate from within it; like a mental boxing ring, it locks in those who take it on."[315]

The IPAT equation conceals more than it reveals. "P" reduces population to sheer human numbers, irrespective of their distribution between city and country or the distribution of wealth and power amongst them. "A" makes no distinction between the consumption necessary for a decent life and conspicuous luxury consumption. "T" averages across everything else, lumping together the environmental impacts of multinational corporations, international financial institutions, and militaries alongside working families and small farmers. There are no real agents here, just mathematical units so amorphous that they tell us nothing about who is doing what to whom, why they have the power to do it, and what different behaviors mean for the environment.

The IPAT equation draws a one-dimensional picture of human beings as purely *takers from*, rather than *positive contributors to*, the natural environment. Sustainable agriculture and resource use practiced by peasant and indigenous communities, urban gardens, soil enhancement, the reclamation of public space, ecological restoration, conservation measures, advances in renewable energy, and other green technologies figure nowhere in the model, just as they do not figure into notions of carrying capacity.[316] Instead, IPAT posits, the more of us humans, the worse things get. It's as simple—that is, as simple-minded—as that.

Like IPAT, computer simulations of population-environment interactions, such as the Club of Rome's famous project "Limits to Growth," can lock us into stultifying oversimplifications. Founded in 1968, the Club of Rome was a group of Western government, business, and science leaders that came together to study "the predicament of mankind." In deciding how to study such a huge and intractable problem, those who favored a more dynamic and democratic approach, engaging a group of actual stakeholders in discussions of poverty, pollution, population, nuclear proliferation, and a host of other global challenges, lost out to an elite team of systems engineers at MIT whose backgrounds were in defense and private industry. Using computer simulations to forecast over 100 years into the future, the MIT crew studied interactions between five key aggregates: population, resources, industrial output, food supply, and pollution.[317]

Their model assumed that growth in all these realms would be exponential. As critics pointed out, the model neglected the effects of technological change and price movements on resource use. Not surprisingly, the basic message of the model was that humanity was headed toward a fatal crash unless population and consumption growth were brought rapidly under control. Published in book form in 1972, *Limits to Growth* became an instant bestseller. The early mystique of computers in that era may help to explain its popularity.[318] Many environmentalists also welcomed its attention to the impact of unfettered consumption. With sales of 12 million copies, the book is still the best-selling environmental title ever published.[319]

Such models not only bolster the power of experts, turning them into high priests who tell us what's best for the planet; their approach towards population also lays the ground for authoritarian prescriptions. The mathematical abstractions mask a moral economy that implicitly, if not explicitly, blames and punishes the poor, especially poor women, for society's many ills.[320]

The gravest result of this phenomenon was the one-child policy adopted by the government of China in 1979. Anthropologist Susan Greenhalgh has recounted a fascinating history of how the policy in part grew out of the Club of Rome's computer model. Chinese scientists first learned about *Limits to Growth* on delegations to the West in the late 1970s. Back home, they crunched the numbers to show that China's population growth posed a looming crisis, one that required a draconian response. In the ensuing policy debates, the systems modelers won out over social scientists who advocated a voluntary approach to family planning. Thanks to the authority of science, coupled with the coercive power of China's one-party state, "the numbers themselves gained new and formidable powers over people's minds and women's bodies."[321] Setting unrealistic demographic targets, the government launched a highly coercive population control campaign in 1983, forcing millions of women to be sterilized or undergo abortions against their will. Coercion became, and still is, built into the structure of the family planning program.

The one-child policy has had terrible gender outcomes. China's 2010 census shows a sex ratio at birth of 119 males per 100 females, reflecting the widespread practice of sex-selective abortions.[322] The normal sex ratio at birth is about 106 males per 100 females. These figures are typically blamed on traditional cultural norms of son preference, but research has shown that many Chinese families want daughters too. It was the one-child policy, not "tradition," that pressured them into the grim calculus of sex selection. The policy also forced many parents who had daughters to abandon or conceal them so that they wouldn't be counted against the one-child quota.[323] In the end, the policy has had negative outcomes for men as well, especially poor men in rural areas who can't find brides, and who are then stigmatized as "bare branches."[324]

In 2015 the Chinese government finally announced the end of the one-child policy, but many China experts worry that the new two-child policy will maintain authoritarian state control over people's reproductive decisions. The huge population control bureaucracy has a financial incentive toward coercion, since its employees benefit from fines leveled on over-quota births and their salaries and prestige are dependent on surveilling others.[325]

The Chinese government has frequently credited the one-child policy with preventing the birth of 400 million Chinese. At first glance, this claim might seem to make sense. However, the 400 million figure is now disputed by Chinese demographers, who point out that most of China's demographic transition was accomplished *before* the implementation of the one-child policy. The total fertility rate fell from 5.8 children in 1970 to 2.8 in 1979. Moreover, in the 1980s and 1990s, other countries at a similar level of development experienced a fertility decline much like China's *without* imposing a one-child policy. If China had promoted two-child families instead, demographers argue, it probably would have yielded the same result—a current fertility rate of 1.5 children per woman. "History will remember China's one-child policy as the most extreme example of state intervention in human reproduction in the modern era," three Chinese demographers write in the *Population and Development Review*. "History will also likely view this policy as a very costly blunder, born of the agency of a political system that planned population numbers in the same way that it planned the production of goods. It showcases the impact of a policymaking process that, in the absence of public deliberations, transparency, debate, and accountability, can do permanent harm to the members of a society."[326]

Malthusian models tell us precious little about human relationships with the environment, let alone with other humans. And, as in the case of China, they can do great harm. Yet they persist. Their graphs and simulations give them a superficial appearance of sophistication. Once they achieve the status of received truth, it can be hard to see through them. But sometimes people do. In 1994 I organized a panel on population at an ecological economics conference in Costa Rica. Among the panelists was Patricia Hynes, who presented her critique of IPAT. The environmental scientist Donella Meadows, one of the principal authors of *Limits to Growth*, was in the audience. As she listened to Hynes, she grew more and more outraged. "IPAT was the lens through which I saw the environmental situation," Meadows later wrote about the experience. "It's neat and simple. I didn't want to see it any other way."

But then she began to feel uneasy. Hynes's point about how IPAT ignores economic and political power rang true. "There are no *agents* in the IPAT equation, said Patricia Hynes, no identifiable *actors*, no genders, colors, motivations. Population growth and consumption and technology don't just happen. Particular people make them happen, people who shape and respond to rewards and punishments, people who may be acting out of desperation or love or greed or ambition or fear," Meadows recounted. "Unfortunately, I said to myself, I agree with this." She began to think about the disproportionate environmental impact of the military and of large corporations, and about how much damage done to the Earth comes from vanity as opposed to necessity. "Use a different lens," she concluded, "and you see different things, you ask different questions, you find different answers."[327]

POPULATION AND SCARCITY

Anxiety about scarcity runs deep in the American psyche. Some of the reasons are understandable. Growing up during the Great Depression of the 1930s, my parents' generation experienced what happened when the bottom fell out of the economy, and worried that it could happen again. Many poor Americans live with real scarcity, not sure where the next meal is going to come from. In 2014, one in seven American households suffered from food insecurity at some point during the year, according to the US Department of Agriculture.[328] Meanwhile, the boom-and-bust cycle of financial markets, cuts in government spending on safety nets, the high price of health insurance, and the rising cost of living keep all but the richest Americans on edge.

There are also more irrational fears of Scarcity with a capital "S." Americans often read periodic shortages of food, water, or energy as harbingers of a population and environment apocalypse that will make our bellies ache, mouths go dry, and houses go dark. And even if we stockpile food, water, and fuel against this specter, we worry that desperate hordes of poor people will come to loot them.

Such fears of scarcity derive in large part from the America syndrome, especially our fractured relationship with nature. Puritan guilt at our profligacy elicits dread of the revenge that an angry Nature, like Jonathan Edwards's angry God, will make us suffer for our sins. Or, as Paul Ehrlich puts it, "It's the top of the ninth inning and humanity has been hitting nature hard, but you've always got to remember that nature bats last."[329] Ehrlich makes a straight line to Malthus, thinking our population numbers ultimately force nature to take its final revenge.

Overlaid with this trepidation is the peculiarly American geographical anxiety about shrinking space—too many people, too little room—that also predisposes us to Malthusian ideas. I began writing this chapter having just returned from a cross-country trip from California to Massachusetts. Anyone who has made that journey knows how long the country stretches from coast to coast, and that along the route there are vast empty spaces where you have to plan where to stop for gas since the next station will be many miles away. I used to think it was sort of crazy, given all those empty miles, that Americans worry so much about population pressure, much more in fact than Europeans who live in more densely populated lands. Gradually, I have come to understand that how we occupied this great and beautiful continent, and what we did and didn't learn from that history, accounts for much of our claustrophobia. It's less about craziness than about enduring national myths.

When I was a child, I was taught that when the Europeans arrived in North America, they found a wilderness. While there were a few Native Americans lurking around, they were savages whose presence didn't tame the landscape. Recent historical research has blown apart this wilderness myth. In his book *1491*, author Charles Mann draws on this scholarship to paint a very different picture of what the country looked like before the Europeans showed up. In the 16th century, New England alone may have been home to 100,000 or more Native Americans. Much earlier than that, from 950–1250, the Native American town of Cahokia, on the banks of the Mississippi, not far from what is now St. Louis, was a thriving population center. It grew to a size of at least 15,000 people, similar to the size of London at that time.

Across the continent, Native Americans managed fields and forests to sustain their livelihoods. They used fire to turn the Great Plains and Midwest prairies into "prodigious game farms" for bison and other large animals; in the eastern forests, they cut the underbrush to facilitate hunting, cleared land for farming, and managed tree species. "Rather than the thick, unbroken, monumental snarl of trees imagined by Thoreau," Mann writes, "the great eastern forest was an ecological kaleidoscope of garden plots, blackberry rambles, pine barrens, and spacious groves of chestnut, hickory, and oak."[330] Native Americans enjoyed longer life expectancies, and quite possibly a higher quality of life, than most Europeans. But the new diseases, like smallpox, that arrived with the Europeans depopulated the continent. Early settlers found the New England woodlands littered with human bones and skulls.[331]

On their divine errand into this wilderness, the Pilgrims saw this depopulation as a gift from God. Later generations of Americans simply forgot that the land had been populated in the first place. The wilderness became a romantic, sublime, quasi-religious force, and its loss a source of profound nostalgia. "For many Americans," writes historian William Cronon, "wilderness stands as the last remaining place where civilization, that all too human disease, has not fully infected the earth."[332]

The "wilderness ethic" became a cornerstone of American environmentalism, locating Nature in places without people, rather than in the places where people live. John Muir, iconic father of the wilderness movement and first president of the Sierra Club, saw no place for Native Americans in the "pure wildness" of Yosemite. Those that lived there were "most ugly, and some of them altogether hideous," he wrote, and "they seemed to have no right place in the landscape." The government agreed, and they were expelled to make way for the national park. Ironically, the Native Americans had carefully managed that landscape through controlled burns, giving Yosemite Valley the park-like appearance that so enchanted Muir. Once they were gone, the ecosystem declined. Muir's prejudices didn't allow him to see the people for the trees.[333]

In 1893, the US Census Bureau officially announced there was no more unsettled land in the country. Historian Frederick Jackson Turner lamented "the closing of a great historic moment," and declared that American history was largely about the colonization of the Great West: "The existence of an area of free land, its continuing recession, and the advance of American settlement westward, explain American development." The frontier transformed the pioneers from Europeans into rugged Americans. "The wilderness masters the colonist," Turner wrote.[334]

There is a conundrum here. For if both the wilderness and the frontier are fundamental to American identity, what happens if advancing the latter means destroying the former? And when we reach the limits of both—a vanished wilderness, a closed frontier—what then? Imperial adventures overseas, or into outer space, may extend the frontier, but our continental dream is dashed. In its place arise the nightmares of Scarcity. The land can no longer hold all of us, at least not in the manner to which we believe we are entitled.

Combined with the fear of shrinking space come periodic racial panics about overcrowding, especially in urban areas where black and immigrant communities are viewed as an ominous threat. In the 1960s and '70s, population control advocates purposefully placed articles and images about overcrowding in popular media to build support for their cause. "How many people do you want in your country?" one of Hugh Moore's ads asked, painting a picture of cities "packed with youngsters—thousands of them idle, victims of discontent and drug addiction . . . You go out after dark at your peril. Birth Control is an answer."[335] In fact, framing the population issue in terms of overcrowding was an important factor in building a public consensus for population control interventions in the US and overseas.[336] It still is. To warn Americans about the perils of overpopulation, the recent coffee table book *Overdevelopment, Overpopulation, Overshoot*, produced by the Foundation for Deep Ecology and the Population Media Center, features photographs of dark-skinned crowds struggling to get on urban transport or squashed together in a "human tide" on a beach. These representations of the "collected weight of a bloated humanity" almost never include any white people.[337] No photographs of businessmen at rush hour in Manhattan's Grand Central Station.

Our economic system breeds further scarcity fears. Modern textbooks define economics as being about the allocation of scarce resources among competing ends. *Homo economicus* rationally pursues his self-interest, with little room for other values like altruism, sharing, and caring, and this is exalted as rational behavior. Capitalism enshrines greed as the holy grail. In his book *Scarcity and Modernity*, political scientist Nicholas Xenos tells the story of how capitalism came to reframe our view of human nature so that to be human is to have unlimited wants and desires, defined in relation to the next guy's, that outstrip our actual needs. We don't just need an adequate roof over our heads, but a bigger and bigger house in a never-ending quest to keep up with the Joneses.[338]

These insatiable appetites that are the engine of American consumerism are bred into us by Madison Avenue and the purveyors of credit. As a result, most Americans are constantly pushing against another frontier, the bottom line of their bank accounts. The anxiety this creates has intensified in recent years due to deepening wealth inequality and the instability and corruption of a financial system that runs on risk and speculation. Globally, the bottom 50 percent of adults on the wealth scale now own less than 1 percent of the world's total wealth, while the richest 10 percent own almost 90 percent of total wealth. The top 1 percent alone owns 50 percent.[339] The US is no stranger to this pattern. The top 0.1 percent—approximately 160,000 families—owns almost a quarter of the nation's wealth, a figure that is almost as high as before the 1929 stock market crash.[340] With so much wealth in so few hands, the specter of the 2008 global financial crisis still fresh in many people's minds, and a volatile labor market where workers are easily expendable, it's hard for most Americans to feel economically secure. Scarcity looms, if not today, then certainly tomorrow.

In an article written 20 years ago, but equally applicable to today, historian Andrew Ross contends that many Americans have come to conflate such economic scarcities with natural ones. We live in an era, he argues, when American capitalism is pushing natural limits in terms of guzzling resources, generating waste, and degrading the environment. At the same time, in thrall to the neoliberal ideology of competitive individualism and free markets, the government has imposed cuts on health, education, and social services, enforcing an austerity regime that hits the working and middle classes the hardest. While the root causes of both kinds of scarcity—natural and economic—lie in particular features of our economy and political system, we are told instead that they result from Malthusian population pressures: because there are too many of us, there's not enough money or natural resources to go around. This potent "scarcity cocktail" dulls the critical senses, preventing us from seeing what's really going on.[341]

DUELS AND DUALISMS

Challenging the hold of Scarcity on the American imagination is thus no easy task. Doing so is complicated by the either/or dualism that is part of the America syndrome and that pervades so much of our thinking. In the name of balance, the media typically frame debates in terms of two competing views. When it comes to scarcity, the battle is between doomsday predictors on one side and cornucopian free marketeers on the other. Epitomizing this dualism is the bet made in 1980 between biologist Paul Ehrlich and economist Julian Simon on what would happen over the next decade to the prices of five scarce metals (copper, chromium, nickel, tin, and tungsten). Ehrlich bet their prices would go up, while Simon wagered they would go down. Simon won.

The bet, which featured as a cover story in the *New York Times* magazine, was about much more than the price of metals. Simon maintained that shortages of resources simply spur the development of new techniques to find them, so that, in the end, we're better off than if the temporary shortage had never occurred. Moreover, population growth is a good thing since people are the "ultimate resource," provided they live in a free market economy where they can come up with the new ideas to make the system work. Simon's positive view of human potential didn't extend to government, however. In his libertarian view, government regulation was a break on progress. If capitalism creates some environmental damages along the way, then capitalism will also find the means to fix them.[342] We don't need the likes of the Clean Air Act and the EPA.

Simon's techno-hubris and disdain for environmental protection made Ehrlich appear to be the responsible conservationist. Simon and Ehrlich's contrasting positions came to demarcate differences between the Democratic and Republican parties on environmental issues and to deeply influence perceptions of population in the wider culture.[343] This duality has made it difficult to critique Malthusianism without being cast as an enemy of the environment. If you disagree with Ehrlich, you must be in Simon's camp. The notion that one could be in favor of environmental protection and *not* espouse population control is hard for people to fathom.

Cast as a duel between two alpha male experts, the competition between Ehrlich and Simon shut out women's voices and turned reproduction into a political football tossed by men. While Ehrlich's arguments were harnessed to support population control, Simon's were used to encourage pro-natalist policies: the more babies women have, the better. Simon himself wasn't against family planning, but the anti-abortion movement seized upon his arguments. At the International Conference on Population held in Mexico City in 1984, the Reagan administration announced that population wasn't a problem. In what is now known as the global gag rule, it then proceeded to deny US government funds to any private family planning organization overseas that included abortion as an option or even just counseled women about it, marking the beginning of a full-scale attack on contraception and abortion access.[344] The result was yet another dualism—this time between population control on the one hand and the anti-abortion movement on the other. In both scenarios, women lack agency. Instead, they are to be acted upon in the service of either preventing scarcity or guaranteeing abundance. Either way, they lose the right to chart their own reproductive destinies.

THE WAR ON MOTHERS AND OTHERS

Since its inception, Malthusianism has drawn on powerful stereotypes. While Malthus reduced his own parishioners to abstract
numbers, his imagination roamed further when it came to the
impoverished people of distant lands. In his famous essay, he
embellished the dismal arithmetic of scarcity with over-heated
colonialist narratives about the barbaric practices of inferior races
(as well as less-than-flattering views of women almost everywhere). In rereading Malthus, scholar Carole McCann found this
passage about the mating practices of "races of savages":

> He steals upon her in the absence of her protectors, and
> having first stupefied her with the blows of a club, or
> wooden sword, on the head, back, every one of which is
> followed by a stream of blood, he drags her through the
> woods by one arm, regardless of the stones and broken
> pieces of trees that may lie in his route, and anxious only
> to convey his prize in safety to his own party, where a
> most brutal scene occurs.[345]

While the nations of northern Europe had some chance of
reducing population pressure by means of moral restraint, Malthus viewed violence as endemic to the lesser cultures.[346] He
naturalized not only poverty, but violence, linking the latter
explicitly to ethnicity and race.

Fear of the dark and menacing Other has passed down through
successive generations in the "Church of Malthus," along with
loathing of the poor and the mothers who breed them. While
numbers provide the arithmetic of population apocalypse, it is
these more emotional undercurrents that turn believers into

crusaders.[347] In a classic inversion of victim and perpetrator, population crusaders justify violence against the poor by convincing themselves that the poor, especially poor men, are naturally violent.[348] Malthusian violence against the poor takes three main forms: *structural, reproductive,* and *nativist.*

Structural violence refers to the violence of routine inequalities, embedded in the institutions and social arrangements that govern people's lives. The exorbitant infant and child mortality rates we witnessed in Bangladesh in the 1970s were an example of structural violence: no single individual pulled the trigger, but lack of access to health care, clean water, and food condemned many children to an early death. By masking the power relationships that determine who has the right to live and who doesn't, Malthusian ideology feeds into this structural violence. Politically, it often acts as a brake on reforms that could make things better. When the Bangladesh government devoted over one-third of the country's health budget to curbing birth rates in the 1980s, this diverted resources from primary health care and the prevention and treatment of common diseases.[349]

A century earlier, British colonial authorities in India allowed a severe drought to turn into the massive famine of 1876–1878, in which between five and eight million people perished, by shipping existing food stocks to Britain, failing to curtail speculation and hoarding, and not mounting relief efforts in the countryside. Afterward, British finance minister Sir Evelyn Baring told Parliament, "Every benevolent attempt made to mitigate the effects of famine and defective sanitation serves but to enhance the evils resulting from overpopulation."[350] Such views also influenced the British non-response to the Irish potato famine of 1846–1849, during which food was exported to England while the Irish peasants starved.[351]

Reproductive violence directly targets sexuality, fertility, and child-bearing. One of the most dramatic forms is forced sterilization. This, too, has a long history. In the US in the early 20th century, eugenics, the science (or pseudo-science) of improving human heredity, was widely preached and often practiced. Proponents of racial hygiene called for improvement of the white race not only through controls on immigration and anti-miscegenation laws, but also through compulsory sterilization of prisoners, the mentally disabled, and poor women deemed to be a burden on the state by having too many children.[352] Eugenics began as a private venture, funded by the likes of Andrew Carnegie and the wealthy Harriman and Kellogg families, but by 1932, 30 states had mandatory sterilization laws. Between the turn of the century and the end of World War II, some 70,000 Americans were forcibly sterilized.[353] When Nazi Germany adopted eugenic laws, they were based in part on the Model Eugenic Sterilization Law developed by the US Eugenics Record Office.

Although the Nazi holocaust gave eugenics a bad name, 27 US states kept eugenic laws on the books into the 1970s, and Americans continued to be sterilized against their will. Black, Native American, and Latina women were the main targets. In the early 1970s, hundreds of Mexican-origin women were sterilized without their knowledge or consent at the University of Southern California–Los Angeles County Medical Center.[354] In 1976 the US General Accounting Office revealed that the federally-funded Indian Health Services had sterilized 3000 Native American women over a four-year period without informed consent.[355]

Concerns about population "quality" and "quantity" have often mingled. A number of the pioneers of population control, including Clarence Gamble (of the Procter and Gamble fortune), biologist Garrett Hardin, and Frederick Osborn of the Population Council, had strong ties to eugenics, as did Margaret Sanger, founder of Planned Parenthood, who forsook her earlier radical feminist roots to forge an unsavory political alliance with the eugenics movement.[356] Hardin, famous for his essay "Tragedy of the Commons" and his advocacy of lifeboat ethics—don't let the poor onto the proverbial lifeboat if they'll swamp and sink it— never gave up his eugenic ties, accepting money in the 1990s from the Pioneer Fund, the major funder of eugenics research in the US.[357]

Like eugenics, population control at first was privately funded by wealthy individuals like Gamble and Dixie Cup magnate Hugh Moore, as well as private foundations such as Ford and Rockefeller. By the 1960s, however, it had become a major component of America's Cold War foreign policy. In an important about-face, instead of reasoning that economic development would bring down birth rates, influential demographers began to reverse this logic and identify rapid population growth in poor countries as a serious impediment to development. Reducing birth rates, they argued, was a prerequisite for, rather than a consequence of, successful modernization. And if poor countries didn't develop quickly, they would be susceptive to Communist takeover. By 1967, the US government had become the largest funder of population control programs in the world.[358]

In the 1970s, the US government pushed sterilization over temporary contraceptive methods in many of the programs it supported. Coercion became a matter of course. As in the case of eugenics, victims of this social engineering were overwhelmingly poor, non-white mothers. In subsequent years, the technology shifted to long-acting forms of contraception, such as the IUD, hormonal implants, and injectables. While these methods were an improvement over forced sterilization, they were often delivered in coercive environments that denied women contraceptive choice and took dangerous risks with their health.[359]

The reproductive violence of population control sparked an international women's health movement against it. As a member of this movement, I advocated (and still advocate) voluntary family planning as part of comprehensive health services, as opposed to family planning as a weapon of population control. In 1994, at the UN international population conference in Cairo, the women's health movement succeeded in shifting policy away from coercion and toward respect for reproductive rights, but reforms proved easier on paper than in practice. Only a few years later, the Fujimori dictatorship in Peru launched a brutal campaign that sterilized some 300,000 indigenous women. When the scandal broke, the US government pleaded ignorance, though it supported Fujimori financially and approved of his population control targets.[360]

The Campaign to Stop Torture in Health Care, an initiative of George Soros's Open Society Foundations in New York, defined forced sterilization as a form of medical torture. If we don't condone torture in other arenas, why should it be acceptable in this most intimate realm of women's bodies and lives? Today, five US states—California, Oregon, Virginia, and North and South Carolina—have issued public apologies to the victims of eugenic sterilization. No such apology has been forthcoming from the US federal government for its role in forced sterilization overseas.

Panic over saving the planet from overpopulation, meanwhile, encourages people to turn a blind, or half-open, eye to coercion: Well, we had to get those birth rates down *somehow*. While many Americans find the Chinese practice of forced abortions and sterilizations distasteful, there has been a willingness to tolerate them because, after all, aren't there already *too many* Chinese gobbling up the world's resources? Or if only it could be done a little more humanely, wouldn't the one-child policy be a great model for the rest of the world?[361]

Such attitudes were unfortunately bolstered by the failure of major international family planning organizations to speak out against the Chinese policy. In fact, both the UN Fund for Population Activities (UNFPA) and the International Planned Parenthood Federation (IPPF) actively *aided* China in implementing it. In 1983, during the initial wave of heavy coercion, the UN bestowed its first Population Award to China's family planning minister. (He shared the award with Indian Prime Minister Indira Gandhi, who, along with her son Sanjay, was responsible for forcibly sterilizing over six million men during the Emergency Rule she imposed in 1975–76.)[362] Only now is there belated recognition that the one-child policy ranks among the world's most serious human rights violations of the past 35 years.[363]

Nativist forms of Malthusian violence explicitly target foreigners—and their babies—as national enemies. During the Cold War, the poor in developing countries were regarded as potential Communists. Today, they are portrayed as potential terrorists or dangerous migrants, or both rolled up into one. National security pundits warn about new kinds of population bombs, often with an Islamic cast. Too many Palestinian babies, too few Israeli ones, or "youth bulges" of angry, urbanized Muslim young men who are easy recruits for political extremism. In the face of these challenges, aging white Western populations just can't keep up.[364]

In Europe, declining fertility and aging populations are stoking fears of a "demographic winter," in which the barren white population is overwhelmed by dark-skinned immigrants from Africa and the Middle East. In the words of author Kathryn Joyce, demographic winter is "a more austere brand of apocalypse than doomsdayers normally trade in, evoking not a nuclear inferno but a quiet and cold blanket of snow in which . . . Western civilization is laying itself down to die."[365] In the US, the prospect that whites may become a minority by 2050 sparks similar anxieties.

The scapegoating of immigrants for environmental degradation gives nativism an environmental twist. I first encountered this phenomenon, which I've called the greening of hate, when I was invited to debate a woman named Virginia Abernethy at an environmental law conference in Oregon in 1994. Abernethy, a professor at Vanderbilt University, was representing an organization called the Carrying Capacity Network. The topic of our debate was supposed to be women and population stabilization, but I soon realized I wasn't debating a fellow environmentalist or family planning advocate, but instead an anti-immigrant zealot for whom "population control" and "carrying capacity" meant circling our wagons and closing our borders. I later learned that Abernethy worked with the white supremacist Council of Conservative Citizens. In 2011, she joined the neofascist American Third Position Party, now renamed the American Freedom Party, the largest racist political party now operating in the US.[366]

In the person of Abernethy I encountered a well-funded nativist network, founded by Michigan ophthalmologist and neo-eugenicist John Tanton, that cloaks itself in green language to lure liberal environmentalists into its conservative fold. Its main contention is that immigration, by spurring US population growth, drives environmental degradation. When they come to the US, the argument goes, immigrants cause everything from traffic congestion to deforestation to accelerated greenhouse gas emissions. This environmental burden compounds the supposed economic burden they place on taxpayers, schools, hospitals, and other public services. In the late 1990s and early 2000s, this nativist movement sought to take over the Sierra Club by becoming members *en masse* in order to get the Club to take a stand against immigration and put nativists on the board. Fortunately, they were beaten back, but they have hardly faded away. The Federation for American Immigration Reform, which has helped to orchestrate the greening of hate, took an active role in drafting Arizona's draconian anti-immigration law. New front groups, with names like Progressives for Immigration Reform, continue to woo environmentalists with Malthusian arguments.[367]

The structural, reproductive, and nativist violence condoned and espoused by the "Church of Malthus" makes apocalyptic fear of overpopulation more than an eccentric preoccupation, and more than a diversion from efforts to understand and address the real causes of poverty, environmental degradation, and war. The violence moves beyond sins of omission to the more dangerous terrain of actively committed transgressions against human dignity and lives. This makes it ethically imperative to confront and challenge its core beliefs. What is more, freeing ourselves from population fundamentalism allows us to imagine, and start to create, a more peaceful, equitable, and sustainable future.

KEEPING TIME

In addition to images of ticking time bombs depicting overpopulation, there are actual clocks that register each new birth as if it were a potential disaster. One such clock is posted on a medical building at a busy intersection in New Delhi. On the website of the Population Media Center in the US, a similar clock tells how many human beings were added to the planet during your visit.[368] The countdown to doom is measured one birth at a time. Humanity is heading backwards, not forwards.

Sometimes the population time keepers raise the rhetoric to fever pitch. As the year 2000 millennium approached, Population Connection, the group formerly called ZPG, launched a campaign that tried to link the birth of the world's six billionth child to the coming Y2K global computer crash, a disaster that never materialized despite all the hype. In his 2013 book *Countdown*, author Alan Weisman warns that the population crisis could lead humanity to extinction. "Either we decide to manage our own numbers, to avoid a collision of every line on civilization's graph," he writes, "or nature will do it for us, in the form of famines, thirst, climate chaos, crashing ecosystems, opportunistic disease, and wars over dwindling resources that finally cut us down to size." He believes our numbers have reached a point "where we've essentially redefined the concept of original sin."[369]

How do we rid ourselves of the ticking time bombs, the countdown clocks, the dismal models, and the dystopic dread that the Reverend Malthus set in motion two centuries ago? With birth rates dropping and family size shrinking around the world, his church's time has passed, but the bells in the belfry are still ringing loudly. Their latest clamor concerns climate change.

Some American population and environment groups now argue that reducing population growth in developing countries is the key to mitigating climate change. The Sierra Club urges people to "fight climate change with family planning."[370] A private American philanthropist even financed a climate scientist to come up with a model that would show the purported linkage between the two.[371] Yet industrialized countries, with 20 percent of the world's population, are responsible for 80 percent of the carbon dioxide that has accumulated in the atmosphere. In 2010, the US emitted 17.6 metric tons of carbon dioxide per person, compared to 6.2 in China, 0.4 in Bangladesh, and 0.1 in Uganda.[372] In the few countries in the world where population growth rates remain high, most of them in sub-Saharan Africa, carbon emissions per person are the lowest on the planet.[373]

Others, like Johns Hopkins philosopher Travis Rieder, are grabbing media attention by arguing that the looming climate catastrophe means that we should socially engineer a reduction in birth rates, not just in developing countries but at home, too. Curbing women's fertility is supposedly easier than other measures to reduce greenhouse gas emissions. New parents in the US should be financially penalized for having children, Rieder maintains, while mothers in developing countries should have their birth control refills paid for. "Maybe we should protect our kids by not having them," he told NPR.[374] The absurd notion that babies cause climate change is a convenient way to obscure its structural causes, including the economic and political clout of the fossil fuel industry. It's also yet another way to scapegoat women and children for global crisis.

Equally worrying is the way powerful interests in the international family planning field are turning the clock back toward population control, undoing a lot of the progress made at the 1994 international population conference in Cairo. They are reintroducing numerical targets, promoting long-acting contraceptives over other methods, and brushing aside critical health, safety, and human rights concerns. For example, despite mounting evidence that the injectable contraceptive Depo-Provera significantly increases the risks of acquiring and transmitting HIV/AIDS, it is being energetically promoted in parts of Africa where there are high HIV rates among young women. This is the work of a coalition of donors led by the Bill & Melinda Gates Foundation, and includes the pharmaceutical giant Pfizer, the UNFPA, and the US and British governments.[375]

Here in the US, population interests are targeting low-income young women and women of color with long-acting reversible contraceptives (LARC for short), notably the IUD and hormonal implants. These methods are being touted as a technical fix for high rates of adolescent pregnancy and a solution to endemic poverty. While these methods should be part of the mix, the LARC strategy restricts poor women's access to a wider range of contraceptives and opens the door to pressure and coercion. There are now reports of poor women on Medicaid not being able to get their IUDs removed unless they pay privately out of their own pocket. Concerned about such restrictions on reproductive choice, a number of women's health groups, including Planned Parenthood, have signed onto a Statement of Principles to guide LARC distribution. The statement notes that "A one-size-fits-all focus on LARCs at the exclusion of a full discussion of other methods ignores the needs of each individual and the benefits that other contraceptive methods provide."[376]

Meanwhile, the anti-abortion movement very cleverly plays the moral high ground card whenever the international family planning establishment fails to speak out against coercion or sweeps contraceptive risks under the rug. This happened with China's one-child policy, and it is happening now with Depo-Provera.[377] In these instances, the anti-abortion movement falsely bills itself as the true defender of women. Instead, in working to deny women access to abortion, contraception, and reproductive health care—through defunding Planned Parenthood, for example—the movement undermines women's health and human rights. The election of Donald Trump puts reproductive rights, including the legal right to abortion, granted in the 1973 Supreme Court decision *Roe v. Wade*, in serious jeopardy. One of his earliest acts as president was to reinstate the global gag rule first imposed by Ronald Reagan.

Given the hyperbole on both sides, it's important to remember that the population issue shouldn't be defined by the two ideological poles of population control on the one hand and the anti-abortion movement on the other. You can promote reproductive rights and support access to birth control, including the right to safe, legal abortion, *without* supporting population control. You can be an environmentalist, too, *without* subscribing to Malthusian notions of Scarcity.

From the time of the Puritans onwards, the vision of Armageddon-style battles between good and evil, God and the Devil, has predisposed Americans to simple-minded dualisms and extremist ideologies. Malthusianism is one of them. The overpopulation fears it ignites help keep the larger American apocalyptic fire burning, and that fire in turn helps keeps Malthusianism alive. It's a vicious cycle that we have to break.

Before leaving Malthus, I'd like to follow him back to Okewood, where he began his career. I think of him visiting the home of one of his poor parishioners. I imagine him as an inexperienced young man, standing in the doorway, peering in, aghast at the squalor and the emaciated children. Perhaps the woman of the house is breastfeeding a newborn baby. He's invited in, but politely declines. He has seen enough, thank you. Incapable of making that basic human connection, he retreats to his study and the neat, comforting world of numbers. What if he had dared to stay, dared to ask a few sympathetic questions of both husband and wife, dared to get to the bottom of what caused their predicament?

He could have made another choice. So can we.

Chapter Five

CLIMATE CHANGE: TIP OF THE MELTING ICEBERG

In 1947, as the Cold War began to escalate, the movement of nuclear scientists against the bomb inaugurated the Doomsday Clock on the cover of their journal, *Bulletin of the Atomic Scientists*. The intent was to use "the imagery of apocalypse (midnight) and the contemporary idiom of nuclear explosion (countdown to zero), to convey threats to humanity and the planet."[378] The clock is still ticking today. The initial countdown was seven minutes until the stroke of midnight and the end of the world. Shortly after Donald Trump became president in 2017, the clock moved from three minutes to midnight to only two and a half. To the threat of nuclear weapons, the scientists have added the serious risks posed by unchecked climate change, and Trump is considered dangerous on both counts.[379] After a childhood lived under the shadow of the bomb, will I now grow old with the hands on the clock drawing ever closer to a climate catastrophe of similar proportions?

I'm very worried about climate change. In the 1990s, I was invited to join an international committee on the human dimensions of climate change. Which people were likely to be most vulnerable to its effects, and what could be done to reduce that vulnerability, were the central questions the group addressed. Growing out of that work, in 2005 I co-authored a report for the United Nations Environment Programme (UNEP) on how to bring women's needs more fully into environmental assessments and early warning systems.[380]

Teaching courses on climate change, I educated myself along with my students about its scientific, cultural, and social complexities. As I watched the increasing militarization of climate change—its portrayal as a national security threat in the media and official reports—I began to consider the dangers of this approach. In the growing hype about "climate wars," I heard the echo of old Malthusian refrains about poor dark-skinned people as naturally disposed to violence and environmental destruction. To my relief, I also got to know the emerging movement for climate justice that advocates policies which combine protection of the planet with respect for the rights of its most vulnerable people.

As a gardener, I've been observing the subtle changes in my own backyard as New England winters grow shorter and a little less harsh. Spring bulbs poke up earlier, new species of weeds appear, and the grass needs mowing later into the fall. The growing season at our community-supported farm down the road extends longer each year. Freak local weather events—a tornado in western Massachusetts, a surprise blizzard at Halloween that toppled trees and branches onto roofs and power lines, a forest fire alert in the ordinarily cold and damp month of March, and in 2016 a summer of severe drought—seem to portend more disruption to come.

Despite the loud claims of climate change deniers, the scientific evidence is unequivocal and overwhelming that the world's climate is changing as the result of human activities, above all the burning of fossil fuels and the felling of forests. Between 1970 and 2012, carbon dioxide emissions from fossil fuel combustion and other industrial processes accounted for 78 percent of greenhouse gas emissions worldwide. The years from 1983 to 2012 were reportedly the warmest 30-year period in the last 1400 years. The oceans are warming, snow and ice are melting, and the sea level is rising.[381]

The accelerating shrinking of Arctic sea ice, coupled with the thermal expansion of ocean waters, is causing a rise in sea levels that already affects many low-lying coastal areas and islands. Sea level rise is perhaps the single most threatening aspect of climate change. If, as now seems possible, we see major reductions in the West Antarctic and Greenland ice sheets, the sea level could rise 10 meters or more, flooding major coastal cities around the globe.[382] Another worrying prospect is the melting of permafrost in the Arctic region, and the subsequent release of large quantities of carbon dioxide and methane into the atmosphere. That release would probably occur slowly, over the course of a century or more, but once the decomposition began, it would be impossible to stop.[383]

In the shorter term, climate change is disrupting rainfall patterns, increasing the incidence of droughts and floods, and intensifying heat waves and hurricanes. Scientists are cautious about pinning any single event, such as Hurricane Katrina's devastation of New Orleans in 2005 or Hurricane Sandy's destruction in the New York area in 2012, on climate change. But what is clear is that the frequency and severity of such events are increasing. To be sure, climate change could bring benefits in some places, like a longer growing season in temperate regions, but its overall effects are more negative than positive, in part because human societies are adapted to the world as it has been, not the changed world as it will become.[384]

What has most seized the public imagination in the US—at least among those who acknowledge the reality of climate change—is the threat of abrupt and potentially catastrophic destabilization. This could occur when some development, even a relatively minor one, pushes the climate system over a threshold (popularly referred to as a "tipping point"), into a new state "so rapidly and unexpectedly that human or natural systems have difficulty adapting to it."[385] Such an outcome is not impossible, but it probably can still be averted if we take concerted action to reduce greenhouse emissions *now*.

The current scientific consensus is that we need to limit global warming to a maximum temperature increase of 2 degrees Centigrade (3.6 degrees Fahrenheit) to avoid such a tipping point. To achieve that goal, greenhouse gas emissions worldwide would need to peak within the next ten years and decline to half their current level by mid-century. Without significant reductions in emissions, the world could face a much greater temperature rise by the end of the century—not exactly the end of the world, but the end of the world as we know it. Some scientists argue that even a 2 degrees Centigrade limit may not be enough to stave off catastrophic changes, and that the target should be 1.5.[386]

As I write these words, there are some signs of hope but also many reasons to be pessimistic. The Paris climate conference in December 2015 yielded an important international agreement on reducing emissions so as to keep temperature rise below 2 degrees Centigrade. 175 countries have signed on to the Paris accord, but many environmentalists argue that it didn't go nearly far enough. Moreover, whether or not the major greenhouse gas-emitting countries will actually comply with it is an open question.[387] So far, the political will to curb the use of fossil fuels has been sorely lacking, especially in the US, where climate change is a partisan football. The election of Trump has set the clock dangerously backwards on climate policy. Not only has he denied the reality of climate change, but politically he's in bed with the fossil fuel industry. On the campaign trail, he threatened to renegotiate US terms in the Paris accord.[388]

While the scientific realities of climate change are depressing enough, the failure of national and international leaders to respond can really drive one to despair. The resulting sense of powerlessness provides fertile ground for apocalyptic fantasies. In popular movies and fiction, as well as in the pronouncements of prominent scientists and environmentalists, climate change is portrayed as the latest harbinger of doom for humankind and nature.

I understand that feeling. I really do. Yet I'm not willing to go down that road. The "climate apocalypse" is a dead end in more ways than one. It can paralyze efforts to forge social, economic, political, and technological solutions to climate change. And it ends up boosting the authority and power of the military-industrial complex, encouraging responses that call out the troops and beef up our borders to prepare for the coming crisis. The risks of apocalyptic rhetoric about climate change far outweigh the benefits.

Fear of a climate apocalypse is in many ways a response to climate change denial. If the fossil fuel industry and its acolytes hadn't poured vast sums of money into denial of the problem, today we might be debating the fine points of a national climate policy and how to implement it. We might be moving far more rapidly to curb carbon emissions, embrace energy efficiency, and invest in clean and renewable energy technologies. Instead, the obstinacy of the denial lobby pushed many well-meaning climate scientists and advocates to adopt apocalyptic arguments as a counter-strategy. The national conversation about climate change—if you can call it a conversation—descended into the either/or extremes of US political discourse. The choice between denial and doomsday leaves little space in between for constructive maneuver. If the US were a small country with a small carbon footprint, this political impasse might not matter so much. Instead it has far-reaching consequences for the entire world.

FOLLOW THE DRILL

As late as 1998, before the climate deniers mustered their forces, opinion polls showed that a large majority of Americans saw global warming as a real problem that required action. They supported ratification of the Kyoto Protocol, the 1997 international agreement in which developed nations pledged to reduce greenhouse gas emissions. But while President Clinton supported the treaty, the Senate refused to ratify it. When George W. Bush took office, he announced that the US would not sign, nor would he make any plans to reduce carbon dioxide emissions by American power plants.[389] In fact, his administration proposed to construct over a thousand new power plants, mainly fired by coal.[390]

The US government's refusal to join the Kyoto accord was a major setback to national and international action on climate change. The US has been responsible for almost 30 percent of the total emissions of carbon dioxide into the atmosphere since 1850, ranking first among all nations in its historical responsibility for climate change.[391] Although China surpassed the US as the largest emitter in 2007, on a per capita basis China still emits much less carbon dioxide than the US—6.2 metric tons compared to 17.6 metric tons by the US.[392] The American public got it right in the

1990s: we need to do something about climate change. But the politicians were dancing to the tune of a different drummer.

Call it a conspiracy or just a concerted effort, but since the 1990s a powerful combination of Big Coal and Big Oil corporations and conservative free enterprise think tanks joined together to convince the American public that man-made climate change is a myth. In many cases it was money from the fossil fuel industry that underwrote the think tanks' climate work. By 2003, Exxon-Mobil was providing a million dollars a year to conservative think tanks.[393] Scratching each other's backs and reinforcing each other's messages, the corporations and think tanks threw their weight behind a coterie of scientists who were willing to play the role of climate skeptics, giving them power and influence well beyond their modest numbers and even more modest professional reputations. Most of them didn't publish in peer-review journals, a litmus test for credibility in the scientific community, nor did they have training or expertise in climate science.[394] Taking a page from the public relations playbook of the tobacco industry—for which some of them had earlier worked to deny the link between smoking and cancer—the skeptics attacked climate science, seizing on its careful acknowledgement of uncertainties as a weakness rather than a strength.[395]

The 2000 election, which brought George W. Bush and Dick Cheney to office, gave the fossil fuel industry and its backers easy access to the White House. Along with the growing influence of right-wing media, the new administration further politicized and polarized the climate debate. Over the first decade of the 21st century, public opinion on climate change bifurcated increasingly along party lines, with Democrats generally supportive of doing something about it, and Republicans in the skeptic camp.[396]

With the rise of the Tea Party, financially backed by the Koch brothers whose $35 billion business empire includes industries that refine and distribute oil, positions hardened further.[397] In the 2010 Congressional elections, climate change denial became a litmus test for Republican candidates.[398] Those Republican lawmakers who had pro-environmental inclinations before were forced to abandon them, or to abandon office altogether.

Christian fundamentalists have also played their part. Some see climate change as a sign of the end times predicted in the Book of Revelation, where environmental disaster is a prelude to the battle of Armageddon. If climate change is real, it's God's will. Others reject scientific evidence of climate change because scientists believe the Earth to be billions of years old, whereas the literalist interpretation of the Bible sets a 6000-year limit.[399]

Not all evangelicals subscribe to these views. Some are conservationists, who take seriously their mission to steward God's creation. In 2006 a group of religious leaders launched the Evangelical Climate Initiative, issuing a statement supportive of action on climate change and highlighting the ethical concern that it will hit the poor the hardest. The document was a hopeful sign that, in the name of "creation care," the divide between evangelicals and environmentalists could be breached. Even televangelist Pat Robertson, who previously depicted environmentalists as evil, godless, and un-American, started changing his tune on global warming. Harvard biologist E.O. Wilson issued an impassioned plea to work with the evangelical community.[400]

The Evangelical Climate Initiative withered, however, in the face of a concerted counter-attack by groups like the conservative Cornwall Alliance.[401] The Alliance's declaration states,

> We believe Earth and its ecosystems—created by God's intelligent design and infinite power and sustained by His

faithful providence—are robust, resilient, self-regulating, and self-correcting, admirably suited for human flourishing, and displaying His glory. Earth's climate system is no exception. Recent global warming is one of many natural cycles of warming and cooling in geologic history.[402]

But environmentally inclined evangelicals are fighting back. By 2014 the Evangelical Environmental Network, which spreads the message that climate change is real and that Christians need to protect God's handiwork, had grown to 300,000 members in the space of five years.[403] Meanwhile, for Catholics, Pope Francis's 2015 papal encyclical on the environment, *Laudato si'*, is a rousing call to arms for climate justice. Denialism is starting to pass from favor, except that now Trump may give it another big boost.

If climate change denial was Plan A for the fossil fuel corporations, Plan B is a can-do message that they are taking action on climate change by investing in renewable energy technologies. The bottom line, however, is still drill, baby, drill. They are loath to see their proven reserves of oil, coal, and natural gas—five times more than scientists think is safe to burn without triggering a catastrophic temperature rise—left in the ground as stranded assets. In reality, fossil fuel companies are investing precious little in renewable energy.[404] Instead, they are pursuing ever dirtier and ever riskier forms of extraction—fracking for natural gas and oil, mining tar sands and shale oil, and deep sea-drilling—what energy and security scholar Michael Klare has termed "extreme energy." Unfortunately, harvesting fuels from "geologically and geographically forbidding environments" tends to produce ever more extreme accidents and pollution—the 2010 BP Deepwater Horizon disaster off the coast of Louisiana being a case in point.[405]

The politics remain dirty too. After embarrassing exposés, most major oil companies, even ExxonMobil, the most egregious of the bunch, have pledged to stop financing the climate denial activities of conservative think tanks. Yet there's a fuzzy line between direct and indirect funding. ExxonMobil is now a major finance arm of the Republican Party. In the 2010 elections, its Political Action Committee gave 90 percent of its money to the Republicans, with only a small fraction left over for a few Democrats.[406]

Meanwhile, the Democrats' climate record has been less than inspiring. The Obama administration largely supported drilling, mining, and fracking our way to national "energy independence." On the campaign trail in 2012, Obama promised voters, "You have my word that we will keep drilling everywhere we can . . . That's a commitment that I make."[407] The Waxman–Markey bill, introduced during President Obama's first term when the Democrats controlled both houses of Congress, sought to reduce US emissions by means of a "cap and trade" scheme that would have given free emission permits to Big Coal, Big Oil, and electric utilities, bringing them windfall profits. Even so, the bill died in the Senate. Following that defeat, Obama focused on executive actions rather than trying to pass legislation. In 2014 and 2015, he announced new EPA regulations to cut pollution from motor vehicles and power plants, though the Supreme Court has stayed the implementation of his Clean Power Plan pending judicial review.[408] In an agreement with China, Obama pledged to cut US carbon emissions by 28 percent from 2005 levels by 2025, while China pledged to stop increasing emissions by 2030.[409] In 2015 Obama vetoed a bill that would have approved the construction of the Keystone XL pipeline, and in 2016 the Army Corps of Engineers put a temporary halt to the passage of the Dakota Access pipeline through the lands of the Standing Rock Sioux. These promising developments under Obama have been swiftly revoked by Donald Trump, who has launched a full-scale attack on the EPA and environmental regulation more generally.

Fortunately, there is still some progress on the state level. California is cutting emissions under its Global Warming Solutions Act. The Regional Greenhouse Gas Initiative of the northeastern states is capping power plant emissions and auctioning the permits, rather than giving them away, yielding revenue that can be returned to the public or used for investments in clean energy and energy efficiency. But lack of progress at the federal level continues to help spawn apocalyptic visions of climate change. After all, this is an eminently time-sensitive issue: the less we do now, the worse it will be. True enough, but how helpful is it to paint the future in dark and dismal hues?

ENDGAMES

Climate apocalypse comes in many flavors. Sometimes they're mixed together, sometimes they're served separately. The first apocalyptic warnings came from climate scientists who were battling the denial industry. NASA climatologist James Hansen, now at Columbia University's Earth Institute, is known for his heroic efforts to put climate change on the agenda for urgent public action. Frustrated by the lack of progress, he began to warn about the certainty of catastrophe, even though climate science prides itself on clearly articulating the *uncertainties* involved in predictions about the future. Hansen's 2009 book, *Storms of My Grandchildren: The Truth About the Coming Climate Catastrophe and Our Last Chance to Save Humanity*, concludes with a dystopian sci-fi scenario in which more technologically advanced creatures from another solar system fly to Earth on a spaceship called the Mayflower II to explore whether they can migrate their civilization here, as their own sun threatens to burn them up. Alas, Earth is no longer habitable. Boiling oceans and scorched deserts are all that remain. "The above scenario—with a devastated, sweltering Earth purged of life—may read like far-fetched science fiction," Hansen writes. "Yet its central hypothesis is a tragic certainty . . ."[410] James Lovelock, of Gaia theory fame, similarly warned that climate change would kill most of us and leave just a few sturdy couples to live a Stone Age existence in the Arctic, though he has since recanted these doomsday views.[411]

Apocalyptic climate change scenarios often draw inspiration from computer simulation models. Though the models' findings can only be suggestive, never definitive, they come to be misinterpreted as literal truth. "By their very nature," climate scholars Mark Maslin and Patrick Austin write in the journal *Nature*, "models cannot capture all the factors involved in a natural system, and those that they do capture are incompletely understood."[412] Indeed, as climate models become ever more complex, they reveal greater uncertainties about possible outcomes. Does this make the models useless? Not at all. Climate modeling has advanced our knowledge of the links between carbon dioxide emissions, temperature changes, and environmental conditions. But acknowledging uncertainties is both scientifically honest and politically smart. Misrepresenting models to predict certain catastrophe bolsters skeptics who like nothing better than to ridicule such forecasts when they fail to materialize. Throwing caution to the wind risks counterproductive blowback.

Al Gore's 2006 award-winning documentary, *An Inconvenient Truth*, combines classic disaster imagery—glaciers melting with thunderous sound effects, the swirling chaos of Hurricane Katrina, harrowing scenes of flood and drought in Asia, power plants spewing pollution—with the scientific appeal of charts and graphs and the personal touch of Gore's love for his family home in Tennessee. Calling this approach "tempered apocalypticism," one critic writes that, even though the film takes you on "a nature hike through the Book of Revelations," it ends with the upbeat message that we can do something about global warming.[413] Yet the recommendations that roll with the film credits—like buying more energy-efficient light bulbs—seem pretty lame compared to the scale of the problem. How much Gore's tempered apocalypticism inspired constructive action is hard to say, but it did help him win the 2007 Nobel Peace Prize that he shared with the UN's Intergovernmental Panel on Climate Change (IPCC).

One of the film's strongest legacies was to make disaster imagery a common staple of our cultural imagination of climate change, along with the poor polar bear floating around on a piece of ice. Climate change disasters in turn mesh well with what social scientist Michael Barkun calls the current era of disaster obsession, "where large numbers of people become convinced they live in an insecure world on the verge of cataclysmic events."[414] Along with disaster imagery, the possibility of a tipping point that will cast the planet into abrupt and catastrophic climate change also feeds into a larger cultural fascination with points of no return. Many believers in peak oil, for example, see the peak and subsequent decline of oil reserves as heralding the end of modern civilization and the need for a more primitive, rural survivalism.[415]

In recent years the proliferation of apocalyptic films and books on climate change has spawned a new genre: "cli-fi."[416] The plots differ, but many share a dark vision of the end of Western civilization, together with the jeremiad-style message that we sinners will get what we deserve. Historians Naomi Oreskes and Erik Conway, authors of *Merchants of Doubt*, an excellent book on tobacco and climate denial, have unfortunately gone off the cli-fi deep end with their more recent publication, *The Collapse of Western Civilization*. In their nightmarish tale, climate change spurs all manner of disasters from political chaos, including the imposition of martial law in the US, to urban food riots all over the world, to "mass migration of undernourished and dehydrated individuals," to "widespread outbreaks of typhus, cholera, dengue fever, yellow fever, and viral and retroviral agents never before seen."[417]

The 2004 Hollywood film *The Day After Tomorrow* depicts the submergence of New York City in a flood of biblical proportions. The rest of the country doesn't do too well either. In one of the film's campier scenes, refugees from the US stream toward the Mexican border, a novel twist on the "climate refugee" trope. *Earth 2100*, a made-for-TV movie, painted a similarly lurid picture, in which half the world's population dies from a climate-induced new plague and New York City also goes under. This time, though, it's the Mexicans who storm our borders. In *Elysium*, a higher-end production starring Matt Damon and Jodie Foster, the ravaged environment is Los Angeles which is poor, overpopulated, violent, and Hispanicized. The rich have fled to a luxurious space-station habitat. The film manages to promote immigrant rights and universal health care, but people of color in Los Angeles don't come off looking real good—their violence and squalor amount to slum porn.

These kinds of cli-fi (not all cli-fi is so dystopian) speak to the deep undercurrent in white American culture that sees the big city, and especially multiracial, multiethnic megalopolises like New York and Los Angeles, as evil, unhealthy places. In *The Ecology of Fear*, Mike Davis writes that, in disaster fiction, this "urge to strike out and destroy, to wipe out an entire city and untold thousands of its inhabitants—is rooted in racial anxiety."[418] It's worth pondering whether the popularity of climate dystopia is related to demographic trends. By 2050, non-Hispanic whites are projected to be a minority in the United States. Worldwide, people of European descent are already a distinct minority. Is this why some of the "doomer discourse" seems to derive a certain satisfaction from predicting that millions or billions of people in the Third World and our own inner cities are going to die in the coming climate apocalypse?[419]

A brighter version of climate apocalypse forecasts the arrival of a new millennium, as capitalism is once and for all relegated to the dustbin of history. In her book, *This Changes Everything*, Naomi Klein writes how climate change

> could be the best argument progressives have ever had to demand the rebuilding and reviving of local economies; to reclaim our democracies from corrosive corporate influence; to block harmful new free trade deals and rewrite old ones; to invest in starving public infrastructure like mass transit and affordable housing; to take back ownership of essential services like energy and water; to remake our sick agricultural system into something much healthier; to open borders to migrants whose displacement is linked to climate impacts; to finally respect Indigenous land rights—all of which would help to end grotesque levels of inequality within our nations and between them.

As a political wish list, this has much to recommend it. But to think that the threat of climate change will jumpstart this great transformation has more than a faint taste of pie in the sky. Klein's bright-side vision never strays too far from the dark side. The choice, she tells us, is stark: "allow climate disruption to change everything about our world, or change pretty much everything about our economy to avoid that fate."[420] To be fair, Klein is more nuanced in her climate activism, supporting organizational efforts for energy conservation and renewable energy technologies.[421]

In the left millennial view, climate change often substitutes for the working class and the role it was supposed to play in bringing down the system.[422] There's a jeremiad version too. Climate change not only stands in for the missing-in-action proletariat, but is an environmental avatar of Christ who will redeem us of our sins. Those who embrace the radical apocalypse will be saved. Coming together to fight climate change is the next "Great Awakening."[423]

Alongside apocalyptic rhetoric about climate change, the term "Anthropocene" has been coined to demarcate a new geological epoch in the planet's history. Derived from the Greek word for humans, the Anthropocene label infers that our species now has such a vast impact on the Earth system, especially through man-made climate change, that it operates like one of the great forces of nature. This formulation runs the risk of downplaying differential power relations among human beings because of its emphasis on the supposedly greater struggle between Humans and Nature. "The unfolding of man into a single story, with a single past and a single future, is the most powerful (and problematic) aspect of the discourse," writes political theorist Matthew Lepori. "The specter of catastrophe looms over the entire species."[424] That some people bear more responsibility for climate change than others can get left out of the picture, along with the fact that not all will be equally affected by it.

Prophets of climate apocalypse think of it as an incentive to action. It proceeds via a kind of inverted logic: "Ask not what you can do about climate change, but what climate change can do to you." At meetings where I've spoken about ways to engage constructively in climate policies and politics, I've sometimes been attacked for not being sufficiently apocalyptic. Like the Puritans of an earlier era, some seem to find in the specter of doom an opportunity to evidence their own moral superiority. By forgoing a plane journey, or not having a child, they are saving the world, while others who don't follow in their carbon-reducing footprints are unworthy sinners. But holier-than-thou elitism doesn't help to win many others to the cause.

Instead, raising the specter of climate apocalypse can be a real turn-off. Disaster images may grab attention, but in the end they often disempower, generating fears of faraway people and places that make people feel distant or helpless or numb. Communication strategies that appeal to hope and a vision of the common good are more compelling. "Communicators can serve the emergence of such a vision," writes American climate researcher Susanne Moser, "first, by ceasing to conjure a doomsday scenario in people's imagination; second, by pointing to the many positive efforts underway; and finally, by providing fora where people can engage in the visioning process."[425]

Recent polls suggest that climate denial may finally be burning out in the US. In a March 2016 Gallup poll, 64 percent of US adults (including 40 percent of Republicans) said they worried a great deal or fair amount about global warming, and 65 percent attributed climate change to human activities.[426] Solid majorities of women, blacks, Latinos, and young people say they would support candidates for office who favor action on climate change.[427] Even if Trump stokes climate denialism during his administration, it won't last forever. There's a political opportunity to build a broad coalition for effective climate policy, an opportunity that isn't well served by doomsday thinking.

That's the good news. The bad news is that powerful vested

interests stand to gain from perpetuating the climate apocalypse in our political and cultural imaginations. Among them is the national security state, which capitalizes on the premise that climate change will lead to violent conflict among peoples deemed less civilized than ourselves. Poor Africans, for example, are predicted to descend into a Hobbesian state of human nature where they kill each other over scarce resources. Unsubstantiated claims proliferate that climate change will create millions of "climate refugees" who will roam the globe and threaten our borders. Alarm bells over the coming "climate wars" find a powerful echo chamber in the military-industrial complex.

A PERFECT STORM

In 2004, a Pentagon-commissioned report called *An Abrupt Climate Change Scenario and Its Implications for United States National Security* hit the news. The authors, Global Business Network consultants Doug Randall and Peter Schwartz (Schwartz was former head of scenario planning for the fossil fuel giant Royal Dutch/Shell), trotted out the trusty old Malthusian model to argue that abrupt climate change, by diminishing carrying capacity, would provoke scarcities of food, water, and energy. These would trigger violent conflicts and drive desperate people to wash up on Western shores. Better-off nations will be forced "to build fortresses around their countries, preserving resources for themselves." US borders will be strengthened "to hold back unwanted starving immigrants from the Caribbean islands (an especially severe problem), Mexico, and South America." The one glimmer of hope is that massive die-offs of poor people from war, starvation, and disease will cull the human population, "which over time, will re-balance with carrying capacity."[428]

Given the report's provenance, this sanguine view of annihilation perhaps should come as no surprise. The report was the product of the Defense Department's secretive Office of Net Assessment (ONA), run for over four decades by security strategist and futurist Andrew Marshall. He retired in 2015 at the age of 93. Marshall is a legendary figure in national security circles. His nickname is Yoda, after the Jedi Grand Master in the Star Wars films. His influence has lasted from the Cold War to the War on Terror. In the 1990s, he was the leading proponent of the "Revolution in Military Affairs" that promoted new information technologies and long-range precision strike weapons as the cutting edge of 21st-century warfare.[429]

Marshall is well-known for his apocalyptic tendencies. "The old joke about the Office of Net Assessment is that it should be called the Office of Threat Inflation," Dr. Barry Posen, director of Security Studies at MIT, told the *Washington Post*. "They go well beyond exploring the worst cases," he explained. "They convince others to act as if the worst cases are inevitable."[430] During the Cold War, Marshall focused ONA's work on Doctor Strangelove-style doomsday nuclear scenarios. More recently, he ran war games that hyped up the threat of war with China. "We tend to look at not very happy futures," he once told an interviewer.[431]

In researching this book, I sometimes came upon a perfect storm where all the elements converged into an apocalyptic extreme weather pattern. Marshall's "abrupt climate change scenario" was the first gust in the perfect storm of climate militarization. Most ONA reports remain confidential, hidden from public view. This one was unclassified, and let out of the bag before it was cleared by Marshall's superiors in the Defense Department or the Bush administration.[432]

While the report garnered criticism for being over-the-top—even the Pentagon tried to distance itself from its more outlandish speculations—it set the tone for a slew of lurid scenarios that portrayed climate change as a dangerous national security threat rivaling terrorism. The authors of these scenarios typically had little to no knowledge of the low-income people and societies they were stereotyping.[433] These threat-mongering fictions were often accepted, even in liberal circles, as plausible scientific predictions. The public was already primed for such messages. "The perennial alarmism of a large and vocal wing of the environmental movement," writes international security scholar Richard Matthew, "has had considerable success in convincing people that the world is an inherently dangerous place, perilously close to catastrophe and chaos."[434]

By 2007, the perfect storm had swept up many voices into its swirling vortex. That year, fears of climate chaos reached fever pitch. For example, the NGO Christian Aid released a report entitled *Human Tide: The Real Migration Crisis* that warned of millions of climate refugees roaming the globe, wreaking havoc, and creating "a world of many more Darfurs."[435] The war in Darfur, in western Sudan, was depicted as the harbinger of the coming era of climate wars. First, the American magazine *Atlantic Monthly*, then UNEP, and then UN Secretary General Ban Ki-moon attributed the violence in Darfur to the interaction of climate change, population pressure, and resource scarcity. The British government brought the climate conflict issue before the UN Security Council for the first time, citing the Darfur case.[436] In awarding the 2007 Nobel Peace Prize to Al Gore and the IPCC, the prize committee warned that climate-induced migration and scarcities could cause violent conflict and war.[437]

The blitz was on because climate militarization served so many interests: journalists and pundits were hungry for headlines; NGOs and researchers were looking for new winds to shake money trees; the UN sought to divert attention from its failure to resolve the conflict in Darfur by shifting the narrative from a shortage of political will to a shortage of rainfall; and with the end of the Cold War, national security interests needed new threats to replace the Soviet enemy. Add to these interests the temptation for environmentalists to invoke national security as a way to get climate policy more attention at the highest levels of government. In 2009, backers of the Waxman–Markey climate bill used the security argument to woo conservative votes in the US Senate. The *New York Times* editorialized that this was "pretty good politics—especially on Capitol Hill, where many politicians will do anything for the Pentagon."[438] One can imagine that under a Trump administration that denies or downplays climate change, the environmental lobby's inclination to play the national security card will be even stronger.

Each of these interests draws on the other's dire predictions to legitimize their own. In deploying images of desperate refugees and starving children in Africa, writes Harry Verhoeven,

> NGOs and think tanks play a vital role in shaping the policy consensus around climate change and violence. Their reports intend to be prescient by warning governments, international organizations, and parliaments about probably violent long-term consequences of global warming, but in part do so by quoting the dystopian warnings of the very policymakers they are seeking to inform; (inter)national politicians in turn draw on alarmist warnings from NGOs and think tanks to bolster their admonitions.[439]

This self-reinforcing dynamic depends in turn on deeply held and widely shared colonial prejudices about race and climatic determinism that still influence Western views of the developing world. In their starkest form, hardy, hard-working white Europeans from colder climates are deemed innately superior to the lazy black savages of the enervating tropics. Whites get to make history, while blacks are part of nature. The colonial imagination linked climate to conflict too. In the early part of the 19th century, American geographer Ellsworth Huntington argued that drought and famine caused by climate changes rendered Asian societies permanently unstable and uncivilized.[440] Even today in books like Jared Diamond's *Collapse*, the ruin or disappearance of entire civilizations like the Mayans is mainly attributed to an overly deterministic combination of bad weather and population growth.[441]

In international policy circles, these prejudices intersect with "crisis narratives" that draw a simple causal chain between poverty, overpopulation, environmental degradation, and violent political unrest in poor countries.[442] Despite numerous critiques leveled by scholars and development practitioners, crisis narratives have proved a hardy justification for Western economic and military interventions: The situation is getting so bad that if we don't go in and fix it immediately, all hell is going to break loose. The narratives tap into and reinforce racialized fears of the poor, fears now epitomized by the so-called threat of climate wars and climate refugees.

THE PARABLE OF THE HERDSMAN AND
OTHER TALL TALES

Stephan Faris, the *Atlantic Monthly* journalist who ascribed the conflict in Darfur to climate change, claimed that the real fault lines there are between "settled farmers and nomadic herders fighting over failing lands." The main reason those lands are failing, he writes, is because climate change is reducing rainfall. "With countries across the region and around the world suffering similar pressures, some see Darfur as a canary in the coal mine, a foretaste of climate-driven political chaos."[443]

No one knows the precise figure, but the best estimates are that, since the Darfur conflict flared in 2003, upwards of 300,000 people have died from direct violence or illness, and many more have been displaced. The simple climate war story ignores the exploitative relationship between Sudan's rulers and the impoverished people of Darfur that is at the root of the violence. In a world of gross inequalities in wealth and power, Sudan stands out. Beginning in the 1970s, the government seized land from peasants and pastoralists alike, handing it over to big industrial farms that proceeded to degrade the environment through unsustainable irrigation and agricultural practices. In the 1990s, the regime also forcibly relocated Nuba farmers in Darfur into so-called "peace villages" where they became a source of captive labor for mechanized farms. When protest movements began to emerge in Darfur, the Sudanese government sent in the army. It also played the ethnic card, supporting the Janjaweed militia, composed of mainly Arab nomads, in their genocidal attacks on the local population. Oil revenues greased a war machine whose origins go back to the Reagan administration's support for the government's disastrous agricultural policies, nascent oil industry, and military.[444]

In a chapter on human security, the IPCC's Fifth Assessment Report found that most scholarly studies of the Darfur conflict have found government practices to be far more influential drivers than climate variability. The report further notes that "similar changes in climate did not stimulate conflicts of the same magnitude in neighboring regions," and "in the past people in Darfur were able to cope with climate variability in ways that avoided large-scale violence."[445] These facts get lost in the climate conflict version of events. Precisely for that reason, the Sudanese government "loves the 'climate war' rhetoric" because it obscures the regime's role in causing the conflict through policies of exclusion, patronage, and violence.[446]

From Darfur, the phantasm of climate conflict has spread to large swaths of Africa's drylands, with the itinerant herder playing the role of the ignoble savage. A report on climate and security by the Science Board of the US Department of Defense identifies pastoral landscapes in Darfur, the margins of the Sahel, and southern Africa as sites of future climate conflict.[447]

Why does so much anxiety center on the African herder? These are some of the poorest people in the world. Why have they become the harbinger of the apocalyptic climate chaos to come? Perhaps they evoke fears of roving tribes in biblical times. Perhaps the fact that they are not fully tamed by governments and constrained by national borders makes herders a metaphor for instability. But there's another prejudice at work, too: for many environmentalists, herders are a potent symbol of ecological destruction.

The late Garrett Hardin's "Tragedy of the Commons" is among the most commonly assigned essays in American environmental studies courses. It is not only used to illustrate the ostensible perils of overpopulation, but also to make the case for private property or state control to protect the environment. Along the way, it paints herders in a most unflattering light:

> Picture a pasture open to all. It is to be expected that each herdsman will try to keep as many cattle as possible on the commons. Such an arrangement may work reasonably satisfactorily for centuries because tribal wars, poaching,

and disease keep the numbers of both man and beast well below the carrying capacity of the land. Finally, however, comes the day of reckoning, that is, the day when the long-desired goal of social stability becomes a reality. At this point, the inherent logic of the commons remorselessly generates tragedy.

As a rational being, each herdsman seeks to maximize his gain . . . [and] concludes that the only sensible course for him to pursue is to add another animal to his herd. And another; and another... But this is the conclusion reached by each and every rational herdsman sharing a commons. Therein is the tragedy. Each man is locked into a system that compels him to increase his herd without limit—in a world that is limited. Ruin is the destination toward which all men rush, each pursuing his own best interest in a society that believes in the freedom of the commons. Freedom in a commons brings ruin to all.[448]

Hardin's parable of the herdsman embodies a very dim view of human nature as "every man out for himself." It also obscures the fact that people have been managing common resources cooperatively for centuries, successfully negotiating the tension between private gain and the public good. Cooperation in the commons doesn't always happen of course, but it's a lot more common than Hardin and his intellectual successors admit. The late Elinor Ostrom, the first woman to win the Nobel Prize in economics, documented many cases from around the world where individuals have created stable institutions of self-governance that make and enforce rules that protect natural resources and provide mutual protection against risk.[449]

Case studies of African pastoralists bear out Ostrom's findings. Furthermore, it turns out that herders—and other people—often respond to environmental stress by cooperating to manage it, with the result that there can be less conflict, not more. In the drylands of northern Kenya, for example, researchers have found that in times of drought and water scarcity, violence among poor herders is less frequent. Despite poverty and population growth in the region, common property regimes help the herders to adjust to water scarcity. "If at any time a conflict over a scarce natural resource like water exists," the researchers report, "it can be a sign that local resource users themselves have been made powerless and that their negotiating system has been paralyzed, either by external agencies or local elites."[450]

In the Sahel, Africa's semi-arid region which stretches across the continent between the Sahara desert to the north and more humid areas to the south, evidence for a link between climate change and higher violence rates is similarly weak. Recent periods of drought have not been followed by greater violent conflict. The real crisis is the ongoing political and economic marginalization of poor communities by powerful national and global interests, and the political violence perpetrated by them. Almost half of violent events in the Sahel involve government security forces; militias, rebel groups, and transnational militaries comprise the rest.[451]

More and more field research in Africa is showing just how biased and inadequate the climate conflict story is. Yet these insights do not seem to be flowing, or even trickling down, to pundits and policymakers. Ignorance isn't the only reason. An African exceptionalism is at work. While it's commonly assumed that resource scarcities and environmental stress can lead to institutional and technological innovations in the Global North, the idea that this could be true for poor Africans is inconceivable. Instead scarcity supposedly turns them into victims and villains, incapable of innovation and intrinsically prone to violence. Ironically, the main trigger of violent conflict in Africa, going back to colonial times, is resource *abundance*—struggles for control over oil, gold, diamonds, and other valuable minerals.[452] Corporations and governments may enlist poor soldiers to do their dirty work, but it's mainly the rich who pull the strings.

Writing in *Nature Climate Change*, geographer Clionadh Raleigh and colleagues describe how this exceptionalism stretches beyond African borders to other developing regions. They contrast the expectation of climate conflict with the reality that

> [o]n the ground in developing countries, climate change and ecological stress is treated as a problem to be solved, not a harbinger of apocalyptic violence as it is viewed by many analysts. Indeed, during periods of hardship, higher levels of cooperation are found between erstwhile competitors . . . Yet cooperation is far less likely to make headline news. Alternative livelihoods, migration, and changing agricultural patterns are all examples of how individuals and communities adapt to new and volatile circumstances . . . In terms of predicting and interpreting future insecurity in developing states, it is probably more critical to understand the "nature of the state" than the "state of nature" . . . People in poor countries do not respond to bad weather by attacking each other.[453]

The strongest linkages between climate change and violence are not to be found in the behaviors of the poor, but of the rich and powerful, especially the fossil fuel corporations that significantly drive global warming and politically thwart the transition to renewable energies. Here again the concept of structural violence is useful—the ways inequalities in wealth and power, embedded in the institutions and social arrangements that govern people's lives, cause undue suffering and death. Sociologist Eric Bonds calls attention to the prediction by the World Health Organization that climate change will indirectly cause a quarter of a million excess deaths per year from 2030–2050. Most of these deaths will be in developing countries, resulting from heat waves, the spread of tropical diseases, and childhood malnutrition. The focus on armed conflict misses the boat. "After all," Bonds asks, "can we say that, if global warming continues unabated, the increasing numbers of children who will die from waterborne diseases is somehow peaceful, even if it does not trigger armed conflict?"[454]

Other researchers point to how armed conflict itself, through destruction of local environments and livelihoods, increases people's vulnerabilities to climate change. In the wrong hands, climate change adaptation and mitigation schemes can also end up violently displacing local communities from their lands, effectively operating as "green grabs" by government and corporate interests. In a supreme irony, once ecologically sustainable peasant and pastoral landscapes are being turned over to commercial farming, biofuel plantations, and ecotourism for the rich.[455] When it comes to understanding the relationship between climate change and conflict, it makes much more sense to start by looking at what the people at the top of the social ladder are doing to the people on the bottom rung than what the people on the bottom are doing to each other.

THE CLIMATE REFUGEES THAT WEREN'T

That the effects of climate change—from sea level rise to severe storms to droughts and floods—may force or induce people to migrate, temporarily or permanently, isn't in question. But the way the term "climate refugee," like "climate conflict" and "climate war," is being bandied about has more to do with apocalyptic grandstanding than it does with realities on the ground.

The first quantitative estimates of future climate refugees came from British environmental writer Norman Myers, who has made something of a cottage industry of pulling numbers out of a hat. In the mid-1990s, Myers and a few colleagues conjured up the figure of 25 million "environmental refugees" who posed a threat to international security. As scholars subsequently pointed out, this figure had little evidence behind it, but nevertheless it circulated so widely in the international policy arena that it became an accepted "fact."[456] In 2005, Myers announced that there would be 50 million climate refugees by 2010 and 200 million by 2050. The 50 million figure, quickly embraced by UNEP and the UN University, soon made its way into the media and policy documents. On its website, UNEP posted a map showing where the refugees were likely to come from.[457] The 200 million figure gained wide currency, too, and like the size of the fish the man once caught, it kept getting bigger—700 million climate refugees were possible by 2050, according to one author.[458]

In 2011, UNEP quietly took down its map when the prediction of 50 million climate refugees proved incorrect. But the genie was already out of the bottle. A 2010 documentary, *Climate Refugees*, showed in film festivals across the globe. Along with the usual environmental pundits, it featured Democratic Senator John Kerry and Republican ex-Speaker of the House Newt Gingrich, both warning of the dire threat these migrants pose. Maybe the Halloween-style graphics on the film's website enhanced its bipartisan appeal.[459]

The enumeration of climate refugees is a cautionary tale of how such inflated statistics, if politically useful, come to assume a life of their own. The problem with climate refugees isn't just about the math, however. It's about the concept itself. Most serious migration researchers are loath to use the term, preferring more accurate descriptors like "climate-related migration" instead. The IPCC's Fifth Assessment Report notes how the notion of climate refugees is "scientifically and legally problematic."[460]

At this point no one can predict the precise extent to which climate change will force migration.[461] Even when climate change affects an area, decisions to migrate will be influenced by many other factors, too. A study of the impact of desertification on migration from the highlands of northeastern Ethiopia found that decisions to stay or go hinged on whether residents had other livelihood options apart from agriculture at home, and whether they had opportunities and connections in urban areas. It also depended on the influence of ethnic politics in terms of whether the new area would be hospitable or not. With the possible exception of sea level rise, migration is too complex a process to label as simply climate-induced.[462]

Even on the islands and atolls threatened by rising seas, decisions to migrate are not one-dimensional. Take the small Pacific island of Tuvalu which, along with its neighbor Kiribati, has become an international symbol for climate refugees. Journalists and filmmakers flock to the island to film the approaching disaster, often mistaking periodic high tide flooding with sea level rise. People *are* migrating today from Tuvalu—but they always have been. Migration is a way of life in the Pacific. Current pressures to migrate have less to do with sea level rise than with the lack of employment opportunities and other environmental stresses. The media also tends to overlook the detailed planning the islanders are doing to adapt to climate change. "Tuvalu becomes a space where the fate of the planet is brought forward in time and miniaturized in space," writes scholar Carol Farbotko, "reduced to a performance of rising seas and climate refugees played out for those with most control over the current and future uses of fossil fuels." She calls this "wishful sinking," in which the islanders are cast as desperate victims, "something to fear and/or control."[463] It's not surprising that the islanders themselves don't appreciate being called climate refugees.[464]

The extent to which climate change will increase future migration depends on what we do now to reduce carbon emissions and implement adaptation measures such as better drought and storm preparedness. In some cases, migration may make sense as an adaptation strategy, although whether it's temporary, seasonal, or permanent will be context-specific. In many agricultural regions, people already migrate seasonally to urban or peri-urban jobs to earn cash to invest back in farming or in their children's education. The greatest climate-related humanitarian emergencies, according to a Norwegian government report, may be in places "where people *cannot* afford to move, rather than the places to which they do move."[465] Fearful narratives about climate refugees are not helpful in making plans to strengthen the capacities of communities and to improve physical infrastructure to prepare for the risks of climate change.

Most experts agree that climate-related displacement and migration are likely to happen mainly within national borders, not across them.[466] Yet you wouldn't know that from the climate refugee literature. In the case of Africa, political scientist Gregory White points out how current threat projections about roaming climate refugees serve the larger aim of security forces in the region, as well as NATO, to build up borders in northern African transit states through the construction of fences, patrols, and detention centers.[467]

In the event that people do have to cross international borders due to climate change, we need to question the assumption that they pose a security threat. Painting Bangladesh as the scene of the coming climate apocalypse, where the "Four Horsemen" are already gathering their forces, an article in the American environmental magazine *OnEarth* warned that sea level rise could turn millions of destitute Muslims into refugees and Islamic terrorists.[468] Blending fear of climate refugees together with the threat of terrorism not only reduces empathy for those at risk of displacement, but further militarizes the environmental imagination.

ADDING SYRIA AND TERRORISM TO THE MIX

In 2015 the Syrian conflict replaced Darfur as the new climate war. Setting the process in motion was an article in the *Proceedings of the National Academy of Sciences* in March that year. The authors argued that the drought that afflicted Syria from 2007–2010 was made two to three times more likely by human-induced climate change. They then asserted that the drought caused a mass exodus of peasants from rural to overcrowded urban areas, and that these migrants helped to trigger the civil war. While the authors provided nothing more than a single farmer's testimony in support of this latter claim, they reached the conclusion that human-induced climate change is strongly implicated in the current Syrian conflict.[469]

Like the *Atlantic* story on Darfur eight years earlier, the Syria article hit the media jackpot, spurring headlines in major news outlets that climate change was an important cause of the war.[470] It was only a small step from that claim to seeing people displaced by the conflict, almost eight million within the country, and five million outside, as climate refugees. As the refugee crisis in Europe escalated over the summer and fall of 2015—by the end of the year a million people had arrived by boat—so did the climate refugee hyperbole. "How Climate Change is Behind the Surge of Migrants to Europe" was the title of a September *Time* magazine article.[471] That same month the Canadian *National Observer* carried the iconic photograph of a drowned Syrian boy on a Turkish beach with the headline, "This is what a climate refugee looks like."[472]

President Obama and Secretary of State Kerry took up the mantle. In a May 2015 graduation address to the US Coast Guard Academy, Obama spoke about the role of climate change in the Syrian civil war as well as in the rise of Boko Haram in Nigeria.[473] At an international climate conference in Alaska several months later, Kerry raised the specter of millions of "climate refugees" leaving their countries. "You think migration is a challenge to Europe today because of extremism," he said, "wait until you see what happens when there's an absence of water, an absence of food, or one tribe fighting against another for mere survival." He likened the challenge to World War II, when "all of Europe was overrun with evil and civilization itself seemed to be in peril."[474]

A day after the deadly Islamic State attacks in Paris, even the progressive senator Bernie Sanders, then a Democratic presidential hopeful, told a national TV audience that "climate change is directly related to the growth of terrorism." Citing the CIA as his source, he went on to say that climate change was likely to cause international conflict because of struggles over "limited amounts of water, limited amounts of land . . . to grow crops."[475]

There was a certain breathless quality to the way the Syria climate war/climate refugee story became conventional wisdom almost overnight. It was if there was no time to pause, take a deep breath, and carefully consider the evidence. The causes of the Syrian civil war are enormously complex—there's no straightforward, simple narrative to explain them, no easy "good guys versus

bad guys" storyline. For a start, one has to take into account the
authoritarian character of the Assad regime, neoliberal economic
policies that increased poverty and financial insecurity in the
country, regional and global geopolitics, and the legacy of the
Arab Spring. Just parsing the competing foreign interests involved
in the civil war—Russian, American, Iranian, Saudi Arabian,
Turkish, Lebanese—requires considerable knowledge of history
and international relations. Add to that the competing players in
the Syrian opposition, from fundamentalist ISIS to secular, democratic forces.[476]

A new study by climate scholars and regional experts carefully
assesses the evidence behind the Syria-as-climate-conflict thesis
and finds it seriously flawed. For one, the drought was three
years in duration, not five, and the meteorological data do not
support the finding that it was due to climate change. Secondly,
drought-related migration was nowhere near the scale claimed by
the *PNAS* article and others like it. There is no meaningful foundation for the statistic that 1.5–2 million Syrians migrated as a
result of drought; the figure is based on one humanitarian news
report and does not align with much lower estimates by UN and
government agencies. Moreover, it wasn't just the drought *per se*
that induced migration from rural areas. Other factors, like the
government's decision to reduce agricultural subsidies, must be
taken into account. Thirdly, field research among migrants who
did leave because of drought has found little evidence of their participation in the 2011 political protests against the Assad regime
that triggered the civil war.[477]

Another article by Francesca de Châtel, an expert on Middle
Eastern water issues, also argues that the climate conflict thesis is
not borne out by the facts. She points to how, for 50 years, successive Syrian regimes have mismanaged the country's water and

land resources, allowing, for example, the depletion and pollution of aquifers. And while drought conditions may have contributed to political unrest, it was less the drought specifically that was the trigger than the Assad regime's failure to provide relief to the people most affected by it. De Châtel cautions against seeing the drought "as a harbinger of catastrophic climate change and conflict scenarios."[478]

Today, more than ever, it is important to be skeptical about these scenarios, and to ask whose interests they ultimately serve. Linking the current refugee crisis in Europe with climate change, for example, creates the impression that such a mass migration is a "new normal" which will continue even after the Syrian war ends. Rather than seeing the current crisis as politically rooted and time-limited, we are encouraged to believe that we're entering a world of "permanent emergency" due to climate change in which nations should retreat from their commitments to harbor refugees and instead beef up their borders and surveillance.[479]

Focusing the lens so much on the "climate refugees" trying to enter Europe also diverts attention from the real dynamics of forced displacement. The UN High Commissioner for Refugees (UNHCR) estimates that by the end of 2015, 65.3 million people worldwide had been forcibly displaced by "persecution, conflict, generalized violence, or human rights violations." Of that number, 21.3 million are refugees, 40.8 million internally displaced, and 3.2 million asylum seekers. More than half of all refugees come from the war-torn countries of Syria, Afghanistan, and Somalia. Developing regions—*not* Europe or North America—host 86 percent of refugees under the UNHCR mandate. The top hosting countries are Turkey, Pakistan, Lebanon, Iran, Ethiopia. and Jordan.[480] The financial burden of refugees is not shared equally either. At a time of great need, the UNHCR, the World Food Programme, and the World Health Organization are facing serious shortfalls in funding from UN member countries. The resulting deteriorating conditions in refugee camps and settlements in Lebanon, Jordan, and Turkey are driving refugees and asylum seekers to make the dangerous trip to Europe. "Governments need to prioritize," a World Food Programme official in the Middle East told the *New York Times*. "If they can't prevent and stop the wars, at a minimum they need to help the victims—Europe should not be surprised if people from the region are deciding to come here if they're not being helped where they are."[481]

We need to resist the sense of a new normal and permanent emergency, and instead look to why, in the words of António Guterres, former UN High Commissioner for Refugees and now UN Secretary-General, "on the one hand there is more and more impunity for those starting conflicts and on the other there is seeming utter inability of the international community to work together to stop wars and build and preserve peace."[482] These political and institutional failures should not be laid at the door of the amorphous mega-agent of climate change. When we do so, we ignore the very real human agency behind war and bolster the power of the warmongers. We scare ourselves to death, or rather into accepting death, destruction, and massive dislocation as the inevitable apocalypse that awaits us in the era of climate change.

The international relations field uses the term "securitization" to refer to the process by which challenging issues that should be resolved by civilian institutions come to be (re)defined and (mis) handled as national security problems. The term is inelegant, but germane. We are in a securitization moment now with climate change as the Pentagon and other national security interests seek to expand their dominion over Africa, disaster relief, and foreign policy more broadly.

WHEN THE SAINTS COME MARCHING IN

There are good reasons for the Pentagon to be concerned about climate change. After all, as the largest institutional consumer of petroleum in the world, it is a major driver of global warming. A single B-52 bomber mission over Afghanistan burns up 47,000 gallons of fuel.[483] And the Pentagon expends vast quantities of fuel (and dollars) to protect US access to oil and gas reserves around the world. The cost of US military force projection from 1976–2007 in the Persian Gulf alone has been estimated at a staggering $7.3 trillion, equivalent to roughly half the US national debt.[484] There are arguably better uses for these resources, among them investing in climate change mitigation.[485]

In response to mounting political pressure on the defense budget, the US military is now trying to cut costs by reducing its dependence on oil. A further motive is that fuel trucks make an easy target in hostile places like Afghanistan. For a while, a "DoD Goes Green" page on the Department of Defense website featured a bright green "SUSTAINABILITY" banner along with a spinning windmill.[486] The Pentagon boasts that it's a leader in green innovation, and to a certain extent it is. The Nellis Air Force base in Nevada, for example, has one of the largest solar energy projects in the US. But this begs the question of why public resources for green innovation should flow through the military instead of to civilian scientists, engineers, and businesses. There is no particular reason to think that the Pentagon will give us more green bang for the buck.[487]

The Pentagon's more immediate practical concerns about climate change, such as how sea level rise could affect its military bases, are laid out in its 2014 *Climate Change Adaptation Roadmap* report.[488] In terms of strategic doctrine, the 2014 *Quadrennial*

Defense Review asserts that, while climate change may not by itself cause conflict, it's an important "threat-multiplier":

> The pressures caused by climate change will influence resource competition while placing additional burdens on economies, societies, and governance institutions around the worlds. These effects are threat multipliers that will aggravate stressors abroad such as poverty, environmental degradation, political instability, and social tensions— conditions that can enable terrorist activity and other forms of violence.[489]

The DoD's Science Board goes further, describing climate change as "Mother Nature's weapon of mass destruction."[490] A 2014 report by the influential Center for Naval Analyses (CNA) think tank concludes that the "threat multiplier" language is too weak and that climate change impacts will be "catalysts for instability and conflict," as distressed populations become more vulnerable to extremist and revolutionary influences. Endorsing the report's findings, Secretary of State John Kerry pulled out his tribal stereotype, telling the press that "tribes are killing each other over water today."[491]

The securitization of climate change fits into broader developments in US national security policy. In recent years, the military has increasingly occupied what was once mainly civilian territory. In what is billed as the "whole-of-government" approach, the Pentagon is exerting authority over international development assistance and humanitarian aid, once the preserve of the State Department and USAID. The war in Iraq spurred the creation of this aid-military complex,[492] which continued under the Obama administration. In 2013, a report by the US intelligence community, *Climate and Social Stress*, called for the immediate development of "a systematic and enduring whole-of-government strategy for monitoring threats connected to climate change."[493]

The "whole-of-government" approach coincides with the increasing privatization of development assistance. Over the period 1990–2008, USAID experienced a 40 percent reduction in staff, while outsourcing to for-profit international development contractors (IDCs) increased significantly. This privatization has reduced USAID's accountability to the public. Today in a new twist, private defense contractors like Tetra Tech, L-3 Communications, and DynCorp International are buying up IDCs, ever more closely moving aid into the military orbit. In 2011, for example, Tetra Tech, which consults regularly for the US Missile Defense Agency, received $400 million from USAID for climate change, forestry, and sanitation projects in Africa.[494]

The weapons, border control technology, and surveillance industries are also getting into the game. Airbus Military is promoting its defense aircraft as dual-use with the claim that it will bring "hope for 375 million people worldwide" who need assistance because of conflict, climatic disasters, and "unstable borders."[495] Climate and security think tanks are also part of the feeding frenzy.

Civilian proponents of the "whole-of-government" approach argue that influence cuts both ways, and that it's important for civilian agencies to weigh in on military strategy. They also argue that it could lead to better coordination of responses to international crises. Reform-minded military leaders, too, want to move away from deployment of brute force towards a more humanitarian agenda. But these good intentions only go so far, as long as the overarching goal remains US military dominance worldwide and the country is locked in a state of permanent war. Moreover, if military operations and development assistance are undertaken by the same private contractors, there's little to no firewall between them.

Defining climate change as a security threat also meshes neatly with the shift in US defense policy in recent years toward a greater focus on counterinsurgency and "stability operations" such as local policing and aid delivery. In order to win over potentially hostile communities, these operations employ "military-civilian teams" that include representatives of NGOs, international agencies, and the private sector.[496] A 2016 DoD directive on climate change adaptation and resilience calls for the Assistant Secretary of Defense for Special Operations/Low-Intensity Conflict to incorporate "climate risks into stability operations policy, doctrine, and planning, including the impact of climate trends on conflict and state fragility." It notes the "increased instability sparked by competition for limited natural resources" as a result of climate change. It also calls for joint exercises and war games with partners and allies that incorporate climate change considerations, such as "geopolitical and socioeconomic instability."[497]

In Afghanistan, the stabilization strategy has not been a resounding success, but today it soldiers on, so to speak, in Africa. In 2007, the Pentagon launched a regional military command for Africa, AFRICOM, which blurs military/civilian boundaries. Senior officials from USAID serve on its staff. So far, no African country has been willing to host AFRICOM, and so its headquarters, at least for the moment, are in Stuttgart, Germany. The largest US military base on the African continent is Camp Lemonnier in Djibouti, but in recent years the Pentagon has set up a number of smaller air bases for drones and surveillance as part of what the military calls a "lily pad" strategy—like frogs, troops will be able to hop from one base to another in pursuit of their prey. With the drawdown of US forces in Afghanistan, Africa may become the Pentagon's new frontier—what the *Economist* magazine cutely calls "Afrighanistan."[498] A 2013 investigative report found evidence of US military involvement in 49 African nations. "Africa is the battlefield of tomorrow, today," explained one officer.[499]

AFRICOM's primary raisons d'être are to combat Islamic terrorism and to ensure access to the continent's rich energy and mineral resources. But the Pentagon also welcomes other justifications to step up its presence in the African theater. Climate conflict widens public support for the mission by appealing to apocalyptic fears.[500] Threat language around climate change also furthers the military's goal of exercising more authority over the delivery of humanitarian aid during natural disasters, not just in Africa but all over the globe.[501]

A 2010 report by the CNA think tank argues that global warming threatens to tip "marginally stable" countries into instability and violence and prevent them from adapting to climate change: "Large-scale events, such as hurricanes or typhoons, or poorly managed responses might tip a country where adaptation is ongoing into an unstable state where adaptation is less possible. The need to stabilize these countries, and to decrease violence so that adaptation may proceed, may drive the US military into simultaneous disaster relief and security missions."[502] The recent history of American military interventions suggests that they are unlikely to "decrease" violence.

The report also highlights military planning for "potential futures" through scenario-building and gaming exercises, to prepare, in particular, for "black swan" events—low-probability, high-impact results of abrupt climate change. There's nothing wrong in planning for such events, but entrusting this task to the military poses a number of risks. One is that the military comes to see itself—and comes to be seen by the public—as the white knight best positioned to neutralize the black swan. And the more black swan scenarios the military organizes, the more real and possible they seem to become. Since our cultural default button is already set on apocalypse, people both inside and outside the military begin to believe that these worst case scenarios are what actually lie in store. In its latest report on climate change, CNA warns that "[w]hen it comes to climate change, we must guard against a failure of imagination."[503] What we really need to guard ourselves against are the dark fantasies of the national security state.

The escalating rhetoric about climate change, war, and disaster helps to justify military interventions on home territory, too. After 9/11, the Federal Emergency Management Agency (FEMA) was incorporated into the new Department of Homeland Security. This wasn't just a bureaucratic shift. An "all hazards" planning strategy was put into effect, lumping together terrorist attacks with natural disasters and other emergencies, with terrorism the top priority.[504] What does it mean when national security objectives, rather than meeting urgent human needs, come to dominate emergency response? The first test of these new arrangements came in September 2005, after Hurricane Katrina struck New Orleans.

When Katrina hit, I, like many other Americans, sat glued in front of the TV set, watching the horror scenes of cataclysmic flooding, flattened homes, and floating corpses. If these images were meant to pull on my heart strings—which they certainly did—another set of images seemed designed to have the opposite effect, pictures of young black men apparently running amok, shattering glass, and looting stores. I remember thinking then how similar these visuals and associated commentary were to American TV coverage of African conflicts. Others noted the same parallel.

The Army Times observed on September 2, 2005 that "combat operations are now underway on the streets . . . This place is going to look like little Somalia . . . We're going to go out and take the city back."[505] Private security personnel from the firm Blackwater, notorious for its undisciplined actions in Iraq, were brought in, sporting assault weapons. Innocent people were shot and others were left to die as law enforcement personnel were ordered to focus their efforts on looting instead of search and rescue.[506]

When the floodwaters receded, and reporters were able to investigate the stories behind the images, it turned out that many of the "looters" were ordinary people engaged in a desperate search for necessities like water, food, and diapers. There was no increase in the murder rate in New Orleans during the week after Katrina.[507] The most serious crimes were committed by the forces of law and order that treated the poor black population as the enemy rather than as disaster victims they should be assisting. The government put security first. "The rhetoric was all-hazards," writes political scientist Michael Barkun, "but the reality was homeland security."[508]

In environmental quarters, Katrina was portrayed as a climate catastrophe spectacle. Scientists cannot say what role, if any, climate change played in Katrina, but its swirling mass of clouds came to portend many more such climate disasters to come.[509] New Orleans residents displaced by the disaster were depicted as climate refugees. "The first massive movement of climate refugees has been that of people away from the Gulf Coast of the United States," proclaimed environmentalist Lester Brown.[510] Never mind that they might have been able to stay home if the Army Corps of Engineers had maintained the city's levees.

Through the securitization of climate change and disaster response, we are being taught to fear the dark people global warming will supposedly set loose, on the move, whether from across the seas or within the borders of our own nation. The more we accept that racialized apocalyptic vision of the future, the more we cede control to the military. Catastrophic thinking also plays into the hands of the would-be "climate engineers"— entrepreneurs and scientists who are dreaming up drastic-fantastic technological fixes. One such proposal involves pumping sulfur particles into the atmosphere so that more sunlight radiates back into space. Another is seeding the oceans with iron to induce enormous algal blooms that will suck carbon from the atmosphere. Another would try to redirect hurricanes by means of satellite-based microwaves. The sky's no limit.

These proposals are the latest in a long line of grandiose schemes to control the climate, closely intertwined with the military's efforts to weaponize the weather during the Cold War and Vietnam. Some advocates of climate engineering are veterans of Cold War atomic research. Former weapons designer Lowell Wood has pushed the development of a 25-mile long "sky hose" connected to a military super blimp that will spray the upper atmosphere with reflective particles.[511] Even if such climate engineering projects turn out to be techno-fantasies, the publicity around them serves to convince some people that the situation is so dire that such projects are the only hope and that doing anything on a smaller and more realistic scale is useless. Why bother with energy efficiency or solar panels if the atmosphere can be re-engineered?

As if this prospect isn't wacky enough, a trio of researchers from Oxford University and New York University have suggested re-engineering humans as a way to fight climate change. In the journal *Ethics, Policy and the Environment*, the authors propose a menu of pharmaceutical and genetic interventions to modify the species. These include creating intolerance to red meat since livestock-raising contributes to global warming; breeding smaller humans who will consume less energy; breeding smarter humans so they will have fewer babies; and dosing the population with oxytocin and other drugs to make them more altruistic.[512] When the apocalypse threatens, nothing remains unthinkable.

BREAKING THROUGH

Maybe we are barking up the wrong tree when we frame climate change as a mega-problem demanding a mega-solution. "By constructing climate change as the 'mother of all problems,' perhaps we have out-maneuvered ourselves," writes British climate scholar Mike Hulme. "We have allowed climate change to accrete to itself more and more individual problems in our world—unsustainable energy, endemic poverty, climatic hazards, food security, structural adjustment, hyper consumption, tropical deforestation, biodiversity loss . . . We have created a political log-jam of gigantic proportions, one that is not only insoluble, but one that is perhaps beyond our comprehension."[513]

Is there another way forward? If there's a log-jam, maybe it's time to chart other routes. One way for Americans to think outside the box is to look more outside the country. We can learn a lot, for example, from countries like Germany which began taking climate change seriously years ago. Germany is attempting to reduce its greenhouse gas emissions to 40 percent below 1990 levels by 2020, a decade ahead of the target set by the European Union. This commitment is visible to the naked eye. Windmills stretch along the Autobahn highway system and solar panels seem to be everywhere. Germany's policies include serious energy efficiency requirements for new buildings, "feed-in" tariffs that provide even small and residential producers of renewable energy with guaranteed access to the power grid and favorable payment rates, and low-interest loans for solar roof installations. Investment in renewable energy technologies has created thousands of jobs, and given Germany an edge in the global market for green technology. In the wake of Japan's Fukushima disaster, Germany has accelerated plans to phase out nuclear power in favor of an energy future that is both low-carbon and non-nuclear. Although environmentalists criticize the present government for backsliding and still depending too much on coal, Germany's example shows that slow and steady progress is possible.[514]

Why not have windmills along America's interstate highways, solar panels on roofs and over parking lots across the nation, public and private investments in clean, renewable energy on a scale comparable to past investments in fossil fuels and nuclear power, and a train system at least as efficient and extensive as those in Europe or Japan? Not drastic engineering of the planetary climate, but practical engineering to achieve the transition away from fossil fuels. Why do so many Americans find it harder to imagine that kind of future than an apocalyptic future of climate chaos and conflict?

Breaking down the challenge of climate change into tractable components, rather than treating it as a single, gigantic, intractable problem, would open up the many synergies between climate policies and other social, economic, and environmental objectives. For example, reducing our use of fossil fuels not only mitigates global warming, but also leads to cleaner air and healthier environments for all, especially for those who live closest to coal mines, power plants, refineries, and polluting industries.[515] It can also lead to cleaner politics, as our energy dollars would no longer be lining the pockets of corrupt rulers in petroleum states like Nigeria, Angola, and Saudi Arabia, and greasing the palms of lobbyists and politicians at home. Investments in decentralized, renewable energies and energy efficiency can also create millions of jobs.[516] In fact, even if there were no climate change, there would still be compelling reasons to wean ourselves from fossil fuels.

Addressing climate change also provides an opportunity to rethink business as usual. Whether one likes it or not, capitalism may come up with many of the means to mitigate climate change. Innovative firms are already profiting from new markets in green technologies. But alternative ways of organizing the economy have the advantage of helping to mitigate climate change while simultaneously reducing inequality, supporting workers' rights, and advancing environmental justice. Many people who are already developing such alternatives don't expect a revolution to happen overnight, however. In the short run some tools from the capitalist toolbox will be needed to keep global temperature rise to a minimum. Since investors and consumers respond to prices, a crucial policy is to make fossil fuels more costly compared to renewables and energy efficiency.

Once we move beyond the national "debate" as to whether climate change is real or not, it will become clear that the real political fault line is between who wins and who loses when we finally get serious about capping carbon emissions. Will fossil fuel companies and utilities reap windfall profits from carbon permit giveaways, or will revenues from auctioning the permits flow back to the public to offset the effect of rising fuel prices? Instead of reading climate change as the Book of Revelation, we need to get literate, fast, about the finer details of climate policy.

We're going to have to get more comfortable with uncertainty, too. Climate science has progressed to the point where we have a pretty good idea of what's happening now and what could happen in the future if we don't reduce greenhouse gas emissions. But scientists can never tell us with absolute certainty what the future holds. We have to live with this uncertainty without using it as an excuse for inaction. And along with reducing emissions, we need to strengthen the capacities of our communities to adapt to climate change and respond to natural disasters.

All this entails developing a new and different mindset, less prone to fear and more prone to action. Rebecca Solnit's book, *A Paradise Built in Hell*, reminds us that "the image of the selfish, panicky, or regressively savage human being in times of disaster has little truth to it."[517] It is more often the minority in power who respond with savagery. Ordinary people tend to come together to help one another during disasters, often displaying their best, most selfless behavior. By exposing the deep inequalities that make some people more vulnerable than others, and by helping people cross social divides, disasters can awaken positive economic and political transformation. That doesn't mean we should hope for more disasters. But it does provide one less reason to lie awake at night worrying about impending catastrophes.

In the end, the mindset I'm describing comes down to a question of who we trust. We have to trust ourselves, and others here and abroad, to rise to the multiple challenges posed by climate change. If instead we trust the military to protect us, what we will get is more violence, war, and bloated defense budgets that rob resources from pressing human and environmental needs. Breaking free of apocalyptic thinking can help restore faith in our common humanity and solidarity with those most affected and afflicted by climate change, wherever they may be.

NOTES

PREFACE

1   President Richard Nixon, "Address to the Nation on the Situation in Southeast Asia, 1970," April 30, 1970, reprinted as an online feature of the television series *American Experience: Nixon*, PBS, at http://www.pbs.org/wgbh/americanexperience/features/primary-resources/nixon-asia/, accessed December 11, 2014.

2   kainah, "Prelude to Kent State: Nixon Invades Cambodia," April 26, 2006, at http://www.dailykos.com/story/2006/04/26/205304/-Prelude-to-Kent-State-Nixon-Invades-Cambodia#, accessed December 11, 2014; Nixon quote from *American Experience: Nixon*, Program Transcript, 42, at http://www-tc.pbs.org/wgbh/americanexperience/media/uploads/special_features/download_files/nixon_transcript.pdf, accessed December 11, 2014.

3   Evan Osnos, "Survival of the Richest: Why Some of America's Wealthiest People are Prepping for Disaster," *New Yorker*, January 30, 2017, 36–45.

INTRODUCTION: END TIMES AND ENDLESS WAR

4   The Pew Center for the People and the Press, "Life in 2050: Amazing Science, Familiar Threats," June 22, 2010, at http://www.people-press.org/files/legacy-pdf/625.pdf, accessed December 12, 2016; Chris Michaud, "One in Seven Thinks End of World is Coming: Poll," Reuters, May 1, 2012, at http://www.reuters.com/article/2012/05/01/us-mayancalendar-poll-idUSBRE8400XH20120501, accessed November 5, 2014; and Emma Green, "Half of Americans Think Climate Change is a Sign of the Apocalypse," *Atlantic*, November 22, 2014, at http://www.theatlantic.com/politics/archive/2014/11/half-of-americans-think-climate-change-is-a-sign-of-the-apocalypse/383029/, accessed August 25, 2015.

5   Kate Mather, "December 21, 2012: Fearful 'End of World' Callers Flood NASA," *Los Angeles Times* blog, December 19, 2012, at http://latimesblogs.latimes.com/lanow/2012/12/dec-21-2012-fearful-end-of-world-callers-flood-nasa-phonelines-.html, accessed November 5, 2014.

6   Elaine Pagels, *Revelations: Visions, Prophecy, and Politics in the Book of Revelation* (New York: Viking, 2012), 7.

7　*The Revelation of St. John the Divine*, reprinted in Lois Parkinson Zamora, ed., *The Apocalyptic Vision in America: Interdisciplinary Essays on Myth and Culture* (Bowling Green, Ohio: Bowling Green University Popular Press, 1982), 17:16, 234.

8　*The Revelation of St. John the Divine*, 19:13, 19:15, 19:16, 237–38.

9　*The Revelation of St. John the Divine*, 22:1, 240.

10　Robert N. Bellah, "Civil Religion in America," *Daedalus* 96(1) (Winter 1967), 1–21, reprinted at http://www.robertbellah.com/articles_5.htm, accessed on December 10, 2014.

11　Guy Gugliotta, "New Estimate Raises Civil War Death Toll," *New York Times*, April 2, 2012, at http://www.nytimes.com/2012/04/03/science/civil-war-toll-up-by-20-percent-in-new-estimate.html, accessed December 10, 2014.

12　Harry S. Stout, *Upon the Altar of the Nation: A Moral History of the American Civil War* (New York: Viking, 2006), xvii.

13　Drew Gilpin Faust, *This Republic of Suffering: Death and the American Civil War* (New York: Alfred A. Knopf, 2008), xiii.

14　Ernest Lee Tuveson, *Redeemer Nation: The Idea of America's Millennial Role* (Chicago: University of Chicago Press, 1968), vii.

15　Cited in Michael Northcott, *An Angel Directs the Storm: Apocalyptic Religion and American Empire* (New York: I.B. Taurus, 2004), 26.

16　President Dwight Eisenhower, "Text of the Address by President Eisenhower, Broadcast and Televised from His Office in the White House, Tuesday Evening, January 17, 1961," reprinted at the Dwight D. Eisenhower Presidential Library, Museum and Boyhood Home website, at https://www.eisenhower.archives.gov/research/online_documents/farewell_address/1961_01_17_Press_Release.pdf, accessed September 1, 2016.

17　Andrew J. Bacevich, *The New American Militarism: How Americans are Seduced by War* (Oxford: Oxford University Press, 2013 ed.), 1. Also see Rosa Brooks, *How Everything Became War and the Military Became Everything: Tales from the Pentagon* (New York: Simon & Schuster, 2016).

18　White House, "The National Security Strategy of the United States of America" (Washington, DC: September 2002), 15, at http://www.state.gov/documents/organization/63562.pdf, accessed Oct. 16, 2014.

19　*9/11 Commission Report* (Washington, DC: 2004), 362, at http://www.9-11commission.gov/report/911Report.pdf, accessed on October 20, 2014.

20　Jimmy Carter, "State of the Union Address," January 23, 1980, at http://www.jimmycarterlibrary.gov/documents/speeches/su80jec.phtml, accessed August 22, 2016.

21　Greg Grandin, *Empire's Workshop: Latin America, the United States, and the Rise of the New Imperialism* (New York: Metropolitan Books, 2006), 51.

22　Grandin, *Empire's Workshop*, 150.

23　Robert P. Jones, *The End of White Christian America* (New York: Simon and Schuster, 2016), 204.

24　See Jones, *The End of White Christian America*, for more on this strategy.

25　Lisa McGirr, *Suburban Warriors: The Origins of the New American Right* (Princeton: Princeton University Press, 2002).

26　James Mills, "The Serious Implications of a 1971 Conversation with Ronald Reagan: A Footnote to Current History," *San Diego Magazine*, August 1985,

140–141, cited in Paul Boyer, *When Time Shall be No More: Prophecy Belief in Modern American Culture* (Cambridge, MA: Harvard University Press, 1992), 162.

27   DeLay cited in Paul Boyer, "Afterword: The Geopolitics of End-Time Belief in the Era of George W. Bush," in *Mapping the End Times: American Evangelical Geopolitics and Apocalyptic Visions*, eds. Jason Dittmer and Tristan Sturm (Burlington, VT: Ashgate, 2010), 238.

28   Bacevich, *The New American Militarism*.

29   Grandin, *Empire's Workshop*, 134.

30   Dan Baum, "Legalize It All: How to Win the War on Drugs," *Harper's Magazine*, April 2016, at http://harpers.org/archive/2016/04/legalize-it-all/, accessed August 22, 2016.

31   Michelle Alexander, *The New Jim Crow: Mass Incarceration in the Age of Colorblindness* (New York: The New Press, 2012).

32   Alexander, *The New Jim Crow*, 5.

33   See Alexander, *The New Jim Crow*.

34   Mathew Coleman, "Immigration Geopolitics Beyond the Mexico–US Border," *Antipode* 39(1) (2007), 54–76.

35   See Alexander, *The New Jim Crow*, 2, and the Sentencing Project, "Fact Sheet: Trends in U.S. Corrections," at http://sentencingproject.org/wp-content/uploads/2016/01/Trends-in-US-Corrections.pdf, accessed August 30, 2016.

36   See, for example, Giles Tremlett, "Al-Qaida Leaders Say Nuclear Power Stations were Original Targets," *Guardian*, September 8, 2002, at https://www.theguardian.com/world/2002/sep/09/september11.afghanistan, accessed September 8, 2016.

37   Jackie Orr, "Making Civilian-Soldiers: The Militarization of Inner Space," in *Making Threats: Biofears and Environmental Anxieties*, eds. Betsy Hartmann, Banu Subramaniam, and Charles Zerner (Lanham, MD: Rowman & Littlefield Publishers, 2005), 49, 62.

38   Elisabeth Bumiller, "A Nation Challenged: The President; Bush Announces a Crackdown on Visa Violators," *New York Times*, October 30, 2001, at http://www.nytimes.com/2001/10/30/us/a-nation-challenged-the-president-bush-announces-a-crackdown-on-visa-violators.html, accessed August 30, 2016.

39   Matthew J. Friedman, "PTSD History and Overview," Department of Veterans Affairs National Center for PTSD, at http://www.ptsd.va.gov/professional/PTSD-overview/ptsd-overview.asp, accessed August 24, 2016.

40   Jane Mayer, *The Dark Side: The Inside Story of How the War on Terror Turned into a War on American Ideals* (New York: Anchor Books, 2009). For more on worst-case scenarios, see Stuart Price, *Worst-Case Scenario?: Governance, Mediation and the Security Regime* (London: Zed Books, 2011).

41   Garrett M. Graff, *The Threat Matrix: The FBI at War in the Age of Terror* (New York: Little, Brown, 2011), 19, 249, cited in John Mueller and Mark G. Stewart, *Chasing Ghosts: The Policing of Terrorism* (New York: Oxford University Press, 2016), 21. Also see Mayer, *The Dark Side*.

42   See Mueller and Stewart, *Chasing Ghosts*, 24–26.

43   Frank Rich, *The Greatest Story Ever Sold: The Decline and Fall of Truth from 9/11 to Katrina* (New York, Penguin Books, 2006).

44   Cited in Rich, *The Greatest Story Ever Sold*, 3.

45   David L. Altheide, *Creating Fear: News and the Construction of Crisis* (New York: Aldine de Gruyter, 2002), 84, 89.

46   Altheide, *Creating Fear.*

47   David Ignatius, "The Dangers of Embedded Journalism, in War and Politics," *Washington Post,* May 2, 2010, at http://www.washingtonpost.com/wp-dyn/content/article/2010/04/30/AR2010043001100.html?sid=ST2010043001134, accessed August 25, 2016.

48   "Costs of War: Iraqi Civilians," Watson Institute of International and Public Affairs, Brown University, at http://watson.brown.edu/costsofwar/costs/human/civilians/iraqi, accessed August 25, 2016.

49   Michael J. Glennon, *National Security and Double Government* (New York: Oxford University Press, 2015).

50   Pei-Sze Cheng and Ann Givens, "I-Team: Port Authority Cops Say Surprise Terror Drills Pose Danger to Officers, Public," NBC New York, April 6, 2016, at http://www.nbcnewyork.com/news/local/Port-Authority-Police-Officers-Surprise-Terror-Drill-Dangers-New-Jersey-Train-Station-374651241.html, accessed August 25, 2016; Sarah Lazare, "Overreation to False Reports of Gunfire at JFK Airport Reveals the Depths of America's Fear Culture," AlterNet, August 15, 2016, at http://www.alternet.org/grayzone-project/overreaction-false-reports-gunfire-jfk-airport-reveals-depths-americas-fear-culture, accessed August 25, 2016; and Marc Santora, "From False Alarm to Panic: Inside Kennedy Airport's Chaotic Night," *New York Times,* August 15, 2016, at http://www.nytimes.com/2016/08/16/nyregion/from-false-alarm-to-panic-inside-kennedy-airports-chaotic-night.html, accessed August 25, 2016.

51   Mueller and Stewart, *Chasing Ghosts,* 7.

52   Bacevich, *The New American Militarism,* 32.

53   Kendall Breitman, "Bush: One Regret about Iraq," Politico, November 7, 2014, at http://www.politico.com/story/2014/11/george-w-bush-iraq-regret-112684, accessed August 25, 2016.

54   Spencer Ackerman, "'Apocalyptic' Isis Beyond Anything We've Seen, Say US Defence Chiefs," *Guardian,* August 22, 2014, at http://www.theguardian.com/world/2014/aug/21/isis-us-military-iraq-strikes-threat-apocalyptic, accessed October 16, 2014; see also Patrick Cockburn, "Why Washington's War on Terror Failed: The Underrated Saudi Connection," TomDispatch.com, August 21, 2014, at http://www.tomdispatch.com/blog/175884/, accessed October 16, 2014.

55   William McCants, "ISIS Fantasies of an Apocalyptic Showdown in Northern Syria," Brookings blog, October 3, 2014, accessed October 16, 2014 at http://www.brookings.edu/blogs/iran-at-saban/posts/2014/10/03-isis-apocalyptic-showdown-syria-mccants, accessed October 16, 2014, at https://www.brookings.edu/blog/markaz/2014/10/03/isis-fantasies-of-an-apocalyptic-showdown-in-northern-syria as of January 27, 2017.

56   J.M. Berger, "The Metronome of Apocalyptic Time: Social Media as Carrier Wave for Millenarian Contagion," *Perspectives on Terrorism* 9(4) (2015), 61–71, at http://www.terrorismanalysts.com/pt/index.php/pot/article/view/444/html, accessed August 26, 2015.

57   Todd Miller, *Border Patrol Nation: Dispatches from the Front Lines of Homeland Security* (San Francisco: City Lights Books, 2014).

58   Michael Flynn, "Where's the U.S. Border? Portraits of an Elastic Frontier," paper
      delivered at the Meeting of the Latin American Studies Association, San Juan,
      Puerto Rico, March 15–18, 2006, at http://www.globaldetentionproject.org/file-
      admin/publications/Flynn_LASA.pdf, accessed October 21, 2014, at https://www.
      globaldetentionproject.org/wp-content/uploads/2006/03/Flynn_LASA-1.pdf as of
      January 27, 2017.

59   Alejandra Marchevsky and Beth Baker, "Why Has President Obama Deported
      More Immigrants Than Any President in US History?" *Nation*, March 31, 2014, at
      http://www.thenation.com/article/179099/why-has-president-obama-deported-
      more-immigrants-any-president-us-history, accessed October 21, 2014.

60   Miller, *Border Patrol Nation*, Chapter Six, 151–176.

61   Alexis de Tocqueville, *Democracy in America*, vol. 2 (New York: 1945), 232–235,
      cited in Ronald T. Takaki, *Iron Cages: Race and Culture in 19th-Century America*
      (Seattle: University of Washington Press, 1982), 74.

62   Sander L. Gilman, *Difference and Pathology: Stereotypes of Sexuality, Race, and
      Madness* (Ithaca, NY: Cornell University Press, 1985), 20.

63   Cited in John Protevi, ed., *A Dictionary of Continental Philosophy* (New Haven:
      Yale University Press, 2006), 275.

64   Sacvan Bercovitch, *The American Jeremiad*, Anniversary Edition (Madison: Univer-
      sity of Wisconsin Press, 2012).

CHAPTER ONE: THE PURITANS: PRIDE AND PREJUDICES OF A CHOSEN PEOPLE

65   Alexis de Tocqueville, *Democracy in America*, Vol. I, Chapter XVII, Part I, Project
      Gutenberg eBook 815 (2006; French orig. 1835), at http://www.gutenberg.org/
      files/815/815-h/815-h.htm, accessed December 5, 2014.

66   Edmund S. Morgan, *The Genuine Article: A Historian Looks at Early America* (New
      York: W.W. Norton, 2004). Also see Mary Beth Norton, *Founding Mothers &
      Fathers: Gendered Power and the Forming of American Society* (New York: Alfred A.
      Knopf, 1996) for an in-depth analysis of the role of gender and family in Puritan
      times.

67   Nathaniel Shurtleff and David Pulsifer, eds., *Records of the Colony of New Plym-
      outh*, 12 volumes (Boston: Press of W. White, 1855–1861), 5:156, 4:34, cited in Caleb
      H. Johnson, *The Mayflower and Her Passengers* (Xlibris: 2006), 207–08.

68   Francis J. Bremer, *The Puritan Experiment: New England Society from Bradford to
      Edwards* (Hanover, NH: University Press of New England, 1995).

69   Bremer, *The Puritan Experiment*, 21. Also see Morgan, *The Genuine Article*, 16–21.

70   George M. Marsden, *Jonathan Edwards: A Life* (New Haven: Yale University Press,
      2003), 28.

71   Marsden, *Jonathan Edwards*, 25.

72   Bremer, *The Puritan Experiment*, 30–34.

73   Bremer, *The Puritan Experiment*, 37–47, and Stephen J. Stein, "Transatlantic
      Extensions: Apocalyptic in Early New England," in *The Apocalypse in English
      Renaissance Thought and Literature: Patterns, Antecedents and Repercussions*, eds.
      C.A. Patrides and Joseph Wittreich (Ithaca, NY: Cornell University Press, 1984),
      266–98.

74 Perry Miller, *Errand into the Wilderness* (Cambridge, MA: Belknap Press of Harvard University Press, 1984), 11.

75 John Winthrop, "A Modell of Christian Charity," in *Sinners in the Hands of an Angry God and Other Puritan Sermons: Jonathan Edwards and Others* (Mineola, NY: Dover Publications, Inc., 2005), 53–65.

76 Cited in C.S. Manegold, *Ten Hills Farm: The Forgotten History of Slavery in the North* (Princeton: Princeton University Press, 2010), 24, 28.

77 Charles Mann, *1491: New Revelations of the Americas before Columbus* (New York: Vintage Books, 2005), 60, 67.

78 Manegold, *Ten Hills Farm*.

79 Bremer, *The Puritan Experiment*, 45.

80 Bremer, *The Puritan Experiment*, 86–93.

81 Quotations from "A Report of the Trial of Mrs. Anne Hutchinson before the Church in Boston," in *The Antinomian Controversy, 1636–1638*, ed. David D. Hall (Durham, N.C.: Duke University Press, 1990), 308–09, 382–83, cited in Norton, *Founding Mothers and Fathers*, 359, 365.

82 Norton, *Founding Mothers and Fathers*, 395.

83 Manegold, *Ten Hills Farm*, 40–43.

84 Bremer, *The Puritan Experiment*, 161.

85 Paul Boyer, *When Time Shall Be No More: Prophecy Belief in Modern American Culture* (Cambridge, MA: Belknap Press of Harvard University Press, 1992), 75.

86 Michael Wigglesworth, *The Day of Doom*, reprinted in the Fire and Ice Sermon Series, at http://www.puritansermons.com/pdf/doom.pdf, accessed December 3, 2014. Also see Bremer, *The Puritan Experiment*, 191.

87 Bercovitch, *The American Jeremiad*, xii.

88 Bercovitch, *The American Jeremiad*, 16–17.

89 Samuel Danforth, *A Brief Recognition of New-Englands Errand into the Wilderness* (1670) in *The Wall and the Garden: Selected Massachusetts Election Sermons*, ed. A. William Plumstead (Minneapolis: University of Minnesota Press, 1968), 64–65, 75–77, cited in Bercovitch, *The American Jeremiad*, 15–16.

90 Andrew R. Murphy and Elizabeth Hanson, "From King Philip's War to September 11: Religion, Violence, and the American Way," in *From Jeremiad to Jihad: Religion, Violence and America*, eds. John D. Carlson and Jonathan H. Ebel (Berkeley: University of California Press, 2012), 35.

91 Morgan, *The Genuine Article*, 268.

92 Increase Mather, *The Day of Trouble is Near* (Cambridge, MA, 1674), cited in Bercovitch, *The American Jeremiad*, 60.

93 Manegold, *Ten Hills Farm*, 90–96, and Bremer, *The Puritan Experiment*, 168–171. For a detailed history of the war, and its role in shaping American identity, see Jill Lepore, *The Name of War: King Philip's War and the Origins of American Identity* (New York: Vintage Books, 1998).

94 Bercovitch, *The American Jeremiad*, 81–83.

95 Murphy and Hanson, "From King Philip's War to September 11," 35.

96 Samuel 15:2–3 and Exodus 17:14, cited in John Corrigan, "New Israel, New Amalek: Biblical Exhortations to Religious Violence," in *From Jeremiad to Jihad*, eds. Carlson and Ebel, 111–27, 112.

97 Cotton Mather, *A discourse delivered unto Some Part of the Forces Engaged in the Just War of New-England* (Boston: 1689), cited in Corrigan, "New Israel, New Amalek," 114.

98 Bercovitch, *The American Jeremiad*, 87, and John Demos, *The Enemy Within: A Short History of Witch-Hunting* (New York: Penguin Books, 2009), 219.

99 Demos, *The Enemy Within*, 41.

100 See Mary Beth Norton, *In the Devil's Snare: The Salem Witchcraft Crisis of 1692* (New York: Vintage Books, 2003). Also see Demos, *The Enemy Within* for a summary of the major historical debates surrounding the causes of the Salem witch trials.

101 Demos, *The Enemy Within*, 225.

102 Demos, *The Enemy Within*, 176.

103 Cited in Demos, *The Enemy Within*, 128, 223.

104 Cited in Demos, *The Enemy Within*, 228.

105 Manegold, *Ten Hills Farm*, 46, 121, 125–144.

106 Manegold, *Ten Hills Farm*, 239–240.

107 Miller, *Errand into the Wilderness*, 233.

108 Marsden, *Jonathan Edwards*, 499–500.

109 Marsden, *Jonathan Edwards*, 135–136.

110 First quote from Jonathan Edwards, "Personal Narrative," *Works* 16:792, cited in Marsden, *Jonathan Edwards*, 42; second quote cited in Marsden, 44; third quote from Edwards, "Personal Narrative," *Reader*, 293, cited in Marsden, 185.

111 Cited in PBS Frontline transcript, *Apocalypse!: The Evolution of Apocalyptic Belief and How It Shaped the Western World*, November 22, 1998, at http://www.pbs.org/wgbh/pages/frontline/shows/apocalypse/, accessed December 3, 2014.

112 Marsden, *Jonathan Edwards*, 121–22.

113 See Mark Valeri, *Heavenly Merchandize: How Religion Shaped Commerce in Puritan America* (Princeton: Princeton University Press, 2010), for an analysis of how Puritan doctrine evolved in step with growing commercialization.

114 Bremer, *The Puritan Experiment*, 213–215.

115 Jonathan Edwards, *Divine and Supernatural Light*, *Works* 17, 408–25, cited in Marsden, *Jonathan Edwards*, 157–58.

116 Jonathan Edwards, "Sinners in the Hands of an Angry God," in *Sinners in the Hands of an Angry God and Other Puritan Sermons*, 171-84.

117 Marsden, *Jonathan Edwards*, 163-69.

118 Marsden, *Jonathan Edwards*, 485.

119 Stephen J. Stein, ed., *Jonathan Edwards, Apocalyptic Writings* (New Haven: Yale University Press, 1977), cited in Bercovitch, *The American Jeremiad*, 116.

120 Mark Twain, *The Mysterious Stranger and Letters from Earth*, cited in Marsden, *Jonathan Edwards*, 500.

121 Bercovitch, *The American Jeremiad*, 105–06.

122 David S. Gutterman, "Stories of Sinfulness: Narrative Identity in America," in *Religion, Politics, and American Identity: New Directions, New Controversies*, eds. David S. Gutterman and Andrew R. Murphy (Lanham, MD: Lexington Books, 2006), 73–96, 82–83.

123   Bercovitch, *The American Jeremiad*. Also see Andrew R. Murphy and Jennifer
       Miller, "The Enduring Power of the American Jeremiad," in *Religion, Politics, and
       American Identity*, 49–72.

CHAPTER TWO: UTOPIAN DREAMS, MILLENNIAL MADNESS

124   Krishan Kumar, *Utopianism* (Minneapolis: University of Minnesota Press, 1991), 3.
125   Donald E. Pitzer, "Introduction," in *America's Communal Utopias*, ed. Donald E.
       Pitzer (Chapel Hill: University of North Carolina Press, 1997), 3–13.
126   Boyer, "Afterword," in *Mapping the End Times*, eds. Dittmer and Sturm, and
       Boyer, *When Time Shall Be No More*, 87–89.
127   Ernest Lee Tuveson, *Millennium and Utopia: A Study in the Background of the Idea
       of Progress* (New York: Harper Torchbooks, 1964), 75.
128   Krishan Kumar, "Apocalypse, Millennium and Utopia Today," in *Apocalypse Theory
       and the Ends of the World*, ed. Malcolm Bull (Oxford: Blackwell Publishers, Ltd.,
       1995), 212.
129   Bercovitch, *The American Jeremiad*, xxii.
130   Oscar Wilde, "The Soul of Man Under Socialism" (1891), in *De Profundis and
       Other Writings*, ed. Hesketh Pearson (Harmondsworth: Penguin Books, 1973), 34,
       cited in Kumar, *Utopianism*, 95.
131   Kumar, *Utopianism*, 1.
132   Mark Holloway, *Heavens on Earth: Utopian Communities in America, 1680–1880*
       (Mineola, New York: Dover Publications, Inc., 1966).
133   Cited in Pitzer, "Introduction," 7.
134   See Hancock Shaker Village website, at http://hancockshakervillage.org/museum/
       historic-architecture/1826-stone-barn/, accessed December 11, 2014; also see Chris-
       tian Goodwillie and John Harlow Ott, *Hancock Shaker Village: A Guidebook and
       History* (Hancock, MA: Hancock Shaker Village, 2011).
135   History of the Shakers is drawn from Holloway, *Heavens on Earth*, and Priscilla
       J. Brewer, "The Shakers of Mother Ann Lee" in *America's Communal Utopias*, ed.
       Pitzer, 37–56.
136   Goodwillie and Ott, *Hancock Shaker Village*.
137   Holloway, *Heavens on Earth*.
138   Hancock Shaker Village website, at http://hancockshakervillage.org/museum/his-
       toric-architecture/1826-stone-barn/, accessed December 11, 2014.
139   G.W.F. Hegel, *The Philosophy of History*, trans. J. Sibree (New York: Dover Publica-
       tions, 1956), 85, cited in Kumar, *Utopianism*, 81.
140   Holloway, *Heavens on Earth*.
141   For a history of the Northampton Association, see Christopher Clark, *The
       Communitarian Moment: The Radical Challenge of the Northampton Association*
       (Amherst: University of Massachusetts Press, 1995).
142   Cited in Holloway, *Heavens on Earth*, 104.
143   Quoted in E.P. Thompson, *The Making of the English Working Class* (London:
       Gollancz, 1963), 789, cited in Kumar, *Utopianism*, 74.
144   Cited in Holloway, *Heavens on Earth*, 106.

145   Holloway, *Heavens on Earth*, 113–116; also see Donald E. Pitzer, "The New Moral
      World of Robert Owen and New Harmony," in *America's Communal Utopias*, ed.
      Pitzer, 88–134.

146   Thoreau cited in William Henry Harrison, "Introduction," in Louisa May Alcott,
      Transcendental Wild Oats and Excerpts from The Fruitlands Diary (Carlisle, MA:
      Applewood Books, 1975), 7. Also see Richard Francis, *Transcendental Utopias:
      Individual and Community at Brook Farm, Fruitlands, and Walden* (Ithaca: Cornell
      University Press, 1997), 3.

147   Alan D. Hodder, *Emerson's Rhetoric of Revelation: "Nature," the Reader, and the
      Apocalypse Within* (University Park, PA: The Pennsylvania State University Press,
      1989), 7.

148   Robert E. Spiller et al, eds., *The Collected Works of Ralph Waldo Emerson*, Vol. 1
      (Cambridge: Harvard University Press, 1971, 1979, 1983, 1987), 10, cited in Hodder,
      Emerson's Rhetoric of Revelation, 78.

149   *The Essential Writings of Ralph Waldo Emerson* (New York: Random House Modern
      Library Classics, 2009), 39; for analysis, see Hodder, *Emerson's Rhetoric of Revela-
      tion*, 24.

150   Alcott, *Transcendental Wild Oats*, 25–28.

151   From letter dated February 15, 1843, in Richard L. Herrnstadt, ed., *The Letters of
      A. Bronson Alcott* (Ames: Iowa State University Press, 1969), 99, cited in Francis,
      Transcendental Utopias, 173.

152   Eve LaPlante, *Marmee & Louisa: The Untold Story of Louisa May Alcott and Her
      Mother* (New York: Simon and Schuster, 2012), 115.

153   See Francis, *Transcendental Utopias*, 206.

154   Alcott, *Transcendental Wild Oats*, 53.

155   Cited in LaPlante, *Marmee & Louisa*, 115.

156   Cited in LaPlante, *Marmee & Louisa*, 119.

157   See Francis, *Transcendental Utopias*.

158   Hawthorne, *Letters, 1813–43*, 558, cited in Francis, *Transcendental Utopias*, 49.

159   Information on Brook Farm from Francis, *Transcendental Utopias*; Holloway,
      Heavens on Earth, and Carl J. Guarneri, "Brook Farm and the Fourierist Pha-
      lanxes: Immediatism, Gradualism, and American Utopian Socialism," in *America's
      Communal Utopias*, ed. Pitzer, 159–80.

160   For a history of the community, see Holloway, *Heavens on Earth*, and Lawrence
      Foster, "Free Love and Community: John Humphrey Noyes and the Oneida
      Perfectionists," in *America's Communal Utopias*, ed. Pitzer, 253-79.

161   Cited in Martin Richards, "Perfecting People: Selective Breeding at the Oneida
      Community (1869–1879) and the Eugenics Movement," *New Genetics and Society*
      23(1) (2004), 50.

162   Richards, "Perfecting People," 58–59.

163   Foster, "Free Love and Community," 266–269.

164   Alcott, *Transcendental Wild Oats*, 55–56.

165   Holloway, *Heavens on Earth*, 212.

166   Karl Marx and Friedrich Engels, *The Communist Manifesto* (New York: Penguin
      Books, 1967), 254–56. Marx and Engels did acknowledge the utopian socialists'
      positive side, in particular how their attacks on the injustices of existing society
      served as valuable materials for enlightening the working class. Engels expanded

further on the positive aspects of the theories of Saint-Simon, Fourier, and Owen in his 1880 essay *Socialism: Utopian and Scientific*.

167   Kate Soper, "Other Pleasures: The Attractions of Post-Consumerism," *Socialist Register* 36 (2000), 117–32. Also see other articles in this volume for an interesting discussion of what could or should comprise a socialist utopia.

168   Raymond Mungo, *Total Loss Farm: A Year in the Life* (New York: Bantam Books, 1971), 173, cited in Timothy Miller, *The 60s Communes: Hippies and Beyond* (Syracuse, NY: Syracuse University Press, 1999), 152.

169   Miller, *The 60s Communes*, 15.

170   Miller, *The 60s Communes*, xxvi.

171   Robyn C. Spencer, "Communalism and the Black Panther Party in Oakland, California," in Iain Boal, Janferie Stone, Michael Watts, and Cal Winslow, eds., *West of Eden: Communes and Utopia in Northern California* (Oakland, CA: PM Press, 2012), 95.

172   Thomas Jefferson, *Notes on the State of Virginia* (Philadelphia: H.C. Carey and I. Lea, 1825), 224, written 1781–82, cited in Tuveson, *Redeemer Nation*, 109.

173   See Mann, *1491*, 350–366.

174   Takaki, *Iron Cages*, 37–64.

175   James D. Richardson, *A Compilation of the Messages and Papers of the Presidents*, 20 vols. (New York: 1897–1917), III, 1084, cited in Reginald Horsman, *Race and Manifest Destiny: The Origins of American Racial Anglo-Saxonism* (Cambridge, MA: Harvard University Press, 1981), 202.

176   Horsman, *Race and Manifest* Destiny, 210.

177   Richard Slotkin, *Gunfighter Nation: The Myth of the Frontier in Twentieth-Century America* (New York: Atheneum, 1992). Also see Bercovitch, *The American Jeremiad*.

178   Felicity D. Scott, "Bulldozers in Utopia: Open Land, Outlaw Territory, and the Code Wars," in *West of Eden*, eds. Boal et al., 67.

179   Janferie Stone, "Our Bodies, Our Communal Selves," in *West of Eden*, eds. Boal et al., 176.

180   Miller, *Errand into the Wilderness*, 207.

181   Miller, *The 60s Communes*, 190, and Fred Turner, *From Counterculture to Cyberculture: Stewart Brand, the Whole Earth Network, and the Rise of Digital Utopianism* (Chicago: University of Chicago Press, 2006), 78.

182   Turner, *From Counterculture to Cyberculture*, 67.

183   Turner, *From Counterculture to Cyberculture*, 22.

184   R. Buckminster Fuller and Robert Snyder, *R. Buckminster Fuller: An Autobiographical Monologue Scenario Documented and Edited by Robert Snyder* (New York: St. Martin's Press, 1980), 12, cited in Turner, *From Counterculture to Cyberculture*, 55. On a critique of Fuller, also see Simon Sadler, "The Dome and the Shack: The Dialectics of Hippie Enlightenment," in *West of Eden*, eds. Boal et al., 72–80.

185   Cited in Turner, *From Counterculture to Cyberculture*, 82.

186   Turner, *From Counterculture to Cyberculture*, 87, and Lee Worden, "Counterculture, Cyberculture, and the Third Culture: Reinventing Civilization, Then and Now," in *West of Eden*, eds. Boal et al., 199–221.

187   Nathaniel Rich, "The Mammoth Cometh," *New York Times Magazine*, February 27, 2014, at http://www.nytimes.com/2014/03/02/magazine/the-mammoth-cometh.html, accessed December 11, 2014.

188 Jesse Drew, "The Commune as Badlands as Utopia as Autonomous Zone," in *West of Eden*, eds. Boal et al., 44.

189 Harvey Wasserman, "Sam Lovejoy, the No Nukes Movement, and the Tower that Toppled a Terrible Technology," *Common Dreams*, February 28, 2013, at http://www.commondreams.org/views/2013/02/28/sam-lovejoy-no-nukes-movement-and-tower-toppled-terrible-technology, accessed December 11, 2014.

190 Stone, "Our Bodies, Our Communal Selves," and Carmen Goodyear, "We Met in Berkeley . . . That Heady Summer of Love," in *West of Eden*, eds. Boal et al., 170–184.

191 See the books of Tom Fels, *Farm Friends: From the Late Sixties to the West Seventies and Beyond* (North Bennington, Vermont: Rural Science Institute Press, 2008) and *Buying the Farm: Peace and War on a Sixties Commune* (Amherst: University of Massachusetts Press, 2012) for an extended account of the legacy of the '60s political communes through the lens of Montague Farm.

192 Howard Zinn, "The Optimism of Uncertainty," *Nation*, September 2, 2004, at https://www.thenation.com/article/optimism-uncertainty/, accessed December 13, 2016.

193 See Sonia Kruks, *Simone de Beauvoir and the Politics of Ambiguity* (New York: Oxford University Press, 2012), 7.

CHAPTER THREE: BOOM AND DOOM: THE MAGIC OF THE ATOM

194 Paul Boyer, *By the Bomb's Early Light: American Thought and Culture in the Atomic Age* (Chapel Hill, NC: University of North Carolina Press, 1994), 304.

195 For a stark representation of all the nuclear explosions that have occurred, see Isao Hashimoto's short video "1945–1998," 2003, at https://www.facebook.com/video.php?v=142342605845178, accessed November 12, 2014.

196 *A Feasibility Study of the Health Consequences to the American Population of Nuclear Weapons Tests Conducted by the United States and Other Nations*, Progress Report prepared for the US Congress by the Department of Health and Human Services, Centers for Disease Control and Prevention, Washington, DC, August 2001, at http://www.cdc.gov/nceh/radiation/fallout/, accessed November 12, 2014.

197 Cited in *A Feasibility Study*.

198 Former Worker Medical Screening Program, Ames Laboratory, at http://cph.uiowa.edu/IowaFWP/documents/Ames.Summary.of.FWP.EEOICPA.flyer.pdf, accessed November 12, 2014; Energy Employees Occupational Illness Compensation Program Act, Ames Laboratory, at http://cph.uiowa.edu/IowaFWP/ames/EEOICPA.html, accessed November 12, 2014; Laurence Fuortes, "The Legacy of the Manhattan Project and Cold War in Iowa," at http://cph.uiowa.edu/IowaFWP/documents/FWP_presentation.pdf, accessed Nov. 12, 2014.

199 Photo at http://en.wikipedia.org/wiki/File:Exercise_Desert_Rock_IV_%28Tumbler-Snapper_Dog%29_001.jpg, accessed November 12, 2014.

200 Sheldon Ungar, *The Rise and Fall of Nuclearism: Fear and Faith as Determinants of the Arms Race* (University Park: Pennsylvania State University Press, 1992), 59; and Sadao Asada, "The Mushroom Cloud and National Psyches: Japanese and American Perceptions of the Atomic-Bomb Decision, 1945–1995," in *Living with*

the Bomb: American and Japanese Cultural Conflicts in the Nuclear Age, eds. Laura Hein and Mark Selden (Armonk, NY: M.E. Sharpe, 1997), 179.

201   See Gar Alperovitz, *The Decision to Use the Atomic Bomb: And the Architecture of an American Myth* (New York: Alfred A. Knopf, 1995).

202   Boyer, *By the Bomb's Early Light*, 184–86.

203   Dwight D. Eisenhower, *Mandate for Change 1953–1956* (Garden City: 1963), 312–13, cited in Gar Alperovitz, "Historians Reassess: Did We Need to Drop the Bomb?" in *Hiroshima's Shadow: Writings on the Denial of History and the Smithsonian Controversy*, eds. Kai Bird and Lawrence Lifschultz (Stony Creek, CT: Pamphleteer's Press, 1998), 11.

204   Boyer, *By the Bomb's Early Light*, 188–89.

205   Ungar, *The Rise and Fall of Nuclearism*, 56.

206   Alfonso A. Narvaez, "Gen. Curtis LeMay, an Architect of Strategic Air Power, Dies at 83," Obituaries, *New York Times*, Oct. 2, 1990, at http://www.nytimes.com/1990/10/02/obituaries/gen-curtis-lemay-an-architect-of-strategic-air-power-dies-at-83.html, accessed January 27, 2017.

207   Asada, "The Mushroom Cloud and National Psyches," 174–79.

208   Mike Wallace, "The Battle of the Enola Gay," in *Hiroshima's Shadow*, eds. Bird and Lifschultz, 317–36.

209   George H. Roeder, Jr., "Making Things Visible: Learning from the Censors," in *Living with the Bomb*, eds. Hein and Selden, 87.

210   Cited in Hugh Gusterson, "Remembering Hiroshima at a Nuclear Weapons Laboratory," *Living with the Bomb*, eds. Hein and Selden, 262.

211   Lane Fenrich, "Mass Death in Miniature: How Americans Became Victims of the Bomb," in *Living with the Bomb*, eds. Hein and Selden, 127.

212   Fenrich, "Mass Death in Miniature,"126.

213   Boyer, *By the Bomb's Early Light*, 187.

214   Fenrich, "Mass Death in Miniature," 126.

215   Roeder, "Making Things Visible,"89.

216   Boyer, *By the Bomb's Early Light*, 67, 106.

217   Cited in Ungar, *The Rise and Fall of Nuclearism*, 65.

218   Ungar, *The Rise and Fall of Nuclearism*, Chapter Six.

219   Kenneth D. Rose, *One Nation Underground: The Fallout Shelter in American Culture* (New York: New York University Press, 2001), 9.

220   A.G. Mojtabai, *Blessèd Assurance: At Home with the Bomb in Amarillo, Texas* (Boston: Houghton Mifflin, 1986).

221   Ungar, *The Rise and Fall of Nuclearism*.

222   Boyer, *By the Bomb's Early Light*, 11–12, 85, 88.

223   See Boyer, *By the Bomb's Early Light*, 91–92.

224   Hubert M. Evans, Ryland W. Crary, and C. Glen Hass, *Operation Atomic Vision: A Teaching-Learning Unit for High School Students* (Washington, DC: 1948), 5–7, cited in Boyer, *By the Bomb's Early Light*, 298.

225   Boyer, *By the Bomb's Early Light*, 295.

226   Dan O'Neil, *The Firecracker Boys: H-Bombs, Inupiat Eskimos, and the Roots of the Environmental Movement* (New York: Basic Books, 2007). Real estate developers also pushed for an underground atomic explosion in the Marin headlands, on the northern side of the Golden Gate Bridge, to create a bowl for the formation

of a new city. See Richard Walker, "A Hidden Geography," Berkeley Geography Working Paper, June 2001, at http://oldweb.geog.berkeley.edu/PeopleHistory/faculty/R_Walker/AHiddenGeography.html, accessed November 12, 2014, at http://geog.berkeley.edu/PeopleHistory/faculty/R_Walker/AHiddenGeography.html as of January 27, 2017.

227   Chuck McCutcheon, *Nuclear Reactions: The Politics of Opening a Radioactive Waste Disposal Site* (Albuquerque: University of New Mexico Press, 2002); also see the WIPP fact sheet, "How Will Future Generations Be Warned?" at http://www.wipp.energy.gov/fctshts/PICs.pdf, accessed November 14, 2014.

228   David Nevin, "Nuclear-Age School: New Mexico Students Pursue Knowledge Underground," *Saturday Evening Post*, January 26, 1963, 64. Also see, Rose, *One Nation Underground*, 138–39.

229   Nevin, "Nuclear-Age School," 65.

230   David Monteyne, *Fallout Shelter: Designing for Civil Defense in the Cold War* (Minneapolis: University of Minnesota Press, 2011), 10–11.

231   Rose, *One Nation Underground*, 23.

232   Boyer, *By the Bomb's Early Light*, 313.

233   Rose, *One Nation Underground*, 79.

234   Cited in Rose, *One Nation Underground*, 3–4.

235   Rose, *One Nation Underground*, 94, 202, 210–12.

236   For example, Monteyne, *Fallout Shelter*; Tracy C. Davis, *Stages of Emergency: Cold War Nuclear Civil Defense* (Durham, NC: Duke University Press, 2007); and Laura McEnaney, *Civil Defense Begins at Home: Militarization Meets Everyday Life in the Fifties* (Princeton: Princeton University Press, 2000).

237   Monteyne, *Fallout Shelter*, 27–29.

238   Samuel W. Matthews, "Nevada Learns to Live with the Bomb," *National Geographic Magazine*, CIII(6) (June 1953), 839–50.

239   Robert Jay Lifton, "The New Psychology of Human Survival: Images of Doom and Hope," Occasional Paper No. 1, Center on Violence and Human Survival, John Jay College of Criminal Justice, CUNY, n.d. [1987], 8; Jackie Orr, "Making Civilian Soldiers,"in *Making Threats*, eds. Hartmann et al., 54–60.

240   William F. Vandercook, "Making the Very Best of the Very Worst: The 'Human Effects of Nuclear Weapons' Report of 1956," *International Security* 11 (Summer 1986), cited in Lifton,"The New Psychology of Human Survival," 8, 9.

241   Sibylle K. Escalona, "Children and the Threat of Nuclear War," in *Behavioral Science and Human Survival*, ed. Milton Schwebel (Palo Alto, CA: Science and Behavior Books, 1965), 204, 206.

242   Mícheál D. Roe, Susan A. McKay, and Michael G. Wessells, "Pioneers in Peace Psychology: Milton Schwebel," *Peace and Conflict: Journal of Peace Psychology*, 9(4) (2003), 305–26.

243   Milton Schwebel, "Nuclear Cold War: Student Opinions and Professional Responsibility," in *Behavioral Science and Human Survival*, ed. Schwebel, 217.

244   Schwebel, "Nuclear Cold War," 219.

245   Schwebel, "Nuclear Cold War," 222.

246   This was suggested by William R. Beardslee and John E. Mack in "Adolescents and the Threat of Nuclear War: The Evolution of a Perspective," *Yale Journal of Biology and Medicine* 56 (1983), 79–81.

247 Beardslee and Mack, "Adolescents and the Threat of Nuclear War," 81.

248 Robert Scheer, *With Enough Shovels: Reagan, Bush, and Nuclear War* (New York: Random House, 1982), cover quote and 18.

249 See Beardslee and Mack, "Adolescents and the Threat of Nuclear War," and David S. Greenwald and Steven J. Zeitlin, *No Reason to Talk about It: Families Confront the Nuclear Taboo* (New York: Norton, 1987). There were also workshops for adults, such as Buddhist eco-philosopher Joanna Macy's Despair and Empowerment exercises with titles such as "Spiritual Exercises for a Time of Apocalypse." See Joanna Rogers Macy, *Despair and Personal Power in the Nuclear Age* (Philadelphia: New Society Publishers, 1983).

250 *Children's Fears of War*, Hearing before the Select Committee on Children, Youth, and Families, House of Representatives, Ninety-Eighth Congress, First Session, Washington, DC, September 20, 1983 (Washington, DC: U.S. Government Printing Office, 1984), 7, 11, 13, at http://njlaw.rutgers.edu/collections/gdoc/hearings/8/84602396/84602396_1.pdf as of January 27, 2017.

251 See, for example, Lawrence S. Wittner, "Reagan and Nuclear Disarmament: How the Nuclear Freeze Movement Forced Reagan to Make Progress on Arms Control," *Boston Review*, April/May 2000, at http://bostonreview.net/BR25.2/wittner.html, accessed November 12, 2014.

252 Robert Jay Lifton and Richard Falk, *Indefensible Weapons: The Political and Psychological Case Against Nuclearism* (New York: Basic Books, 1982), 11. Also see Robert Jay Lifton, *The Broken Connection: On Death and the Continuity of Life* (New York: Simon and Schuster, 1979).

253 Lifton and Falk, *Indefensible Weapons*, 7.

254 Lifton, *The Broken Connection*, 343.

255 Boal et al., eds., *West of Eden*, xxii.

256 Lifton, *The Broken Connection*, 345.

257 Norman Mailer, *Advertisements for Myself* (New York: Signet Nooks, 1960), cited in Lifton, *The Broken Connection*, 347.

258 Cited in Walter Isaacson, "Walker Percy's Theory of Hurricanes," *New York Times Book Review*, August 4, 2015, 32, at https://www.nytimes.com/2015/08/09/books/review/walker-percys-theory-of-hurricanes.html as of January 27, 2017.

259 Lifton and Falk, *Indefensible Weapons*, 67.

260 Lifton, *The Broken Connection*, 365.

261 Lifton and Falk, *Indefensible Weapons*, 115.

262 See Kingston Reif, "Would the United States Ever Actually Use Nuclear Weapons?' *Bulletin of the Atomic Scientists*, September 17, 2013, at http://thebulletin.org/would-united-states-ever-actually-use-nuclear-weapons, accessed November 12, 2014; Hans M. Kristensen, "How Presidents Arm and Disarm," Federation of American Scientists, October 15, 2014, at http://fas.org/blogs/security/2014/10/stockpilereductions/, accessed November 12, 2014; Joe Cirincione, "How Big a Nuclear Arsenal Do We Really Need?" *Los Angeles Times*, October 21, 2014, at http://www.latimes.com/opinion/op-ed/la-oe-cirincione-nuclear-weapons-20141022-story.html, accessed November 12, 2014; William J. Broad, "Which President Cut the Most Nukes?" *New York Times*, November 1, 2014, at http://www.nytimes.com/2014/11/02/sunday-review/which-president-cut-the-most-nukes.html, accessed November 12, 2014; Philip Taubman, "No Need for All

These Nukes," *New York Times*, Sunday Review, January 7, 2012, at http://www.nytimes.com/2012/01/08/opinion/sunday/reducing-the-nuclear-arsenal.html as of January 27, 2017; and David Nakamura, "In Hiroshima 71 Years After First Atomic Strike, Obama Calls for End of Nuclear Weapons," *Washington Post*, May 27, 2016, at https://www.washingtonpost.com/politics/obama-visits-hiro-shima-more-than-seven-decades-after-the-worlds-first-atomic-strike/2016/05/27/c7d0d250-23b6-11e6-8690-f14ca9de2972_story.html, accessed June 17, 2016.

263   "The Finger on the Nuclear Button," editorial, *New York Times*, February 6, 2017, A18.

264   Interview with Condoleezza Rice, "Late Edition with Wolf Blitzer," CNN, September 8, 2002, cited in James Davis, "At War with the Future: Catastrophism and the Right," in Sasha Lilley, David McNally, Eddie Yuen, and James Davis, *Catastrophism: The Apocalyptic Politics of Collapse and Rebirth* (Oakland, CA: PM Press, 2012), 79.

265   Julia Preston, "U.S. Faces Suit Over Tactics at Immigrant Detention Center," *New York Times*, August 22, 2014, at https://www.nytimes.com/2014/08/23/us/us-faces-suit-over-tactics-at-immigrant-detention-center.html as of January 27, 2017. The facility was located in the Federal Law Enforcement Training Center, where Border Patrol recruits are subjected to a grueling and brutal indoctrination process. See Todd Miller, *Border Patrol Nation: Dispatches from the Front Lines of Homeland Security* (San Francisco: City Light Books, 2014).

266   Juan Carlos Llorca, "DHS Secretary Visits Artesia, N.M. Facility; Warns Immigrants 'We Will Send You Back'," *El Paso Times*, July 11, 2014, at http://www.elpasotimes.com/latestnews/ci_26128803/dhs-secretary-visit-artesia-nm-mi-grant-detention-center, accessed November 12, 2014, at http://archive.northjersey.com/news/homeland-secretary-visits-immigrant-holding-center-1.1050266 as of January 27, 2017.

267   Preston, "U.S. Faces Suit."

268   Geoff Brumfiel, "Official Report: Nuclear Waste Accident Caused by Wrong Cat Litter," National Public Radio, March 26, 2015, at http://www.npr.org/sections/thetwo-way/2015/03/26/395615637/official-report-nuclear-waste-accident-caused-by-wrong-kitty-litter, accessed June 12, 2015.

269   Matthew L. Wald, "In U.S. Cleanup Efforts, Accident at Nuclear Site Points to Cost of Lapses," *New York Times*, October 30, 2014, A17, at https://www.nytimes.com/2014/10/30/us/in-us-cleanup-efforts-accident-at-nuclear-site-points-to-cost-of-lapses.html as of January 27, 2017, and Ralph Vartabedian, "Nuclear Accident in New Mexico ranks among the Costliest in U.S. History," *Los Angeles Times*, August 22, 2016, at http://www.latimes.com/nation/la-na-new-mexico-nuclear-dump-20160819-snap-story.html, accessed September 1, 2016.

270   Eric Schlosser, *Command and Control: Nuclear Weapons, the Damascus Accident, and the Illusion of Safety* (New York: Penguin Books, 2014), and Ed Pilkington, "US Nearly Detonated Atomic Bomb over North Carolina—Secret Document," *Guardian*, September 20, 2013, at http://www.theguardian.com/world/2013/sep/20/usaf-atomic-bomb-north-carolina-1961, accessed June 15, 2015.

271   Helen Cooper, "Air Force Fires 9 Officers in Scandal Over Cheating on Proficiency Tests," *New York Times*, March 27, 2014, at http://www.nytimes.com/2014/03/28/

us/air-force-fires-9-officers-accused-in-cheating-scandal.html, accessed June 15, 2015.

272   *Final Report of the Los Alamos Historical Document Retrieval and Assessment (LAHDRA) Project*, Centers for Disease Control and Prevention, National Center for Environmental Health, Division of Environmental Hazards and Health Effects, Radiation Studies Branch, November 2010, ii, at https://nnsa.energy. gov/sites/default/files/nnsa/multiplefiles2/ChemRisk%20et%20al%202010%20 Final%20LAHDRA%20Report.pdf as of January 27, 2017.

CHAPTER FOUR: THE CHURCH OF MALTHUS

273   John Avery, *Progress, Poverty and Population: Re-reading Condorcet, Godwin and Malthus* (London: Frank Cass, 1997).

274   Thomas R. Malthus, *An Essay on Population*, Volume I (New York: E.P. Dutton and Co., 1914), 6.

275   Cited in Avery, *Progress, Poverty and Population*, 72.

276   Thomas R. Malthus, *An Essay on Population*, Volume II (New York: E.P. Dutton and Co., 1914), 260.

277   "Discovery Building Gunman Spoke to NBC News," msnbc.com, September 2, 2010, at http://www.msnbc.msn.com/id/38962968/ns/us_news-crime_and_ courts/t/discovery-building-gunman-spoke-nbc-news/#.UL9d54ZniSom, accessed December 5, 2012.

278   Lisa Hymas, "I Am the Population Problem," *Grist*, September 27, 2011, at http://grist.org/population/2011-09-27-i-am-the-population-problem/, accessed November 19, 2014.

279   Loretta J. Ross, "Fighting the Black Anti-Abortion Campaign: Trusting Black Women," *On the Issues*, Winter 2011, at http://www.ontheissuesmagazine. com/2011winter/2011_winter_Ross.php, accessed November 19, 2014.

280   Betsy Hartmann and James K. Boyce, *A Quiet Violence: View from a Bangladesh Village* (London: Zed Books, 1983).

281   Betsy Hartmann, *Reproductive Rights and Wrongs: The Global Politics of Population Control*, third edition (Chicago: Haymarket Books, 2016).

282   Douglass North and Robert Thomas, *The Rise of the Western World: A New Economic History* (Cambridge, UK: Cambridge University Press, 1973), 8.

283   Erik Millstone, "Chronic Hunger: A Problem of Scarcity or Inequity?" in *The Limits to Scarcity: Contesting the Politics of Allocation*, ed. Lyla Mehta (London: Earthscan, 2010), 179–83, and United Nations Environment Program (UNEP), *The Environmental Food Crisis: The Environment's Role in Averting Future Food Crises* (UNEP: Nairobi, Kenya, 2009), at http://www.grida.no/publications/rr/ food-crisis/, accessed November 19, 2014.

284   Tim Dyson, *Population and Development: The Demographic Transition* (London: Zed Books, 2010), 3. A 2014 video "Don't Panic" by the Gapminder Foundation and Hans Rosling, a Swedish public health professor and statistician, clearly and entertainingly takes apart the myth of exponential population growth and describes the dynamics of demographic transition. At https://www.youtube.com/ watch?v=FACK2knCo8E, accessed June 20, 2016.

285 There can also be negative reasons for declining birth rates, such as rising rates of infertility and the kind of economic and social shocks that occurred in the former Soviet Union after the collapse of Communism. In the US, birth rates declined during the Great Depression.

286 For a longer discussion of the role of family planning, see Betsy Hartmann, Anne Hendrixson, and Jade Sasser, "Population, Sustainable Development, and Gender Equality," in *Gender, Equality and Sustainable Development*, ed. Melissa Leach (New York: Routledge and Earthscan, 2016), 56–81.

287 United Nations, *World Population Prospects: The 2015 Revision*, Key Findings and Advance Tables (New York: U.N. Department of Economic and Social Affairs, 2015), 38, at http://esa.un.org/unpd/wpp/Publications/Files/Key_Findings_WPP_2015.pdf, accessed August 13, 2015.

288 United Nations, *World Population Prospects: The 2015 Revision*, 1–11.

289 Paul R. Ehrlich, *The Population Bomb* (New York: Ballantine Books, rev. ed., 1971), 45, cited in Thomas R. DeGregori, "Apocalypse Yesterday," in *The Apocalyptic Vision in America*, ed. Zamora, 206.

290 Cited in Charles T. Rubin, *The Green Crusade: Rethinking the Roots of Environmentalism* (Oxford: Rowman and Littlefield, 1998), 79.

291 See Thomas Robertson, *The Malthusian Moment: Global Population Growth and the Birth of American Environmentalism* (New Brunswick, NJ: Rutgers University Press, 2012), 144, for a discussion of these apocalyptic scenarios and Ehrlich's war imagery.

292 Cited in John Tierney, "Fanisi's Choice," *Science*, 86 (January–February 1986), 42.

293 Cited in M. Jimmie Killingsworth and Jacqueline S. Palmer, "Millennial Ecology: The Apocalyptic Narrative from *Silent Spring* to *Global Warming*," in *Green Culture: Environmental Rhetoric in Contemporary America*, eds. Carl G. Herndl and Stuart C. Brown (Madison, WI: University of Wisconsin Press, 1996), 40.

294 Clyde Haberman, "The Unrealized Horrors of Population Explosion," *New York Times* Retro Report, May 31, 2015, at http://www.nytimes.com/2015/06/01/us/the-unrealized-horrors-of-population-explosion.html, accessed June 1, 2015. Also see accompanying video.

295 Maurice King, "Health is a Sustainable State," *Lancet* 336(8716) (September 15, 1990), 664–67.

296 Boyer, *By the Bomb's Early Light*, 51.

297 Robert Redfield, "Consequences of Atomic Energy," *Phi Delta Kappan* 27 (April 1946), 223, cited in Boyer, *By the Bomb's Early Light*, 60.

298 Daniel Lang, "A Reporter at Large," *New Yorker*, November 16, 1945, 98, cited in Boyer, *By the Bomb's Early Light*, 70.

299 Quoted in Adam Rome, "'Give Earth a Chance': The Environmental Movement and the Sixties," *Journal of American History* 90(2) (September 2003), 525–54, cited in Robertson, *The Malthusian Moment*, 161–62. Robertson also notes Ehrlich's rock star revivalist techniques.

300 Both quotations from Michael Egan, *Barry Commoner and the Science of Survival: The Remaking of American Environmentalism* (Cambridge, MA: MIT Press, 2007), 125, 130, cited in Ian Angus and Simon Butler, *Too Many People?: Population, Immigration, and the Environmental Crisis* (Chicago: Haymarket Books, 2011), 14.

301 Hartmann, *Reproductive Rights and Wrongs*, 101.

302 Allan Chase, *The Legacy of Malthus: The Social Costs of the New Scientific Racism* (Urbana: University of Illinois Press, Illini Books Edition, 1980), 386.

303 See the prefaces to Population and Development Program, *Population in Perspective: A Curriculum Resource*, second edition (Amherst, MA: Hampshire College Population and Development Program, January 2013), at http://www.population-inperspective.org, accessed November 19, 2014, at http://globalstudies.cmswiki. wikispaces.net/file/view/PiP-Introduction.pdf as of January 27, 2017.

304 Teresa Audesirk and Gerald Audesirk, *Biology: Life on Earth*, 4th ed. (Upper Saddle River, NJ: Prentice Hall, 1996), 865. More recent environmental science textbooks used in the local school system have a similar message about population. For an alternative high school curriculum on population, see Population and Development Program, *Population in Perspective*.

305 See the video "Don't Panic" by the Gapminder Foundation and Hans Rosling for a critique of exponential population growth.

306 Aldo Leopold, "Ecology and Politics," in *The River of the Mother of God and Other Essays by Aldo Leopold*, eds. Susan L. Flader and J. Baird Callicott (Madison: University of Wisconsin Press, 1991), 282–84, cited in Nathan F. Sayre, "The Genesis, History, and Limits of Carrying Capacity," *Annals of the Association of American Geographers* 98(1) (March 2008), 120–34. Sayre notes that, at the same time Leopold was writing, the British colonial administration in Northern Rhodesia, now Zambia, was imposing its own version of carrying capacity on the natives. The disruption caused by the white takeover of black farmland and the migration of male labor to the copper mines led to claims that the colony was overpopulated in some parts and underpopulated in others. Officials calculated "land carrying capacity" for different agricultural systems, and identified those areas where critical population densities would cause land degradation. Based on these calculations, over 50,000 natives were forced to move. Later, range scientists employed similar measurements of carrying capacity to justify the compulsory relocation of African pastoralists and the destocking of their herds.

307 Sabine Höhler, "'Spaceship Earth': Envisioning Human Habitats in the Environmental Age," *GHI Bulletin*, No. 42 (Spring 2008), 65–85, and by the same author, "A 'Law of Growth': The Logistic Curve and Population Control Since World War II," presented at the *Technological and Aesthetic (Trans)Formations of Society* conference, Darmstadt Technical University, Hessen, Germany, October 12–14, 2005.

308 Eugene P. Odum, *Fundamentals of Ecology* (Philadelphia: Saunders, 1953), 123, cited in Sayre, "The Genesis, History, and Limits of Carrying Capacity," 128.

309 Sayre, "The Genesis, History, and Limits of Carrying Capacity."

310 William Vogt, *Road to Survival* (New York: William Sloane Associates, 1948), 16–17, cited in Sayre, "The Genesis, History, and Limits of Carrying Capacity," 130.

311 Thomas Robertson, "Total War and the Total Environment: Fairfield Osborn, William Vogt, and the Birth of Global Ecology," *Environmental History* 17 (April 2012), 351.

312 Paul R. Ehrlich and Anne H. Ehrlich, *The Population Explosion* (New York: Simon and Schuster, 1990), 38–39.

313 H. Patricia Hynes, "The 'Invisible Casualty of War': The Environmental Destruction of U.S. Militarism," *DifferenTakes*, No. 84 (Summer 2014), at http://sites.

hampshire.edu/popdev/the-invisible-casualty-of-war-the-environmental-destruc-tion-of-u-s-militarism/, accessed September 2, 2016. Also see Barry Sanders, *The Green Zone: The Environmental Costs of Militarism* (Oakland, CA: AK Press, 2009).

314 See Population and Development Program, *Population in Perspective*, for a discussion of the limitations of carrying capacity. Also see Angus and Butler, *Too Many People?*, for an expanded critique of Malthusian concepts of the relationship between population and the environment.

315 H. Patricia Hynes, "Taking Population out of the Equation: Reformulating I=PAT," in *Dangerous Intersections: Feminist Perspectives on Population, Environment, and Development*, eds. Jael Silliman and Ynestra King (Cambridge, MA: South End Press, 1999), 40.

316 Hynes, "Taking Population out of the Equation," 51–54. For case studies of positive human-environment interactions, see James. K. Boyce, Sunita Narain, and Elizabeth A. Stanton, eds., *Reclaiming Nature: Environmental Justice and Ecological Restoration* (London: Anthem Press, 2007).

317 Ken Bausch, "Problematique and the Club of Rome," Institute for 21st Century Agoras, n.d., at http://quergeist.net/Problematique_Club-of-Rome.htm, accessed June 26, 2015.

318 See John S. Dryzek, *The Politics of the Earth: Environmental Discourses* (Oxford: Oxford University Press, 1997) for a discussion of the Club of Rome and Limits to Growth; also see Robertson, *The Malthusian Moment*, and for a critique of ecological modeling and a history of systems engineering, Peter J. Taylor, *Unruly Complexity: Ecology, Interpretation, Engagement* (Chicago: University of Chicago Press, 2005).

318 Christian Parenti, "'The Limits to Growth': A Book That Launched a Movement," *Nation*, December 5, 2012, at http://www.thenation.com/print/article/171610/lim-its-growth-book-launched-movement, accessed November 19, 2014.

319 Dryzek, *The Politics of the Earth* and Höhler, "'Spaceship Earth,'" 65–85.

320 Susan Greenhalgh, "Globalization and Population Governance in China," in *Global Assemblages: Technology, Politics, and Ethics as Anthropological Problems*, eds. Aihwa Ong and Stephen J. Collier (Malden, MA: Blackwell, 2005), 361. Also see Greenhalgh, "Science, Modernity, and the Making of China's One-Child Policy," *Population and Development Review* 29(2) (June 2003), 163–96.

321 Carl Haub, "China Releases First 2010 Census Results," Population Reference Bureau, May 2011, at http://www.prb.org/Publications/Articles/2011/china-cen-sus-results.aspx, accessed November 17, 2014.

322 See Kay Ann Johnson, *China's Hidden Children: Abandonment, Adoption, and the Human Costs of the One-Child Policy* (Chicago: University of Chicago Press, 2016).

323 Susan Greenhalgh, "Patriarchal Demographics? China's Sex Ratio Reconsidered," *Population and Development Review* 38 supplement (2012), 130–49.

325 Edward Wong, "Population Control is Called Big Revenue Source in China," *New York Times*, September 26, 2013, at http://www.nytimes.com/2013/09/27/world/asia/chinese-provinces-collected-billions-in-family-planning-fines-lawyer-says.html, accessed November 17, 2014.

326 W. Feng, Y. Cai, and B. Gu, "Population, Policy, and Politics: How Will History Judge China's One-Child Policy?" *Population and Development Review* 38 (2013), 126.

327   "Appendix 2: Donella Meadows Reconsiders IPAT," in Angus and Butler, *Too Many People?*, 213–16.

328   Alisha Coleman-Jensen et al., "Household Food Security in the United States in 2014," US Department of Agriculture, Economic Research Service Report Summary, September 2015, at http://www.ers.usda.gov/media/1896836/err194_summary.pdf, accessed June 20, 2016, at https://www.ers.usda.gov/webdocs/publications/err194/53740_err194.pdf as of January 27, 2017.

329   Jesse Finfrock, "Q & A: Paul Ehrlich," *Mother Jones*, November/December 2008, at http://www.motherjones.com/environment/2008/10/qa-paul-ehrlich, accessed November 19, 2014.

330   Mann, *1491*, 282.

331   Mann, *1491*, 60, 67.

332   William Cronon, "The Trouble with Wilderness; or, Getting Back to the Wrong Nature," in *Uncommon Ground: Toward Reinventing Nature*, ed. William Cronon (New York: W.W. Norton, 1995), 70–90.

333   Muir cited in Eric Michael Johnson, "Fire Over Ahwahnee: John Muir and the Decline of Yosemite," *Scientific American* blog, August 13, 2014, at http://blogs.scientificamerican.com/primate-diaries/2014/08/13/fire-over-ahwahnee-john-muir-and-the-decline-of-yosemit/, accessed November 18, 2014. Also see Mark David Spence, *Dispossessing the Wilderness: Indian Removal and the Making of the National Parks* (New York: Oxford University Press, 2000).

334   Frederick Jackson Turner, "The Significance of the Frontier in American History," cited in David Arnold, *The Problem of Nature: Environment, Culture and European Expansion* (Oxford: Blackwell Publishers, 1996), 100–01.

335   Hartmann, *Reproductive Rights and Wrongs*, 101. For the treatment of population and overcrowding in the popular press of this time, see John R. Wilmoth and Patrick Ball, "The Population Debate in American Popular Magazines, 1946–1990," *Population and Development Review*, 18(4) (December 1992), 631–68.

336   Wilmoth and Ball, "The Population Debate in American Popular Magazines," 641, 649, 660.

337   Tom Butler and William N. Ryerson, *Overdevelopment, Overpopulation, Overshoot* (San Francisco: Foundation for Deep Ecology in partnership with Goff Books, 2015), 73.

338   For analysis of economics and scarcity, see *The Limits to Scarcity*, ed. Mehta, Part II, 69–142, and Nicholas Xenos, *Scarcity and Modernity* (New York: Routledge, 1989).

339   Credit Suisse Research Institute, *Global Wealth Report 2015*, at https://publications.credit-suisse.com/tasks/render/file/?fileID=F2425415-DCA7-80B8-EAD989AF9341D47E, accessed October 30, 2015.

340   Emmanuel Saez and Gabriel Zucman, "Wealth Inequality in the United States since 1913: Evidence from Capitalized Income Tax Data," *Quarterly Journal of Economics*, 131(2) (May 2016), 519–78, at http://gabriel-zucman.eu/files/SaezZucman2016QJE.pdf, accessed February 17, 2016.

341   Andrew Ross, "The Lonely Hour of Scarcity," *Capitalism, Nature and Socialism* 7(3) (1996), 3–26.

342   Julian Simon, *The Ultimate Resource* (Princeton: Princeton University Press, 1981).

343   Cass R. Sunstein, "The Battle of Two Hedgehogs," *New York Review of Books*, 60(19) (December 5, 2013), at http://www.nybooks.com/articles/2013/12/05/battle-two-hedgehogs/ as of January 27, 2017.

344   Hartmann, *Reproductive Rights and Wrongs*, 123.

345   T.R. Malthus, *An Essay on the Principle of Population, Volume I*, ed. Patricia James (Cambridge: Cambridge University Press: 1989), 27, cited in Carole R. McCann, "Malthusian Men and Demographic Transitions: A Case Study of Hegemonic Masculinity in Mid-Twentieth-Century Population Theory," *Frontiers: A Journal of Women's Studies* 30(1) (2009), 152. Also see McCann's book, *Figuring the Population Bomb: Gender and Demography in the Mid-Twentieth Century* (Seattle: University of Washington Press, 2017.)

346   Larry Lohmann, "Malthusianism and the Terror of Scarcity," in *Making Threats*, eds. Hartmann, Subramaniam, and Zerner, 81–98, and McCann, *Figuring the Population Bomb*, Chapter 2.

347   For a psychological analysis of overpopulation fears, see Robert Fletcher, Jan Breitling, and Valerie Puleo, "Barbarian Hordes: The Overpopulation Scapegoat in International Development Discourse," *Third World Quarterly*, 35(7) (2014), 1195–215. For the role of racism, see Kalpana Wilson, *Race, Racism and Development: Interrogating History, Discourse and Practice* (London: Zed Books, 2012), and Jade Sasser, "From Darkness into Light: Race, Population, and Environmental Advocacy," *Antipode* 46(5) (2014), 1240–57.

348   See McCann, "Malthusian Men and Demographic Transitions," 142–71; Betsy Hartmann and Anne Hendrixson, "Pernicious Peasants and Angry Young Men: The Strategic Demography of Threats," in *Making Threats*, eds. Hartmann, Subramaniam, 225–32, and Zerner; and Gayatri Chakravorty Spivak, "Can the Subaltern Speak?" in *Marxism and the Interpretation of Culture*, eds. C. Nelson and L. Grossberg (Urbana: University of Illinois Press, 1988), 271–313.

349   Hartmann, *Reproductive Rights and Wrongs*, Chapter 12.

350   Mike Davis, *Late Victorian Holocausts: El Niño Famines and the Making of the Third World* (London: Verso, 2002). See also Corner House, "The Origins of the Third World: Markets, States and Climate," Briefing 27, Sturminster Newton, UK, December 2002, at http://www.thecornerhouse.org.uk/sites/thecornerhouse.org.uk/files/27origins.pdf as of January 27, 2017. Baring quote is from "Famine Commission – Financial Statement," Parliamentary Papers 1881, 68, cited in Corner House, "The Origins of the Third World," 8.

351   Eric B. Ross, *The Malthus Factor: Poverty, Politics and Population in Capitalist Development* (London: Zed Books, 1998).

352   Nancy Ordover, *American Eugenics: Race, Queer Anatomy, and the Science of Nationalism* (Minneapolis: University of Minnesota Press, 2003), 133.

353   Ordover, *American Eugenics*, 134.

354   Jael Silliman, Marlene Gerber Fried, Loretta Ross, and Elena R. Gutiérrez, *Undivided Rights: Women of Color Organize for Reproductive Justice* (Cambridge, MA: South End Press, 2004), 222.

355   Rosalind P. Petchesky, "Reproduction, Ethics, and Public Policy: The Federal Sterilization Regulations," *Hastings Center Report* 9(5) (October 1979), 29–41.

356   Matthew Connelly, *Fatal Misconception: The Struggle to Control World Population* (Cambridge, MA: Harvard University Press, 2008). Connelly's book is the most

comprehensive history of the population control movement to date. Also see Edmund Ramsden, "Between Quality and Quantity: The Population Council and the Politics of 'Science-making' in Eugenics and Demography, 1952–1965," Rockefeller Archive Center Research Reports Online, at http://www.rockarch.org/publications/resrep/ramsden.pdf, accessed November 19, 2014.

357 Richard Lynn, "Garrett Hardin, Ph.D.: A Retrospective of His Life and Work," The Garrett Hardin Society, at http://www.garretthardinsociety.org/tributes/tr_lynn_2001.html, accessed November 19, 2014; and Jean Stefancic, "Funding the Nativist Agenda," in *Immigrants Out! The New Nativism and the Anti-Immigrant Impulse in the United States*, ed. Juan F. Perea (New York: New York University Press, 1997), 129. For more on Hardin's long espousal of eugenic views, see Chase, *The Legacy of Malthus*.

358 Simon Szreter, "The Idea of Demographic Transition and the Study of Fertility Change: A Critical Intellectual History," *Population and Development Review* 19(4) (1993), 676.

359 See Connelly, *Fatal Misconception*, and Hartmann, *Reproductive Rights and Wrongs*, for a history of population control programs.

360 Betsy Hartmann, "The Changing Faces of Population Control," in *Policing the National Body: Race, Gender and Criminalization*, eds. Jael Silliman and Anannya Bhattacharjee (Cambridge, MA: South End Press, 2002), 268–69; also see the 2010 documentary, *A Woman's Womb*, by French director Mathilde Damoisel, at http://www.cultureunplugged.com/play/4623/A-Woman-s-Womb as of January 27, 2017.

361 In *Countdown: Our Last, Best Hope for a Future on Earth?* (New York: Little, Brown and Company, 2013), author Alan Weisman presents the problems with the one-child policy but advocates more humane versions of it as a way to reach an optimal world population and save the planet.

362 See Connelly, *Fatal Misconception*.

363 Kay Johnson, "China's One Child Policy: Not Yet in the Dustbin of History," *DifferenTakes*, No. 83, Winter 2014, at http://www.scribd.com/doc/202828072/DT-83-China-s-One-Child-Policy-Not-yet-in-the-dustbin-of-history, accessed November 18, 2014.

364 Hartmann and Hendrixson, "Pernicious Peasants and Angry Young Men," and Jack A. Goldstone, "The New Population Bomb: The Four Megatrends That Will Change the World," *Foreign Affairs* 89(1) (Jan./Feb. 2010), 26–30. Also see Anne Hendrixson, "Beyond Bonus or Bomb: Upholding the Sexual and Reproductive Health of Young People," *Reproductive Health Matters* 22(43) (May 2014), 125–34, and Hartmann, Hendrixson, and Sasser, "Population, Sustainable Development, and Gender Equality."

365 Kathryn Joyce, *Quiverfull: Inside the Christian Patriarchy Movement* (Boston: Beacon Press, 2009), 189.

366 See Southern Poverty Law Center, "Extremist Files: Virginia Abernethy," at http://www.splcenter.org/get-informed/intelligence-files/profiles/virginia-abernethy, accessed November 19, 2014.

367 See the report by the Southern Poverty Law Center, *Greenwash: Nativists, Environmentalism and the Hypocrisy of Hate*, July 2010, at http://www.splcenter.org/get-informed/publications/greenwash-nativists-environmentalism-and-the-hypocrisy-of-hate, accessed November 19, 2014, at https://www.splcenter.org/20100701/

greenwash-nativists-environmentalism-and-hypocrisy-hate as of January 27, 2017; and my article in the report, "The Greening of Hate: An Environmentalist's Essay." Also see the Center for New Community's resources on the greening of hate at Imagine 2050: Race, Identity, Democracy, at http://imagine2050.newcomm. org/ as of January 27, 2017, and Sebastian Normandin and Sean A. Valles, "How a Network of Conservationists and Population Control Activists Created the Contemporary US Anti-Immigration Movement," *Endeavour* 39(2) (June 2015), 95–105.

368   Population Media Center, at http://www.populationmedia.org/, accessed August 14, 2015.

369   Weisman, *Countdown*, 40, 42. Also see Annalee Newitz, "Has Humanity's Explosion Become a Population Bomb?" Gizmodo, io9, January 9, 2013, at http://io9. com/5969944/has-humanitys-explosion-become-a-population-bomb, accessed November 19, 2014.

370   Jake Abrahamson, "Fighting Climate Change with Family Planning," *Sierra Magazine* (May/June 2012), at http://vault.sierraclub.org/sierra/201205/climate-change-family-planning-159.aspx, accessed June 29, 2015.

371   Jade Sasser, "The Wave of the Future?: Youth Advocacy at the Nexus of Population and Climate Change," *Geographical Journal* 180 (2) (June 2014):102–10, and Sasser, *Making Sexual Stewards: Population, Climate Activism, and Social Justice in the New Millennium*, unpublished book manuscript, 2016 (to be published by New York University Press). Also see Hartmann, Hendrixson, and Sasser, "Population, Sustainable Development, and Gender Equality."

372   World Bank, "CO_2 Emissions (Metric Tons per Capita)," at http://data.worldbank.org/indicator/EN.ATM.CO2E.PC, accessed November 14, 2014.

373   Kirstin Dow and Thomas E. Downing, *The Atlas of Climate Change* (Berkeley: University of California Press, 2007). For a critique of the population-climate linkage, see David Satterthwaite, "The Implications of Population Growth and Urbanization for Climate Change," *Environment and Urbanization* 21 (2) (October 2009), 545–67.

374   Jennifer Ludden, "Should We Be Having Kids in the Age of Climate Change?" National Public Radio, August 18, 2016, at http://www.npr. org/2016/08/18/479349760/should-we-be-having-kids-in-the-age-of-climate-change, accessed September 2, 2016.

375   Betsy Hartmann, "Converging on Disaster: Climate Security and the Malthusian Anticipatory Regime for Africa," *Geopolitics* 19(4) (2014), 757–83, and for information on the latest study linking Depo-Provera to higher HIV risk, see Guttmacher Institute, "New Review of Evidence on Hormonal Contraceptive Methods and Risk of HIV Acquisition in Women Underscores Differences Between Methods," News Release, August 9, 2016, at https://www.guttmacher.org/news-release/2016/new-review-evidence-hormonal-contraceptive-methods-and-risk-hiv-acquisition-women, accessed December 14, 2016.

376   SisterSong and National Women's Health Network, "Long-Acting Reversible Contraception Statement of Principles," 2016, at https://docs.google.com/document/d/1ID4cEuaV10SAXSWdJmSi4YMs5TLCGhnomjOXoIn5odU/edit, accessed December 14, 2016. See also Coco Jervis, "The Great LARC Debate: Facilitating a Balanced Approach to Education and Promotion of LARCs,"

National Women's Health Network Newsletter, July/August 2015, at https://www. nwhn.org/the-great-larc-debate-facilitating-a-balanced-approach-to-education-and-promotion-of-larcs/, accessed December 14, 2016.

377   See, for example, Human Life International, "Depo-Provera: Injectable Abortion," at http://www.hli.org/resources/depo-provera-injectable-abortion/, accessed September 9, 2016.

CHAPTER FIVE: CLIMATE CHANGE: TIP OF THE MELTING ICEBERG

378   "Top Scientists Ask UN Leaders to Act on Nuclear Weapons, Climate Change," *Bulletin of the Atomic Scientists*, press release, January 13, 2014, at http://thebulletin. org/press-release/top-scientists-ask-un-leaders-act-nuclear-weapons-climate-change, accessed December 21, 2014.

379   Science and Security Board, "It is two and a half minutes to midnight: 2017 Doomsday Clock Statement," *Bulletin of the Atomic Scientists*, http://thebulletin. org/sites/default/files/Final%202017%20Clock%20Statement.pdf, accessed February 9, 2017.

380   Joni Seager and Betsy Hartmann, *Mainstreaming Gender in Environmental Assessment and Early Warning* (Nairobi, Kenya: UNEP, 2005), at http://www.unep.org/ dewa/Portals/67/pdf/Mainstreaming_Gender.pdf as of January 27, 2017.

381   IPCC, *Climate Change 2014: Synthesis Report*, Summary for Policymakers, at http://www.ipcc.ch/pdf/assessment-report/ar5/syr/SYR_AR5_SPMcorr1.pdf, accessed December 15, 2014, at https://www.ipcc.ch/pdf/assessment-report/ar5/syr/ SYR_AR5_FINAL_full.pdf as of January 27, 2017.

382   Richard Z. Poore, Richard S. Williams, Jr., and Christopher Tracey, "Sea Level and Climate," US Geological Survey (USGS), fact sheet, September 2011, at http:// pubs.usgs.gov/fs/fs2-00/, accessed December 15, 2014.

383   Justin Gillis, "As Permafrost Thaws, Scientists Study the Risks," *New York Times*, December 16, 2011, at http://www.nytimes.com/2011/12/17/science/earth/warming-arctic-permafrost-fuels-climate-change-worries.html as of January 27, 2017.

384   IPCC, *Climate Change 2014*.

385   National Research Council, *Abrupt Climate Changes: Inevitable Surprises* (Washington, DC: NRC, 2002), at http://www.nap.edu/openbook.php?record_id=10136&page=14, accessed December 14, 2015.

386   Coral Davenport, "Optimism Faces Grave Realities at Climate Talks," *New York Times*, November 30, 2014, at http://www.nytimes.com/2014/12/01/world/climate-talks.html, accessed December 15, 2014, and Justin Gillis, "3.6 Degrees of Uncertainty," *New York Times*, Science Times, December 16, 2014, D1, at https:// www.nytimes.com/2014/12/16/science/earth/is-a-two-degree-limit-on-global-warming-off-target.html as of January 27, 2017.

387   Jean Chemnick, "Negotiators Try to Figure Out What the Paris Climate Agreement Means," *ClimateWire*, May 17, 2016, at http://www.scientificamerican.com/ article/negotiators-try-to-figure-out-what-the-paris-climate-agreement-means/, accessed June 27, 2016.

388   Chris Mooney, "Why Trump's Idea of 'Renegotiating' the Paris Climate Agreement is So Bizarre," *Washington Post*, May 18, 2016, at https://www. washingtonpost.com/news/energy-environment/wp/2016/05/18/why-trumps-

idea-of-renegotiating-the-paris-climate-agreement-is-so-bizarre/, accessed June 27, 2016.

389 Aaron M. McCright and Riley E. Dunlap, "Defeating Kyoto: The Conservative Movement's Impact on U.S. Climate Change Policy," *Social Problems* 50(3) (2003), 349.

390 Ross Gelbspan, *Boiling Point: How Politicians, Big Oil and Coal, Journalists, and Activists Have Fueled the Climate Crisis—and What We Can Do to Avert Disaster* (New York: Perseus Books, 2004), 41.

391 Kevin A. Baumert, Timothy Herzog, and Jonathan Pershing, *Navigating the Numbers: Greenhouse Gas Data and International Climate Policy* (Washington, DC: World Resources Institute, December 2005), at http://pdf.wri.org/navigating_numbers.pdf, accessed December 21, 2014.

392 World Bank, "CO_2 Emissions (Metric Tons per Capita)."

393 Gelbspan, *Boiling Point*, 51.

394 See McCright and Dunlap, "Defeating Kyoto," for a detailed account of these political processes.

395 Two of the main scientists behind climate denial, physicists Frederick Seitz and S. Fred Singer, had not only previously worked for the tobacco industry, but for the military-industrial complex during the Cold War. Seitz helped build the atomic bomb and Singer developed Earth observation satellites. The two scientists' connections to Cold War weapons programs made them highly respected in Washington, DC, with access all the way to the White House. To boot, they were fierce anti-Communists with a hatred for government regulation. The irony, of course, is that during the Cold War, they had made their money off the government's largesse. See Naomi Oreskes and Erik M. Conway, *Merchants of Doubt: How a Handful of Scientists Obscured the Truth on Issues from Tobacco Smoke to Global Warming* (New York: Bloomsbury Press, 2010).

396 Aaron M. McCright and Riley E. Dunlap, "The Politicization of Climate Change and Polarization in the American Public's Views of Global Warming, 2001–2010," *The Sociological Quarterly* 52 (2011), 179, at http://news.msu.edu/media/documents/2011/04/593fe28b-fbc7-4a86-850a-2fe029dbeb41.pdf as of January 27, 2017.

397 Jane Mayer, "Covert Operations: The Billionaire Brothers Who are Waging a War against Obama," *New Yorker*, August 30, 2010, at http://www.newyorker.com/reporting/2010/08/30/100830fa_fact_mayer, accessed December 21, 2014.

398 McCright and Dunlap, "The Politicization of Climate Change," 179.

399 Timothy B. Leduc, "Fueling America's Climatic Apocalypse," *Worldview* II(3) (2007), 255–83, at http://compocalypse.thelong19th.com/wp-content/uploads/2014/08/ContentServer.pdf as of January 27, 2017.

400 Evangelical Climate Initiative, *Climate Change: An Evangelical Call to Action*, February 2006, at http://www.npr.org/documents/2006/feb/evangelical/calltoaction.pdf, accessed December 21, 2014; on Robertson, see Leduc, "Fueling America's Climatic Apocalypse"; and Edward O. Wilson, "Apocalypse Now: A Scientist's Plea for Christian Environmentalism," *New Republic*, 235 (September 4, 2006), 17–19.

401 Molly Redden, "Whatever Happened to the Evangelical-Environmental Alliance?" *New Republic*, November 3, 2011, at http://www.tnr.com/article/politics/97007/evangelical-climate-initiative-creation-care, accessed December 21, 2014.

402   Cornwall Alliance, "An Evangelical Declaration on Global Warming," May
      1, 2009, at http://www.cornwallalliance.org/2009/05/01/evangelical-declara-
      tion-on-global-warming/, accessed December 21, 2014.

403   Gregg Zoroya, "Taking to the Pulpit against Climate Change," *USA Today*, July
      15, 2014, at http://www.usatoday.com/story/news/nation/2014/07/15/climate-re-
      ligion-kansas-church-global-warming-evangelical/12515665/, accessed December
      16, 2014.

404   Bill McKibben, "Global Warming's Terrifying New Math," *Rolling Stone*, July
      19, 2012, at http://www.rollingstone.com/politics/news/global-warmings-terrify-
      ing-new-math-20120719, accessed December 21, 2014.

405   Michael T. Klare, "The New 'Golden Age of Oil' That Wasn't," *Huffington Post*,
      October 4, 2010, at http://www.huffingtonpost.com/michael-t-klare/domes-
      tic-oil-production_b_1939260.html, accessed December 16, 2014.

406   Steve Coll, "Gusher: The Power of ExxonMobil," *New Yorker*, April 9, 2012, 28–37.

407   McKibben, "Global Warming's Terrifying New Math."

408   Environmental Protection Agency (EPA), "Clean Power Plan for Existing Power
      Plants," n.d., at https://www.epa.gov/cleanpowerplan/clean-power-plan-existing-
      power-plants, accessed June 27, 2016.

409   Coral Davenport, "In Climate Deal with China, Obama May Set 2016 Theme,"
      New York Times, November 12, 2014, at http://www.nytimes.com/2014/11/13/
      world/asia/in-climate-deal-with-china-obama-may-set-theme-for-2016.html,
      accessed December 16, 2014.

410   James Hansen, *Storms of My Grandchildren: The Truth About the Coming Climate
      Catastrophe and Our Last Chance to Save Humanity* (New York: Bloomsbury,
      2009), 269.

411   Joe Romm, "James Lovelock Finally Walks Back His Absurd Doomism, But He
      Still Doesn't Follow Climate Science," ThinkProgress, April 23, 2012, at http://
      thinkprogress.org/climate/2012/04/23/469749/james-lovelock-finally-walks-
      back-his-absurd-doomism-but-he-still-doesnt-follow-climate-science/, accessed
      December 21, 2014.

412   Mark Maslin and Patrick Austin, "Uncertainty: Climate Models at Their Limit?"
      Nature 486 (June 14, 2012), 183–84.

413   See Laura Johnson, "(Environmental) Rhetorics of Tempered Apocalypticism in
      An Inconvenient Truth," *Rhetoric Review* 28(1) (2009), 29–46. "Nature hike" quote
      is from Ted Nordhaus and Michael Shellenberger, *Break Through: From the Death
      of Environmentalism to the Politics of Possibility* (New York: Houghton, 2007), 105,
      cited by Johnson, 35.

414   Michael Barkun, *Chasing Phantoms: Reality, Imagination, and Homeland Security
      Since 9/11* (Chapel Hill: University of North Carolina Press, 2011), 29–30.

415   See Mike Hulme, *Why We Disagree about Climate Change: Understanding
      Controversy, Inaction and Opportunity* (Cambridge, UK: Cambridge Univer-
      sity Press, 2009) for a discussion of abrupt climate change and points of no
      return; on peak oil, see Bryant Urstadt, "Imagine There's No Oil: Scenes from
      a Liberal Apocalypse," *Harper's Magazine*, August 2006, at http://harpers.org/
      archive/2006/08/0081156, accessed December 21, 2015; and Matthew Barrett Gross
      and Mel Gilles, *The Last Myth: What the Rise of Apocalyptic Thinking Tells Us about
      America* (Amherst, NY: Prometheus Books, 2012).

416 Jason Mark, "Climate Fiction Fantasy," *New York Times*, December 10, 2014, A31, at https://www.nytimes.com/2014/12/10/opinion/what-interstellar-and-snowpiercer-got-wrong.html as of January 27, 2017.

417 Naomi Oreskes and Erik M. Conway, *The Collapse of Western Civilization: A View from the Future* (New York: Columbia University Press, 2014), 24–25.

418 Mike Davis, *Ecology of Fear: Los Angeles and the Imagination of Disaster* (New York: Vintage Books, 1998), 281.

419 William A. Stahl, "From Peak Oil to the Apocalypse: Cultural Myths and the Public Understanding of Scientific Models" in *Network Apocalypse: Visions of the End in an Age of Internet Media*, ed. Robert Glenn Howard (Sheffield, UK: Sheffield Phoenix Press, 2011), 34.

420 Naomi Klein, *This Changes Everything: Capitalism vs. the Climate* (New York: Simon and Schuster, 2014), 7, 22.

421 See the website This Changes Everything, at http://thischangeseverything.org/, accessed June 27, 2016.

422 For cogent left critiques of left climate apocalypticism, see Lilley, McNally, Yuen, and Davis, *Catastrophism*, Larry Lohmann, "Fetishisms of Apocalypse," *Occupied Times*, October 30, 2014, at http://theoccupiedtimes.org/?p=13488, accessed December 17, 2014, and Mazen Labban, David Correia, and Matt Huber, "Apocalypse, the Radical Left and the Post-Political Condition," *Capitalism Nature Socialism* 24(1) (2013), 6–8.

423 See, for example, Paul Gilding, *The Great Disruption: Why the Climate Crisis Will Bring on the End of Shopping and the Birth of a New World* (London: Bloomsbury Press, 2011).

424 Matthew Lepori, "There is No Anthropocene: Climate Change, Species-Talk, and Political Economy," *Telos* 172 (Fall 2015), 103–24. Also see Erik Swyngedouw, "Apocalypse Forever?: Post-Political Populism and the Spectre of Climate Change," *Theory, Culture & Society*, 27(2–3) (2010), 213–32.

425 Susanne C. Moser, "More Bad News: The Risk of Neglecting Emotional Responses to Climate Change Information," in *Creating a Climate for Change: Communicating Climate Change and Facilitating Social Change*, eds. Susanne C. Moser and Lisa Dilling (Cambridge, UK: Cambridge University Press, 2007), 75, at http://sciencepolicy.colorado.edu/students/envs_4800/moser_2007.pdf as of January 27, 2017.

426 Lydia Saad and Jeffrey M. Jones, "U.S. Concern About Global Warming at Eight-Year High," Gallup, March 16, 2016, at http://www.gallup.com/poll/190010/concern-global-warming-eight-year-high.aspx, accessed June 27, 2016.

427 Davenport, "In Climate Deal with China."

428 Peter Schwartz and Doug Randall, *An Abrupt Climate Change Scenario and Its Implications for United States National Security*, October 2003, 2, 15, 18, at http://www.climate.org/PDF/clim_change_scenario.pdf, accessed December 18, 2014, at http://eesc.columbia.edu/courses/v1003/readings/Pentagon.pdf as of January 27, 2017.

429 Andrew J. Bacevich, *The New American Militarism: How Americans are Seduced by War* (New York: Oxford University Press, 2013).

430 Quoted in Greg Jaffe, "U.S. Model for a Future War Fans Tensions with China and Inside Pentagon," *Washington Post*, August 1, 2012, at http://www.

washingtonpost.com/world/national-security/us-model-for-a-future-war-fans-
tensions-with-china-and-inside-pentagon/2012/08/01/gJQAC6F8PX_story.html,
accessed December 18, 2014.

431   Craig Whitlock, "Pentagon Weighs Future of Its Inscrutable Nonagenarian
      Futurist, Andrew Marshall," *Washington Post*, October 27, 2013, at http://
      www.washingtonpost.com/world/national-security/pentagon-weighs-fu-
      ture-of-its-inscrutable-nonagenarian-futurist-andrew-marshall/2013/10/27/
      f9bda426-3cac-11e3-b6a9-da62c264f40e_story.html, accessed December 18, 2014.

432   Andrew C. Revkin, "The Sky is Falling! Say Hollywood and, Yes, the Pentagon,"
      New York Times, February 29, 2004, at http://www.nytimes.com/2004/02/29/
      weekinreview/ideas-trends-the-sky-is-falling-say-hollywood-and-yes-the-pentagon.
      html, accessed August 7, 2015.

433   See, for example, the scenario exercise by the defense think tanks, Center for a
      New American Security and the Center for Strategic and International Studies,
      published in K.M. Campbell, ed., *Climatic Cataclysm: The Foreign Policy and
      National Security Implications of Climate Change* (Washington, DC: Brookings
      Institution, 2008), 1–3.

434   Richard A. Matthew, "Bioterrorism and National Security: Peripheral Threats,
      Core Vulnerabilities," in *Making Threats*, eds. Hartmann, Subramaniam, and
      Zerner, 238.

435   Christian Aid, *Human Tide: The Real Migration Crisis*, London, May 2007, at
      http://www.christianaid.org.uk/images/human-tide.pdf, accessed December 21,
      2014, and Christian Aid, "World Facing Worst Migration Crisis," press release,
      May 14, 2007, at http://reliefweb.int/report/world/world-facing-worst-migration-
      crisis, accessed December 21, 2014.

436   Stephan Faris, "The Real Roots of Darfur," *Atlantic Monthly*, April 2007, at http://
      www.theatlantic.com/magazine/archive/2007/04/the-real-roots-of-darfur/5701/,
      accessed December 21, 2014;   United Nations Environment Programme (UNEP),
      Sudan Post-Conflict Environmental Assessment, June 2007, at http://postconflict.
      unep.ch/publications/UNEP_Sudan.pdf, accessed December 21, 2014; Ban
      Ki-moon, "A Climate Culprit in Darfur," *Washington Post*, June 16, 2007, A15, at
      http://www.climos.com/news/articles/aclimateculprit.htm as of January 27, 2017;
      and Fiona Harvey, "UN Climate Panel Detailed Potential for Global Conflict,"
      Financial Times, October 13, 2007, at http://www.ft.com/cms/s/0/8465cfd4-7929-
      11dc-aaf2-0000779fd2ac.html as of January 27, 2017. In the US, the influential
      defense think tank, Center for Naval Analyses (CNA), gathered a team of 11 retired
      US generals and admirals to produce a report which argued that global warming
      could help trigger widespread political instability in poor regions, especially in
      Africa. CNA Corporation, *National Security and the Threat of Climate Change*
      (Alexandria, VA: CNA, 2007), at http://www.cna.org/reports/climate, accessed
      December 21, 2014, at https://www.cna.org/cna_files/pdf/national%20secu-
      rity%20and%20the%20threat%20of%20climate%20change.pdf as of January 27,
      2017.

437   Norwegian Nobel Committee, "The Nobel Peace Prize for 2007," press release,
      October 12, 2007, at http://nobelprize.org/nobel_prizes/peace/laureates/2007/
      press.html, accessed December 21, 2014.

438 *New York Times*, "The Climate and National Security," editorial, August 17, 2009, at http://www.nytimes.com/2009/08/18/opinion/18tue1.html, accessed December 21, 2014.

439 Harry Verhoeven, "Gardens of Eden or Hearts of Darkness? The Genealogy of Discourses on Environmental Insecurity and Climate Wars in Africa," *Geopolitics* 19(4) (2014).

440 David Arnold, *The Problem of Nature: Environment, Culture and European Expansion* (Oxford: Blackwell Publishers, 1996), 28. Also see David N. Livingstone, "The Climate of War: Violence, Warfare and Climate Reductionism," *WIREs Climate Change* 6(5) (September–October 2015), 437–44, and by the same author, "Stop Saying Climate Change Causes War," *Foreign Policy*, December 4, 2015, at http://foreignpolicy.com/2015/12/04/stop-saying-climate-change-causes-war-paris-cop-21-bernie-sanders/, accessed July 25, 2016.

441 Jared Diamond, *Collapse: How Societies Choose to Fail or Succeed* (New York: Viking, 2004). For a critique, see Mann, *1491*.

442 The term "crisis narrative" was coined by Emery Roe. See Emery M. Roe, "Except Africa: Postscript to a Special Section on Development Narratives," *World Development* 23(6) (1995), 1065–69. For further critiques of these narratives, see Simon Milligan and Tony Binns, "Crisis in Policy, Policy in Crisis: Understanding Environmental Discourse and Resource-Use Conflict in Northern Nigeria," *Geographical Journal* 173(2) (June 2007), 143–56; Melissa Leach and Robin Mearns, *The Lie of the Land: Challenging Received Wisdom on the African Environment* (Oxford and Portsmouth, NH: International African Institute with James Currey and Heinemann, 1996); and Betsy Hartmann, "Will the Circle be Unbroken?: A Critique of the Project on Environment, Population, and Security," in *Violent Environments*, eds. Nancy Lee Peluso and Michael Watts (Ithaca, NY: Cornell University Press, 2001), 39–62.

443 Faris, "The Real Roots of Darfur."

444 See Alex de Waal, "Sudan: the Turbulent State," in *War in Darfur and the Search for Peace*, ed. Alex de Waal (Cambridge, MA: Justice Africa and the Harvard University Global Equity Initiative, 2007), 1–38; L. Manger, "Understanding Resource Management in the Western Sudan: A Critical Look at the New Institutional Economics" in *Beyond Territory and Scarcity: Exploring Conflicts over Natural Resource Management*, eds. Q. Gausset, Michael A. Whyte, and T. Birch-Thomsen (Stockholm: Nordiska Afrikainstitutet, 2005), 135–48; and Harry Verhoeven, "Climate Change, Conflict and Development in Sudan: Global Neo-Malthusian Narratives and Local Power Struggles," *Development and Change* 42(3) (May 2011), 679–707.

445 W. Neil Adger et al., "Human Security," Chapter Twelve, in *Climate Change 2014: Impacts, Adaptation, and Vulnerability. Part A: Global and Sectoral Aspects. Contribution of Working Group II to the Fifth Assessment Report of the Intergovernmental Panel on Climate Change*, 773, at http://ipcc-wg2.gov/AR5/images/uploads/WGI-IAR5-Chap12_FINAL.pdf, accessed July 26, 2016.

446 Verhoeven, "Climate Change," 695.

447 *Report of the Defense Science Board Task Force on Trends and Implications of Climate Change for National and International Security* (Washington, DC: Office of the Under Secretary of Defense for Acquisition, Technology, and Logistics, October

2011), xv, at http://www.acq.osd.mil/dsb/reports/ADA552760.pdf, accessed September 7, 2016.

448   Garrett Hardin, "The Tragedy of the Commons," *Science*, December 13, 1968, at http://www.garretthardinsociety.org/articles/art_tragedy_of_the_commons.html, accessed December 21, 2014.

449   See, for example, Elinor Ostrom, "Collective Action and the Evolution of Social Norms," *The Journal of Economic Perspectives* 14(3) (Summer 2000), 137–58.

450   K. Witsenburg and A.W. Roba, "The Use and Management of Water Sources in Kenya's Drylands: Is There a Link between Scarcity and Violent Conflicts?" in *Conflicts over Land and Water in Africa*, eds. B. Derman, R. Odgaard, and E. Sjaastad (Oxford: James Currey, 2007), 235. For other examples, see K. Juul, "Transhumance, Tubes and Telephones: Drought-Related Migration as a Process of Innovation," *Beyond Territory and Scarcity*, eds. Gausset et al.; Oli Brown, A. Hammill, and R. McLeman, "Climate Change as the 'New' Security Threat: Implications for Africa," *International Affairs* 83(6) (2007), 1141–54; and Nils Petter Gleditsch, "Whither the Weather? Climate Change and Conflict," *Journal of Peace Research* 49(1) (2012), 3–9. Also see other articles in this issue of *Journal of Peace Research* for a critique of climate conflict in Africa, as well as the special issue of *Geopolitics* 19(4) (2014) on climate and security.

451   Clionadh Raleigh and Caitriona Dowd, "Governance and Conflict in the Sahel's 'Ungoverned Space,'" *Stability: International Journal of Security and Development*, 2(2) (2013), 1–17, and Raleigh, "Political Marginalization, Climate Change, and Conflict in African Sahel States," *International Studies Review* 12 (2010), 69–86.

452   James Fairhead, "International Dimensions of Conflict over Natural and Environmental Resources," in *Violent Environments*, eds. Peluso and Watts, 213–36.

453   Clionadh Raleigh, Andrew Linke, and John O'Loughlin, "Extreme Temperatures and Violence," *Nature Climate Change* 4 (February 2014), 76–77.

454   Eric Bonds, "Upending Climate Violence Research: Fossil Fuel Corporations and the Structural Violence of Climate Change," *Human Ecology Review* (formatted preprint) (2016), 8, at https://digitalcollections.anu.edu.au/bitstream/1885/96101/2/Bonds%20Upending%20climate%20violence%20research%202016.pdf, accessed July 28, 2016.

455   Halvard Buhaug, "Climate-Conflict Research: Some Reflections on the Way Forward," *WIREs Climate Change* 6(3) (2015), 269–75; and on green grabs, see James Fairhead, Melissa Leach, and Ian Scoones, "Green Grabbing: A New Appropriation of Nature?" *Journal of Peasant Studies* 39(2) (April 2012), 237–61, as well as other case studies in this issue.

456   Norman Myers, *Environmental Exodus: An Emergent Crisis in the Global Arena* (Washington, DC: Climate Institute, 1995); for a critique see Ragnhild Nordås and Nils Petter Gleditsch, "Climate Change and Conflict," *Political Geography* 26(6), 627–38.

457   Oli Brown, "The Numbers Game," *Forced Migration Review* 31 (2008), 8–9, at http://www.fmreview.org/sites/fmr/files/FMRdownloads/en/FMRpdfs/FMR31/08-09.pdf as of January 27, 2017; A. Bojanowski, "UN Embarrassed by Forecast on Climate Refugees," *Der Spiegel*, April 18, 2011, at http://www.spiegel.de/international/world/0,1518,757713,00.html, accessed December 21, 2014; and Fred Pearce, "Searching for the Climate Refugees," *New Scientist*, April 27, 2011, at

http://www.newscientist.com/article/mg21028104.600-searching-for-the-climate-refugees.html, accessed May 15, 2011.

458 Christian Parenti, *Tropic of Chaos: Climate Change and the New Geography of Violence* (New York: Nation Books, 2011).

459 See Bojanowski, "UN Embarrassed"; the film's homepage is http://www.climaterefugees.com/ accessed on December 21, 2014.

460 Adger et al., "Human Security," Chapter Twelve, in *Climate Change 2014: Impacts, Adaptation, and Vulnerability*, 771.

461 A report by the International Institute on Environment and Development (IIED) in London notes that, despite the hype about hundreds of millions of climate refugees, "The relatively high levels of uncertainty on the locally-specific impacts of climate change, combined with limited data on migration, especially internal and temporary movements, make it difficult if not impossible to predict with any precision future mobility patterns, let alone their size and direction." Cecilia Tacoli, "Not Only Climate Change: Mobility, Vulnerability and Socio-Economic Transformations in Environmentally Fragile Areas of Bolivia, Senegal and Tanzania," IIED Human Settlements Working Paper Series, Rural–Urban Interactions and Livelihood Strategies (28), (London: IIED, 2011), at http://pubs.iied.org/10590IIED.html, accessed December 21, 2014.

462 James Morrissey, "Rural–Urban Migration in Ethiopia," *Forced Migration Review* 31 (2008), 28–29.

463 Carol Farbotko, "Wishful Sinking: Disappearing Islands, Climate Refugees, and Cosmopolitan Experimentation," *Asia Pacific Viewpoint* 51(1) (April 2010), 53–54.

464 Jane McAdam and Maryanne Loughry, "We aren't Refugees," *Inside Story*, June 30, 2009, at http://insidestory.org.au/we-arent-refugees, accessed August 7, 2015.

465 Global Environmental Change and Human Security (GECHS) Project, *Disaster Risk Reduction, Climate Change Adaptation and Human Security*, a report commissioned by the Norwegian Ministry of Foreign Affairs (Oslo, Norway: GECHS, 2008), 24, at http://www.preventionweb.net/files/7946_GECHSReport3081.pdf, accessed December 21, 2014.

466 GECHS, *Disaster Risk Reduction*; and International Organization on Migration (IOM), "Migration, Climate Change and the Environment," policy brief, May 2009, at http://www.egypt.iom.int/doc/iom_policybrief_en.pdf, accessed December 21, 2014, at https://www.iom.int/sites/default/files/our_work/ICP/IDM/iom_policybrief_may09_en.pdf as of January 27, 2017.

467 Gregory White, *Climate Change and Migration: Security and Borders in a Warming World* (New York: Oxford University Press, 2011).

468 George Black, "The Gathering Storm," *OnEarth*, May 28, 2008, at http://www.onearth.org/article/the-gathering-storm, accessed December 21, 2014, at http://archive.onearth.org/article/the-gathering-storm as of January 27, 2017.

469 Colin P. Kelley et al., "Climate Change in the Fertile Crescent and Implications of the Recent Syrian Drought," *Proceedings of the National Academy of Sciences* 112(11) (March 17, 2015), 3241–46, at http://www.pnas.org/content/112/11/3241.full.pdf, accessed July 26, 2016.

470 See Alex Randall, "Syria and Climate Change: Did the Media Get It Right?," (London: Climate and Migration Coalition, 2016), at https://climatemigration.atavist.com/syria-and-climate-change, accessed July 26, 2016.

471   Aryn Baker, "How Climate Change is Behind the Surge of Migrants to Europe," *Time*, September 7, 2015, at http://time.com/4024210/climate-change-migrants/, accessed July 26, 2016.

472   Fram Dinshaw, "This is What a Climate Refugee Looks Like," *National Observer*, September 4, 2015, at http://www.nationalobserver.com/2015/09/04/news/ what-climate-refugee-looks, accessed July 26, 2016.

473   David Nakamura, "At Coast Guard Graduation, Obama Warns of Climate Change Threat to National Security," *Washington Post*, May 20, 2015, at http:// www.washingtonpost.com/news/post-politics/wp/2015/05/20/in-coast-guard-commencement-obama-to-link-climate-change-to-national-security/, accessed August 10, 2015. Also see White House Office of the Press Secretary, "Remarks by the President at the GLACIER Conference—Anchorage, AK," August 31, 2015, at https://www.whitehouse.gov/the-press-office/2015/09/01/remarks-president-glacier-conference-anchorage-ak, accessed July 26, 2015.

474   U.S. Department of State, "Remarks by John Kerry at the GLACIER Conference Opening Plenary," August 31, 2015, at http://www.state.gov/secretary/ remarks/2015/08/246489.htm, accessed July 26, 2016, and Julie Hirschfeld Davis and Steven Lee Myers, "Obama Makes Urgent Appeal in Alaska for Climate Change Action," *New York Times*, August 31, 2015, at http://www.nytimes. com/2015/09/01/us/us-makes-urgent-appeal-for-climate-change-action-at-alaska-conference.html, accessed July 26, 2015.

475   Jeremy Schulman, "Bernie Sanders: Yes, Climate Change is Still Our Biggest National Security Threat," *Mother Jones*, November 14, 2015, at http://www.motherjones.com/environment/2015/11/bernie-sanders-climate-change-isis, accessed July 27, 2016.

476   See, for example, Samer N. Abboud, *Syria* (Cambridge, UK: Polity Press, 2016).

477   Jan Selby, Omar S. Dahi, Christiane Frölich, and Mike Hulme, "Climate Change and the Syrian Civil War Revisited," unpublished paper, 2017.

478   Francesca de Châtel, "The Role of Drought and Climate Change in the Syrian Uprising: Untangling the Triggers of the Revolution," *Middle Eastern Studies* 50(4) (2014), 522, 524, at https://blogs.commons.georgetown.edu/rochelledavis/files/ francesca-de-chatel-drought-in-syria.pdf as of January 27, 2017.

479   Betsy Hartmann and Jan Selby, "Time to Drop the Climate War Talk," *Common Dreams*, December 1, 2015, at http://www.commondreams.org/views/2015/12/01/ time-drop-climate-war-talk, accessed September 7, 2016.

480   UNHCR, *Global Trends: Forced Displacement in 2015* (Geneva, Switzerland, 2016), at http://www.unhcr.org/statistics/unhcrstats/576408cd7/unhcr-global-trends-2015.html, accessed July 27, 2016.

481   Steven Erlanger and Kimiko de Freytas-Tamura, "U.N. Funding Shortfalls and Cuts in Refugee Aid Fuel Flight to Europe," *New York Times*, September 20, 2015, 15, at https://www.nytimes.com/2015/09/20/world/un-funding-shortfalls-and-cuts-in-refugee-aid-fuel-exodus-to-europe.html as of January 27, 2017.

482   UNHCR, "Worldwide Displacement Hits All-Time High as War and Persecution Increase," June 18, 2015, at http://www.unhcr.org/en-us/news/ latest/2015/6/558193896/worldwide-displacement-hits-all-time-high-war-persecution-increase.html, accessed September 7, 2016.

483 Nick Turse, "The Military-Petroleum Complex," *Foreign Policy in Focus*, March 24, 2008, at http://www.fpif.org/articles/the_military-petroleum_complex, accessed December 21, 2014.

484 Roger J. Stern, "United States Cost of Military Force Projection in the Persian Gulf, 1976–2007," *Energy Policy* (2010), at http://www.princeton.edu/oeme/articles/US-miiltary-cost-of-Persian-Gulf-force-projection.pdf, accessed December 22, 2014.

485 See H. Patricia Hynes, "The 'Invisible Casualty of War': The Environmental Destruction of U.S. Militarism," *DifferenTakes* (84) (Summer 2014), at http://popdev.hampshire.edu/projects/dt/84, accessed December 22, 2014, at http://traprock.org/wp-content/uploads/2014/06/Militarism-and-the-Environment.pdf?x65644 as of January 27, 2017.

486 Department of Defense website, at http://www.defense.gov/home/features/2010/1010_energy/, accessed December 19, 2014. Apparently, as of July 2016 this site had been archived—see http://archive.defense.gov/home/features/2010/1010_energy/.

487 Emily Gilbert, "The Militarization of Climate Change," *ACME* 11(1) (2012), 1–14, at http://www.acme-journal.org/vol11/Gilbert2012.pdf, accessed December 22, 2014.

488 Office of the Deputy Under Secretary of Defense for Installations and Environment, *2014 Climate Change Adaptation Roadmap* (Alexandria, VA: June 2014), at http://www.acq.osd.mil/ie/download/CCARprint.pdf, accessed December 22, 2014, at http://www.acq.osd.mil/eie/Downloads/CCARprint_wForward_e.pdf as of January 27, 2017.

489 Department of Defense, *Quadrennial Defense Review 2014* (Washington, DC: 2014), at http://www.defense.gov/pubs/2014_Quadrennial_Defense_Review.pdf, accessed December 22, 2014, at http://archive.defense.gov/pubs/2014_Quadrennial_Defense_Review.pdf as of January 27, 2017.

490 Office of the Under Secretary of Defense for Acquisition, Technology and Logistics, *Report of the Defense Science Board Task Force on Trends and Implications of Climate Change and National and International Security* (Washington, D.C.: October 2011), at http://www.acq.osd.mil/dsb/reports/ADA552760.pdf, accessed December 22, 2014.

491 CNA Military Advisory Board, *National Security and the Accelerating Risks of Climate Change* (Alexandria, VA: CNA, May 2014), 8, at http://www.cna.org/sites/default/files/MAB_2014.pdf, accessed December 22, 2014, at https://www.cna.org/cna_files/pdf/MAB_5-8-14.pdf as of January 27, 2017. Kerry cited in Coral Davenport, "Climate Change Deemed Growing Security Threat by Military Researchers," *New York Times*, May 13, 2014, at http://www.nytimes.com/2014/05/14/us/politics/climate-change-deemed-growing-security-threat-by-military-researchers.html, accessed December 22, 2014.

492 William Easterly, "Foreign Aid Goes Military," *New York Review of Books* 55(19) (December 4, 2008), at http://www.nybooks.com/articles/2008/12/04/foreign-aid-goes-military/ as of January 27, 2017.

493 National Research Council (NRC), *Climate and Social Stress: Implications for Security Analysis* (Washington, D.C.: 2013), 10, at https://download.nap.edu/catalog.php?record_id=14682, accessed on April 19, 2013.

494 See Vijay Kumar Nagaraj, "'Beltway' Bandits and 'Poverty Barons': For-Profit International Development Contracting and the Military-Development Assemblage," *Development and Change* 46(4) (July 2015), 585–617.

495 Cited in Mark Akkerman, "Greenwashing Death: Climate Change and the Arms Trade," in *The Secure and the Dispossessed: How the Military and Corporations are Shaping a Climate-Changed World*, eds. Nick Buxton and Ben Hayes (London: Pluto Press, 2016), 243. See this book for a detailed analysis of the securitization and militarization of climate change. Also Sanjay Chaturvedi and Timothy Doyle, *Climate Terror: A Critical Geopolitics of Climate Change* (New York: Palgrave Macmillan, 2015).

496 See Andrew J. Bacevich, *Washington Rules: America's Path to Permanent War* (New York: Metropolitan Books, 2010), and Department of Defense, "Instruction—Stability Operations," Directive 3000.05, September 16, 2009, at http://www.dtic. mil/whs/directives/corres/pdf/300005p.pdf, accessed December 22, 2014.

497 Department of Defense, "DoD Directive 4715.21: Climate Change Adaptation and Resilience," January 14, 2016, at http://www.defense.gov/Portals/1/Documents/ pubs/471521p.pdf, accessed on July 29, 2016.

498 "Afrighanistan?" *Economist*, Jan. 26–Feb. 1, 2013, cover and editorial, 11. On US military strategy for Africa, see David Vine, "The Lily-Pad Strategy: How the Pentagon is Quietly Transforming Its Overseas Base Empire and Creating a Dangerous New Way of War," Truthout, July 16, 2012, at http://truth-out.org/ opinion/item/10347-the-lily-pad-strategy-how-the-pentagon-is-quietly-transform- ing-its-overseas-base-empire-and-creating-a-dangerous-new-way-of-war, accessed December 22, 2014; Nick Turse, "Obama's Scramble for Africa: Secret Wars, Secret Bases, and the Pentagon's 'New Spice Route' in Africa," Truthout, July 12, 2012, at http://truth-out.org/news/item/10296-obamas-scramble-for-africa-secret-wars- secret-bases-and-the-pentagons-new-spice-route-in-africa, accessed December 22, 2014; and Julian E. Barnes and Evan Perez, "Terror Fight Shifts to Africa: U.S. Considers Seeking Congressional Backing for Operations Against Extremists," *Wall Street Journal*, December 7, 2012, A1, at http://www.wsj.com/articles/SB10001 424127887323316804578163724113421726 as of January 27, 2017.

499 Nick Turse, "The Pivot to Africa: The Startling Size, Scope, and Growth of U.S. Military Operations on the African Continent," TomDispatch.com, September 5, 2013, at http://www.tomdispatch.com/blog/175743, accessed September 19, 2013.

500 The Defense Science Board report, for example, notes the high potential for climate-related instability in vulnerable but valuable regions, mostly in Africa, where the US fights terrorism and obtains energy resources and strategic materials. See Betsy Hartmann, "Converging on Disaster: Climate Security and the Malthusian Anticipatory Regime for Africa," *Geopolitics* 19(4) (2014), 757–83.

501 J. Barry with A. Jefferys, *A Bridge Too Far: Aid Agencies and the Military in Humanitarian Response*, Humanitarian Practice Network, Paper 37 (London: Overseas Development Institute, 2002); and C. Hofmann and L. Hudson, "Military Responses to Natural Disasters: Last Resort or Inevitable Trend?" *Humanitarian Exchange*, 44 (2009), 29–31.

502 Ed McGrady, Maria Kingsley, and Jessica Stewart, *Climate Change: Potential Effects on Demands for US Military Humanitarian Assistance and Disaster Response* (Alexandria, VA: CNA, November 2010), at http://www.cna.org/sites/default/

files/research/Climate%20Change%20and%20Military%2013873.pdf, accessed December 22, 2014, at www.dtic.mil/cgi-bin/GetTRDoc?AD=ADA564975 as of January 27, 2017.

503 CNA, *National Security and the Accelerating Risks of Climate Change*, 2. Not all military scenarios about climate change are so apocalyptic. See Chad Michael Briggs, "Climate Security, Risk Assessment and Military Planning," *International Affairs* 88(5) (2012), 1049–64.

504 Barkun, *Chasing Phantoms*, 60–63.

505 Alex de Waal, "An Imperfect Storm: Narratives of Calamity in a Liberal-Technocratic Age" (New York: Social Sciences Research Council, 2006), at http:// understandingkatrina.ssrc.org/deWaal/, accessed December 22, 2014; *Army Times* cited in Havidán Rodríguez and Russell Dynes, "Finding and Framing Katrina: The Social Construction of Disaster" (New York: Social Sciences Research Council, 2006), at http://understandingkatrina.ssrc.org/Dynes_Rodriguez/, accessed December 22, 2014.

506 See Rebecca Solnit, *A Paradise Built in Hell: The Extraordinary Communities that Arise in Disaster* (New York: Viking, 2009), for an account of law enforcement during Katrina.

507 Rodríguez and Dynes, "Finding and Framing Katrina."

508 Barkun, *Chasing Phantoms*, 65.

509 For example, see Al Gore on the Oprah Winfrey show, "A Green 'Truth': Unnatural Disasters," December 5, 2006, at http://www.oprah.com/oprahshow/A-Green-Truth_1, accessed December 22, 2014.

510 Lester R. Brown, "Global Warming Forcing U.S. Population to Move Inland: An Estimated 250,000 Katrina Evacuees are Now Climate Refugees" (Washington, DC: Earth Policy Institute, 2006), at http://www.earth-policy.org/Updates/2006/ Update57_printable.htm, accessed January 5, 2007, at http://www.earth-policy. org/plan_b_updates/2006/update57 as of January 27, 2017.

511 James R. Fleming, "The Climate Engineers: Playing God to Save the Planet," *The Wilson Quarterly* (Spring 2007), 48, at http://www.colby.edu/sts/climateengineers. pdf as of January 27, 2017.

512 S. Matthew Liao, Anders Sandberg, and Rebecca Roache, "Human Engineering and Climate Change," *Ethics, Policy and the Environment* 15(2) (2012), 206–21, at http://www.smatthewliao.com/wp-content/uploads/2012/02/HEandClimateChange.pdf as of January 27, 2017.

513 Hulme, *Why We Disagree about Climate Change*, 333.

514 Madeline Chambers, "Germany Steps Up CO2 Cuts to Meet 2020 Climate Goals," *Reuters*, December 3, 2014, at http://www.reuters.com/article/2014/12/03/ us-germany-climatechange-cabinet-idUSKCN0JH0RZ20141203, accessed December 22, 2014; Stefan Nicola, "Renewables Take Top Share of German Power Supply in First," *Bloomburg*, October 1, 2014, at http://www.bloomberg.com/ news/2014-10-01/german-renewables-output-tops-lignite-for-first-time-agora-says. html, accessed December 22, 2014; and Helmut Weidner and Lutz Mez, "German Climate Change Policy: A Success Story with Some Flaws," *Journal of Environment and Development* 17(4) (2008), 356–78.

515   James K. Boyce and Manuel Pastor, "Clearing the Air: Incorporating Air Quality and Environmental Justice into Climate Policy," *Climatic Change* 120(4) (October 2013), 801–14.

516   Robert Pollin, Heidi Garrett-Peltier, James Heintz, and Bracken Hendricks, *Green Growth: A U.S. Program for Controlling Climate Change and Expanding Job Opportunities* (Washington, DC: Center for American Progress and Political Economy Research Institute, 2014), at https://cdn.americanprogress.org/wp-content/uploads/2014/09/PERI.pdf, accessed August 11, 2015.

517   Solnit, *A Paradise Built in Hell*, 2.

ABOUT THE AUTHOR

Historian, educator, and women's rights advocate BETSY HART-MANN's books and appearances have had an impact on national debates on population control, environmentalism, and national security. Now in its third edition, Hartmann's feminist classic, *Reproductive Rights and Wrongs: The Global Politics of Population Control*, tackles the powerful myth of overpopulation and its negative consequences for women's reproductive health and rights. She is the co-author of *A Quiet Violence: View from a Bangladesh Village* and co-editor of the anthology *Making Threats: Biofears and Environmental Anxieties*. Her political thrillers, *The Truth About Fire* and *Deadly Election*, explore the threat the Far Right poses to American democracy. Hartmann is professor emerita of Development Studies and senior policy analyst of the Population and Development Program at Hampshire College. She lives in western Massachusetts.

ABOUT SEVEN STORIES PRESS

SEVEN STORIES PRESS is an independent book publisher based in New York City. We publish works of the imagination by such writers as Nelson Algren, Russell Banks, Octavia E. Butler, Ani DiFranco, Assia Djebar, Ariel Dorfman, Coco Fusco, Barry Gifford, Martha Long, Luis Negrón, Hwang Sok-yong, Lee Stringer, and Kurt Vonnegut, to name a few, together with political titles by voices of conscience, including Subhankar Banerjee, the Boston Women's Health Collective, Noam Chomsky, Angela Y. Davis, Human Rights Watch, Derrick Jensen, Ralph Nader, Loretta Napoleoni, Gary Null, Greg Palast, Project Censored, Barbara Seaman, Alice Walker, Gary Webb, and Howard Zinn, among many others. Seven Stories Press believes publishers have a special responsibility to defend free speech and human rights, and to celebrate the gifts of the human imagination, wherever we can. In 2012 we launched Triangle Square books for young readers with strong social justice and narrative components, telling personal stories of courage and commitment. For additional information, visit www.sevenstories.com